THE
WORKING-CLASS
REPUBLICAN

THE WORKING-CLASS REPUBLICAN

RONALD REAGAN AND THE RETURN OF BLUE-COLLAR CONSERVATISM

HENRY OLSEN

BROADSIDE BOOKS
An Imprint of HarperCollinsPublishers

HarperCollins books may be purchased for educational, business, or
sales promotional use. For information, please email the Special Markets
Department at SPsales@harpercollins.com.

FIRST EDITION

Designed by William Ruoto

Library of Congress Cataloging-in-Publication Data
Names: Olsen, Henry (Political consultant), author.
Title: The working-class Republican : Ronald Reagan and the return of blue-
collar conservatism / Henry Olsen.
Description: First edition. | New York : Broadside Books, 2017.
Identifiers: LCCN 2017009422 (print) | LCCN 2017016583 (ebook) |
ISBN 9780062475282 (ebk) | ISBN 9780062475268 (hardback) |
ISBN 9780062475275 (pb)
Subjects: LCSH: Reagan, Ronald—Political and social views. | United
States—Politics and government—1989– | Political culture—United States—
History—20th century. | Conservatism—United States—History—20th
century. | Progressivism (United States politics)—History—20th century. |
Right and left (Political science)—United States—History—20th century.
| Republican Party (U.S. : 1854–)—History—20th century. | United
States—Politics and government—20th century. | Presidents—United
States—Biography. | BISAC: HISTORY / United States / 20th Century.
| BIOGRAPHY & AUTOBIOGRAPHY / Presidents & Heads of State. |
POLITICAL SCIENCE / History & Theory.
Classification: LCC E877.2 (ebook) | LCC E877.2 .O46 2017 (print) |
DDC 973.927092—dc23
LC record available at https://lccn.loc.gov/2017009422

17 18 19 20 21 LSC 10 9 8 7 6 5 4 3 2 1

TO MY CHILDREN, SARAH SOPHIA, AND HENRY IV

CONTENTS

INTRODUCTION

I grew up as a conservative Republican in Ronald Reagan's California. To call me "die hard" would be understating my belief and commitment: I was the only volunteer in the Santa Clara County GOP HQ on August 9, 1974, the day Richard Nixon resigned. Working my way up from a volunteer to a young political consultant to a candidate myself, I inhaled the standard California conservative belief in very low taxes, a minimum of government, and a maximum of personal freedom. And like all Californians of that age, I knew who our leader was: Ronald Wilson Reagan.

Leaving the Golden State in my midtwenties didn't make me any less of a California conservative. I was part of the conservative Federalist Society while at law school and clerked for a former Reagan staffer on the US circuit court. The candidate I helped elect to the Pennsylvania state House in 1994 was derided as an extreme right-winger. My postlaw career took me into the free-market think tank world, where for twenty years I held high executive posts in nationally known institutions. Ronald Reagan and limited government were as important to me in my forties as they were in my teens.

Barack Obama's election and the Republican wipeouts of 2006 and 2008 were catastrophic events that shook me to the core. They should not have happened according to everything the conservative movement had been saying for decades. Republicans were increasingly becoming conservative, and increasingly winning more elections at all levels. Polls showed America remained a center-right nation where conservatives outnumbered liberals by about two to one. Yet this country had decisively elected the most liberal man ever to be nominated by a major party for president. How could this happen?

As dark as things looked in early 2009, I remembered they looked even darker in 1977 when Republicans held less than a third of the seats in the House of Representatives—and fewer than half of those Republicans were conservatives. Four years later, led by Reagan, conservatives had taken over the GOP and dethroned liberal Democrats from the political perch they had held for a generation. I resolved to look back to learn what Reagan did so that I could help today's conservatives meet our rendezvous with destiny.

What I found shocked me. Everything I had been told about Reagan's philosophy, by the Right and the Left, had been wrong. And I learned it was his own distinct and original philosophy, not his charisma or his pragmatism, that had allowed him to change his party, his country, and his world.

This book is the story of what I found. It is the story of a young New Dealer who moved to California and became a conservative, but never left his youthful admiration of Franklin Roosevelt behind. It is the story of a man whose conservative conversion did not lead him to abandon his belief that government—preferably state or local, but federal if necessary—should give people in need a hand up to help them pursue their dreams.

It is the story of a man who, while lionized by the Right and demonized by the Left, transcended left and right.

It is the story of the real Ronald Wilson Reagan—and how conservatives today could realize their dreams if only they knew who he was.

This story will revise what most people think about Reagan. It will lay to rest the claims that he sought to tear down the modern entitlement-welfare state in favor of a nineteenth-century "night watchman state" that protects peoples' bodies while being indifferent to their souls. It will show that from the minute Reagan entered the political arena he rejected the idea shared by left and right that the major political question was purely over government power. It will show that while Reagan was suspicious of government power, he always believed that justice and fairness were more important measures of what government did than the simple fact that it did it.

In short, it will show that Reagan was a "working-class Republican"— and that this unique philosophy was the secret to his political success.

We will start our journey at the beginning, those youthful years when Reagan was what his older self called a "hemophiliac liberal." His devotion to Franklin Delano Roosevelt knew no bounds; Reagan's contemporaries remember him as hopelessly committed to the president who remade America and the Democratic Party. Our study will show, however, that his liberalism was not theoretical or ideological. Instead, it came from a deep love for the average individual and Reagan's belief that every person was capable of leading a free and dignified life. His support for the New Deal, then, was based on the thought that Democratic policies were intended to enable people to live that free and dignified life—and that those policies worked.

Reagan's belief came from many sources, but none of them were more important than the lessons he learned from his family and his early life experiences. We will learn that Reagan's father was an Irish Catholic Democrat who preached tolerance, respect for hard work and country, and a belief in the nobility of the working person. His mother was neither Irish nor Catholic, but she shared her husband's core political principles as well as his faith in the Democratic Party. Neither parent graduated from high school, much less attended college. Together with a hardscrabble upbringing—Reagan often said later in life that "we were poor, we just didn't know it"—that included brushes with poverty, unemployment, and government relief, Reagan entered adulthood with a strong knowledge of what average, working Americans thought, felt, and faced in their daily lives.

These Americans also shared Reagan's love of Roosevelt and faith in the New Deal. A large majority of the Americans who worked in factories, mines, and industry were European immigrants. While a large majority of the Irish had been Democrats since before the Civil War, most other immigrants had been progressive Republicans. They had backed the party that promised them prosperity—a "full dinner pail"—through high tariffs that favored industry. But within the GOP, these voters tended to prefer crusaders like Theodore Roosevelt, men who promised to break up big business cartels known as trusts, pass workplace safety and injury compensation laws, and generally back the average person when the big business owner seemed to get in the way of people's ability to lead dignified and free lives. When the economy collapsed in 1929 and continued to sink throughout the presidency of Republican Herbert Hoover, these voters abandoned the GOP in droves and joined forces with the FDR-led Democrats. They would stay loyal to that party until, like Reagan, they came to believe that the Democratic Party had left them in the 1960s and 1970s.

These voters did not want socialism or significant changes to the American way of life. They wanted what the Republicans had promised and delivered for decades—a hand up that gave everyone a chance at dignity, comfort, and respect. Historians and professors argue even today about whether FDR and his staff really wanted to do this or if they secretly wanted to remake America into a less individualistic and more socialistic country. There were certainly those among Roosevelt's coterie who did want to take the latter course—and they carried on their crusade within the Democratic Party for decades after his death. But what Roosevelt told the American people and what he sold them on was exactly what they wanted.

Understanding what I call the "public New Deal" is essential to understanding Reagan's thought, his political journey, and the reason why he was politically successful. Roosevelt and his early heirs did not preach reliance on government or the virtues of an expert elite. Instead, they emphasized the virtue and dignity of the average American. They argued that these "forgotten men" could prosper with a government big enough to help them remove the obstacles in their path. To vote for Roosevelt in the 1930s and 1940s was not to vote to remake America, they argued, but to renew its eternal promise for all.

Reagan was faithful to the party of Roosevelt until the early 1950s. By then, however, he had begun to doubt that the party he had grown up in was still committed to the same ideals. He had learned firsthand in Hollywood that some of those on the left were in fact secret Communists dedicated to overthrowing the America he loved. His long acquaintance with intelligent and decent Republicans had shown him that one could be a moral person without sharing liberal politics. His brush with the extremely high marginal tax rates of that era, rates that reached as high as 94 percent when Reagan's earning power was at its peak, left him cold. Finally he came to the conclusion that Democrats no longer cared for the working person, but instead sought to perpetuate an ever-growing government for its own sake.

He often said that he did not leave the Democratic Party, the party left him. That statement is usually considered to be mere political fluff, a ruse to disguise his own radical shift and make himself politically palatable to the voters who revered or held fond memories of FDR and the New Deal. Yet that view is both condescending and wrong. It assumes, as ideologues left and right do, that the essential political question then and now is the fact of the exercise of governmental power rather than its objective. A close reading of Reagan's thought shows that he was always more concerned with what government sought to do than the fact that government was used to do it.

We shall see that Reagan's increasingly political speeches on behalf of his employer in the mid-1950s, General Electric, focused on the power of the bureaucracy to tell people what to do, not on the cornerstone achievements or aspirations of the New Deal. He did not attack laws that favored labor unions in bargaining. He did not argue against the building of roads, the implicit subsidy of suburban housing provided by the FHA and the GI Bill, or the massive expansion of public universities pushed by New Deal devotees in the states. He never attacked the legitimacy or constitutionality of Social Security, and when subsidized medical care became an issue in the late 1950s he backed the Kerr-Mills Act, a bill that provided federal aid to the states to craft their own plans to support "medically needy" senior citizens.

Reagan's preferences again matched those of working-class Americans. Like him, these men and women had voted for the Republican Dwight Eisenhower in 1952 and 1956. Like him, these voters were increasingly willing to vote for other Republicans who promised to respect the New Deal's achievements while maintaining America's traditional

values. Reagan's political transformation was more thorough and complete than his compatriots, but it occurred at the same time and for the
same reasons.

We can see all these trends clearly in the speech that made Ronald Reagan a shooting political star. Known officially as "A Time for
Choosing" and delivered nationwide on television on October 27, 1964,
this presentation—written solely by Reagan and based on his years of
thought—set forth a unique brand of conservatism, distinct from that
of the man whose candidacy Reagan was endorsing in that talk, Barry
Goldwater. By comparing "the speech" with Goldwater's bestselling
book, *The Conscience of a Conservative*, we shall see that Reagan's conservatism was less doctrinaire, less abstract, and less antigovernment
than was Goldwater's. It was more tolerant of the use of government
power, even federal government power, to help those in true need. It
was, simply put, more rooted in the public New Deal consensus and
less rooted in the hyperindividualistic creed that many of Goldwater's
backers worshipped.

Reagan's interpretation of what the New Deal's promises meant
to 1960s America resonated with that coalition's primary voting bloc,
working-class whites. Upset at rising crime, rising taxes, and a seem-
ing disrespect for simple American virtues, many of these men and
women increasingly backed Republicans for statewide and national office. Republicans made significant gains in the 1966 midterm election
as voters reacted negatively to Democratic president Lyndon Johnson's
ambitious expansion of federal government activity known as the Great
Society.

Reagan was one of those newly elected Republicans, who entered
political life with a massive million-vote victory over the incumbent
Democratic governor of California, Pat Brown. Both during his campaign and for his first two years in office, Reagan sought to contrast his
vision with LBJ's by promoting what he called the "Creative Society."
Again, this vision, promoted when Reagan's ideas were freshest, is quite
different from Goldwater's.

Reagan's Creative Society envisioned a government that in many respects was not too different from that which FDR advocated in the public New Deal. Government would continue to have an important role in providing education, welfare, and other services. Permanent aid would be limited to those who were in genuine need "through no fault of their own," but most of the important—and costly—New Deal and New Deal–inspired programs would remain substantially intact.

The Creative Society would break with the increasing pattern of relying on bureaucrats and government officials to determine how government should work and how society should respond to perceived problems. Reagan's vision extolled the expertise of private citizens such as businesspersons and favored private-sector action to address social needs. Government in Reagan's Creative Society would be limited in its aspirations, but energetic, efficient, and effective in its actions.

Reagan's two terms as governor hewed mainly to this path. He reluctantly agreed to raise taxes by a record amount in 1967 to solve an inherited budget deficit, over the opposition of some of his allies whom he came to refer to as "ultraconservatives." He reformed welfare to require able-bodied recipients to work, but also proudly increased the basic benefit for those who remained on the rolls; he called it "giving them a raise." He tried to limit government growth, but never sought to undo the massive expansion of state government that had been initiated by his liberal predecessor. The "ultras" lost faith in Reagan early on because of this, but most conservatives approved.

All the while, Reagan continued to expound on the principle that had animated him all of his adult life, that government should help but never guide. This comes through clearly in a famous interview he gave in 1975 to a then-new libertarian journal, *Reason*. While many libertarians today repeat Reagan's statement that "the heart and soul of conservatism is libertarianism," it is clear from the piece itself that Reagan himself meant something different by that term. Time and time again the interviewer sought to elicit statements from Reagan that government ought not to be involved in something—providing higher education and regulating drug safety, to name two—and just as persistently Reagan refused to echo those sentiments. Government action that responded to a legitimate need for self-protection or self-advancement was acceptable to the conservative Reagan as much as it had been acceptable to his younger, FDR-loving self so many years before.

Reagan had won his two terms as governor with a large measure of support from traditionally working-class Democrats. As these voters began to move away from other Republicans after their initial flirtation with the GOP in 1966, they remained loyal to Reagan. But while many 1966 winners went down to defeat in subsequent elections, Reagan won reelection by a handsome margin in 1970 and remained popular when he stepped down in 1974. The stage was set for him to launch a national campaign.

Most readers will know Reagan primarily from these later years, the time when he ran for president three times, winning twice. Despite liberal caricatures that he sought to undo the New Deal, Reagan ran for president on essentially the same platform on which he ran for governor. Government would be trimmed but not repealed; taxes would be cut but not slashed; programs or actions that helped the "truly needy" or assisted average Americans achieve their dreams would remain in place. Reagan's two terms did much to halt the growth of a government-directed society, but they did little to undo the legacies of the public New Deal—because the man in charge never sought to do that.

We can best see evidence of that by looking at his most important speeches. This philosophy also came through in the one moment that more than any other propelled him to victory, the famous "there you go again" debate exchange with President Jimmy Carter. Carter tried, as so many opponents had tried before, to "Goldwaterize" Reagan by charging that he opposed Medicare. Reagan replied with the famous line, and then went on to explain that he had opposed Medicare originally because he thought another proposal (the Kerr-Mills Act) "would be better for the senior citizens and provide better care than the one that was finally passed. I was not opposing the principle of providing care for them." Reagan's clear belief that government should help the deserving live decent, dignified lives came through loud and clear. A race that polls had shown tied before that debate became a ten-point Reagan victory less than a week later.

Reagan's victory was again dependent on votes from otherwise loyal, pro–New Deal working-class Democrats. This support was so strong that these voters not only elected Reagan, they also gave the Republican Party control of the Senate for the first time since 1954. While Democrats made a comeback in the late 1980s, these voters again rose up in opposition to modern liberalism in the 1990s when they revolted against Bill Clinton and Al Gore. The same coalition Reagan built starting in 1966 gave Republicans control of the House in 1994 for the first time in forty years and has made the GOP competitive in congressional and state-level elections ever since.

Reagan's unique, New Deal–tinged conservatism dismayed many of his more doctrinaire contemporary antigovernment activists. Determined antigovernment types opposed Reagan in 1980, backing the Libertarian Party ticket of Ed Clark and David Koch (today better known as one of the famous Koch brothers). Other, more ideological conservatives rebelled or voiced frustration with Reagan throughout his presidency. More revealing was the ultimate disillusionment of his first director of the Office of Management and Budget, David Stockman. Stockman penned a behind-the-scenes look at his time in the White House, a look that found Reagan wanting. He criticized Reagan for many things, but his strongest charge was that Reagan was not committed to the "revolution" to undo big government that many were waging in his name. We shall see that Stockman was wrong. As Reagan said many times, publicly and in his diaries, he never sought to "undo the New Deal." He sought to undo only the Great Society, and even here that was true only insofar as the programs he targeted were excessively bureaucratic or inefficient.

If Reagan's New Deal conservatism was so politically powerful, why do Republican presidential candidates lose so often today? The answer is simple: even as every candidate pledges allegiance to Reagan, none clearly conveys his or her genuine love for, and belief in, the average American in the way Ronald Reagan did.

Whether they are of the "establishment" variety (Paul Ryan, Rob Portman) or the Tea Party flavor (Ted Cruz), today's conservatives fundamentally misunderstand Ronald Reagan's legacy, because they remain unreconciled to the New Deal's core principle: the primacy of human dignity sanctions government help for those who need it. Americans believe, and have believed for nearly a century, that a government committed to this allows all Americans to live lives of comfort, dignity, and respect, making the American promise of the pursuit of happiness real for all.

Ryan and Portman err by implicitly disregarding the primacy of human dignity when it comes to the economy. Their approach—cut taxes for the rich and cut entitlements for the rest of us—fails to treat the average American as worthy of recognition. Their view that America is great to the extent it frees the few (the entrepreneurs) to create a better life for the rest of us directly contradicts FDR's and Reagan's view of the relation between the people and the economy.

Cruz misunderstands Reagan differently. He views Reagan as someone who was essentially a libertarian, a person for whom freedom was the ultimate political value. As Reagan said once of liberals, "The problem is not that our liberal friends are ignorant; it's that there's so much they know that isn't so." Reagan loved human freedom and thought it essential to a good life, but he followed FDR in believing that government action was good when pure freedom would lead to some people living lives without dignity or hope.

Cruz's faith in supply-side economics is central to his misunderstanding. This creed holds that low marginal tax rates on the wealthiest Americans is the most important engine for ensuring strong economic growth. Tax policy, then, should not be focused on lowering taxes on all working Americans; instead, it should be focused on lowering that top rate above all else. Indeed, David Stockman got into political hot water in 1981 by saying just that to a *Washington Post* reporter and claiming it was Reagan's true agenda.

But, contrary to popular belief, Reagan was not a "supply-sider." We shall see that Reagan never argued that fostering entrepreneurship and enacting low taxes on the rich were the primary reasons for his tax cuts; nor did he contend that freeing the rich was the best way to spur economic growth. He argued for a "humane economy," one in which everyone's taxes were lowered and one in which everyone's contributions were valued. In doing this, Reagan easily avoided the classic Democratic Party charge that Republicans are the party of the rich and the boss. Today's conservatives are sitting ducks for this charge.

Conservatives like these men and women fail to understand that conservative election victories since 1980 have not been rejections of the New Deal's promises but rather representations of the public's wish for their fulfillment. Correcting that error will give conservatives control of the moral high ground in American public life.

Many conservatives have argued that Donald Trump's election, fueled as it was by blue-collar men and women from all backgrounds, is reminiscent of Reagan's rise. Some contend that he is the new Reagan; others believe that Trump's appeal to American greatness is a Reaganesque clarion call that will lead conservatism into a new century.

These people are wrong when it comes to Trump's not-so-veiled racialism and white nationalism. Ronald Reagan was remarkably free of bigotry. He was raised by his parents to look beyond color or creed at a person's worth, and he showed that he was his parents' son time and time again. Reagan loved Americans from all racial, ethnic, and economic backgrounds. He would no sooner think that an immigrant was any less of an American than he would think communism represented mankind's future.

Trump's backers are right, however, that some of their man's appeal overlaps with Reagan's. Trump's primary appeal was that he would squarely place government on the side of the "forgotten American," the man or woman whose job was lost because of foreign competition, whose life was jeopardized by a feckless fight against terrorism, and whose contributions and beliefs were scorned by America's self-appointed best and brightest. Trump's policies are in many cases the antithesis of Reagan's, but the core thrust of his argument regarding government's ultimate purpose bears poignant similarities to Reagan's

New Deal conservatism. It is thus no surprise that the sons and daughters of the Reagan Democrats, the grandchildren of Roosevelt's voters, find Trump appealing.

The public believes with good reason that government delivers too little and costs too much. It believes with good reason that the academic, business, media, and political elites who govern us have stopped caring about whether their dreams and whims benefit anyone other than themselves. Recovering the real Reagan allows today's conservatives to address those beliefs precisely because it allows us to interpret, modernize, and reapply the cardinal principle enshrined in the New Deal, that government has a limited but strong role to play in helping the average person achieve his or her dreams. Recovering the real Reagan will give conservatives the moral legitimacy to complete our sixty-year journey from the margins of American public life to its center. In so doing, we will finally realize our dream to make America the shining city on a hill that we have wanted for so long.

THE
WORKING-CLASS
REPUBLICAN

CHAPTER 1

REAGAN ENTERS, STAGE LEFT

N ovember 8, 1932, began as any other day, but it ended as a day like no other. Nearly twenty-three million Americans had given Franklin Delano Roosevelt and his Democratic Party one of America's biggest landslides, ending over seventy years of Republican Party rule. Ronald Wilson Reagan was one of them.

One long-ago vote, cast in a time of crisis by a young man voting for his first time, might not matter. Reagan did much more than cast a vote. He was a devotee of FDR, impressing friends and casual acquaintances alike with his passion for the thirty-second president.[1] The young Reagan was always talking about politics, to the point where an early girlfriend from Des Moines broke up with him in part because of his incessant pro–New Deal prattle.[2] Early Hollywood friends and coworkers report that Reagan would easily fill the boring hours on a movie set between takes with political commentary and argument, all from a pro-FDR perspective.[3] The man many label as the twentieth century's most conservative president was more than a casual backer of FDR.

Nor did Reagan's devotion to liberalism cease with FDR's death in 1945. Immediately after World War II, Reagan—whose movie career had gone on hiatus while he spent the war in active service as a member of the army reserves—ramped up his political involvement. No longer content simply to talk, he began to act, joining many liberal causes such as the World Federalists, Americans for Democratic Action, and the American Veterans Committee.[4] He was so articulate and active that he was even asked to run for Congress in 1946 as a Democrat.[5] He was also considered by Democratic Party leaders for a congressional bid in 1952. They decided against wooing him because he was considered too liberal.[6]

Reagan's active liberalism continued for many years, even after he had encountered and successfully fought the Communist Party's attempt to infiltrate the Hollywood film industry. He campaigned for the Democratic nominee, Harry Truman, in 1948 against the Republican Tom Dewey and the leftist Progressive candidate Henry Wallace. He backed the Democrat in California's 1950 US Senate race, Congresswoman Helen Gahagan Douglas, even as she was accused by the Republican nominee, Congressman Richard Nixon, of being the "pink lady" who surreptitiously backed Communist aims.[7] Reagan continued to argue on behalf of New Deal and Democratic policies even into the mid-1950s, when he was a "Democrat for Eisenhower" and became a paid spokesman for the behemoth corporation General Electric.[8] What Reagan called his "hemophiliac liberal" phase lasted well over two decades and was an increasingly important part of his life during that time.

Most observers and Reagan analysts pass over this period of his life when trying to understand how Reagan rose to prominence and power. These men and women assume that the essence of Reagan's philosophy changed in the 1950s as he moved from advocating more government action to pushing for less. They credit his rhetorical power, his pragmatism in governing, his determination, and his luck in explaining how he went from an actor in decline to the most important political figure of the late twentieth century. All these views have their merits and all are to some extent correct. But all are inadequate to explain both how Reagan rose and what Reagan did.

They are inadequate because they fail to take Reagan seriously as a thinker. These writers presume they *know* what Reagan believed after his political evolution and conservative rebirth. They *know* he was no different from Barry Goldwater and a host of other unsuccessful conservatives who called for a repudiation of FDR's New Deal. In their hearts, they know he was right—far right.

This view presumes they understand Reagan better than he understood himself. From the beginning to the end of his conservative career, Reagan always said that he did not leave the Democratic Party, the Democratic Party left him.[9] His political views remained, in his eyes, the same even as he changed his mind about such important things as the value of big business and the virtues of government.[10] If we take him at face value—and we have no reason not to—we must conclude one of two things when evaluating his later success: either all his Republican friends and allies who opposed Roosevelt and his New Deal throughout their lives—and lost politically for decades—were simply less gifted politicians than he, or Reagan's conservatism was different in some important way that allowed him to succeed where they had failed.

I started my studies as one of those who thought I knew Reagan's thought, that he was as antigovernment as I had been told. Years of carefully reading his speeches and writings, however, have convinced me I was wrong. The Gipper's ability to plant the tree of liberty in the garden of Roosevelt rested on the fact that the tree he intended to plant was of a different species from those nurtured by others. It was a tree that could draw nutrients from the New Deal's soil because it was a sapling of the original planting.

To see this clearly, we must first revisit Reagan's youth. Our aim is to uncover not just what he supported but what he *believed*. We must then recover the reasons why a man who held these beliefs would find Franklin Roosevelt's New Deal appealing in the first place. For that, we must turn not to intricate scholarly examinations of FDR's presidency but to what Reagan, and the tens of millions of fellow Americans who shared Reagan's devotion to FDR, would have turned to: the public words of the man himself.

When we do this, we will see why Reagan could both change his partisan outlook later in life and contend he never really changed at all. We will see that a young man with Reagan's views could find FDR's public vision intoxicating, and could also find the Democratic Party of the post-FDR years wanting.

Reagan, in his final autobiography, said he "had become a Democrat, by birth" owing to the advocacy of his father, Jack, "for the working man" and active involvement in local Democratic Party politics.[11] This in itself was unusual: Reagan's hometown of Dixon, Illinois, was so heavily Republican that the county it is located in, Lee County, voted against Roosevelt in every race he ever ran.[12] But both of his parents were ardent and devoted Democrats even as they otherwise blended in with their midwestern, small-town neighbors.[13]

Reagan was born in 1911, so the first presidential election in which he could have voted was the Roosevelt-Hoover battle in 1932.[14] That election was contested at the lowest point in the Great Depression. Republicans had run the country almost continuously since 1896. Their majority rested on the laborer, the person who built cars, made steel, mined coal, and otherwise created America's industrial might. Aside from 1912, when Republicans split between the incumbent, President William Howard Taft, and the former president Theodore Roosevelt, who ran on the Progressive "Bull Moose" ticket, the GOP presidential nominee carried most of America's large industrial cities in all or most presidential races.[15]

These voters supported a Republican Party that was unabashedly protectionist and pro–industrial development. Today's Republican Party preached, pre-Trump, free trade and creating a level playing field among businesses. But the GOP of the early twentieth century was anything but that. It argued that high tariffs on imported goods and other support for industry allowed American business to flourish. This economic interventionism was said to be the cause of the jobs and rising wages that supported the nation's workers, farmers, miners, and loggers. The Republican slogan in 1900 said it all: voting for the GOP gave workers "a full dinner pail."

The Great Depression, however, changed everything. Three years of ineffectual and uninspired leadership from Republicans meant these workers were ready for a change. The Democratic nominee, New York governor Franklin Delano Roosevelt, promised them that and more. He promised them a "new deal."[16]

One can easily understand the appeal such a promise had. Unemployment was over 20 percent. The GDP had dropped by nearly 25 percent. Millions were going hungry. The three years since the Depression started with the stock market crash of October 1929 had been bleak, and by 1932 the economy was getting worse, not better. Moreover, the nation faced this crisis without any of the social insurance programs we now take for granted.

Virtually nothing we now associate with the federal government existed before the New Deal. There was no unemployment insurance—if you lost your job and had no savings or friends to support you, you were broke. There were no entitlements: no Social Security or any other form of government pension given to people in retirement. There was no Medicare, Medicaid, or any other broad government-funded support of medical care. Labor unions were on their own—employers were not required to bargain with them and could fire people who joined them.

The same holds true for other things now commonplace. There were no federal antipoverty or job-training programs. Students looking to attend college had to pay for it themselves; there were no federal grants, scholarships, or guaranteed student loans. It was legal to discriminate against anyone in hiring or in anything else: if you didn't want to hire blacks or women (or, in those days, Catholics or Jews) because you didn't like "them," you were free to do so. No federal agency or law tried to limit the amount of air or water pollution factories belched out.

As a consequence of this, government before the New Deal was small. The federal government spent less than 4 percent of the country's GDP on the eve of the Great Depression, compared with over

21 percent today. State and local government didn't do many of these things either, which meant their budgets were also comparatively tiny: together, they spent only about 8 percent of national GDP, compared with about 14 percent today. Americans were on the whole freer to do what they wanted with their lives and their money; they also had to deal with life's consequences much more on their own. The Great Depression meant those consequences were life changing, and even life threatening.

This had not changed much during the Great Depression. State and local governments had increased spending on "relief," but the amounts paled in comparison to the need. The federal government primarily coordinated private and state action, but despite the record-breaking need, no major new social insurance or spending programs were created. Hoover opposed such efforts and argued that enacting them would essentially change the nature of American government and threaten freedom.

Roosevelt disagreed, arguing that the threat to freedom came from the experience of mass, undeserved poverty. The "New Deal" he promised during the campaign was short on specific programs but long on a diagnosis of the problem and its solution.

The problem, Roosevelt said, was that Republican economic policy had favored the rich few at the expense of the average many. "The forgotten man at the bottom of the economic pyramid" had been abandoned by "the Republican leadership" in the years before the Depression by an economic policy that encouraged wasteful production and financial speculation.[17] When the Depression came, that leadership refused to do everything in its power to mitigate the suffering.[18] The New Deal would end this by both engaging the federal government to provide "immediate relief of the unemployed"[19] and "controlling by adequate planning the creation and distribution of those products which our vast economic machine is capable of producing."[20] Toward these ends he promised "bold, persistent experimentation"[21] and the word Americans wanted to hear more than any other: "action."[22]

Hoover argued that such federal government action was contrary to

American principles. He told the Republican convention upon accepting their nomination that despite the economic calamity,

> it is not the function of the Government to relieve individuals of their responsibilities to their neighbors, or to relieve private institutions of their responsibilities to the public, or the local government to the States, or the responsibilities of the State governments to the Federal Government. . . .
>
> It does not follow, because our difficulties are stupendous, because there are some souls timorous enough to doubt the validity and effectiveness of our own ideals and our system, that we must turn to a State-controlled or State-directed social or economic system to cure our troubles. That is not liberalism; that is tyranny.[23]

Hoover insisted that the federal government could only coordinate and assist the acts of others; it could not act on its own. Its primary responsibility was to ensure that it ran a balanced budget, which included raising new revenues and reducing other expenditures. "It is in reducing taxes from the backs of men that we liberate their powers,"[24] Hoover argued. Roosevelt's proposed spending increases on temporary public works programs, he said, would cost "upwards of $9,000,000,000 a year" and so endanger American liberty itself. He said that current government spending, which caused Americans to "work for the support of all forms of Government sixty-one days out of the year," already threatened "national impoverishment and destruction of [our] liberties."[25] Roosevelt's proposals would increase that amount by an additional forty days; Hoover argued that "our Nation cannot do this without destruction to our whole conception of the American system."[26]

Roosevelt responded to Hoover's attacks the same day, contending that "my New Deal does not aim to change [the fundamental principles of America]. It does aim to bring [them] into effect."[27] He had first explained how his proposed expansion of federal government power fulfilled American principles at a speech delivered in front of the Commonwealth Club of San Francisco. FDR argued in that speech that the American Revolution was part of a worldwide effort by the many to control the power of the few that had sprung up in the late Middle Ages.[28] He argued that this same struggle between a few who sought to control government for its benefit and the mass of average people continued after the American Revolution in the struggle between Alexander Hamilton and Thomas Jefferson. Hamilton, in this telling, favored the rule of "a small group of able and public spirited citizens" while Jefferson favored rule by the whole of the people.

Roosevelt's Jefferson was not, however, a mere advocate of smaller government. "Government to him was a means to an end," he said, and he quoted Jefferson to the effect that in early America most people could through their own effort "extract from the rich and the competent such prices as enable them to feed abundantly, clothe above mere decency, to labor moderately and raise their families." Since the industrial revolution had evolved without a commensurate evolution of government power, he argued, that situation no longer prevailed. "We are steering a course toward economic oligarchy, if we are not there already."

FDR placed the well-being of the average person ahead of the economic liberty of the most successful individuals in his political hierarchy. "Every man has a right to make a comfortable living"; "every man has a right to be assured, to the fullest extent possible, in the safety of his savings." If restricting "the operations of the speculator, the manipulator, even the financier" was needed to bring these rights to fruition, "I believe we must accept the restriction as needful, not to hamper individualism but to protect it." "Faith in America," that "apparent Utopia which Jefferson imagined for us in 1776, and which Jefferson, [Theodore] Roosevelt, and Wilson sought to bring to realization . . . demands we recognize the new terms of the old social contract."

Roosevelt decisively won his contest with Hoover. He received 57 percent of the vote, smashing the incumbent by nearly 18 points. FDR crushed Hoover in the Electoral College 472–59. Working-class Catholics and other immigrants whose votes had sustained the GOP for decades swung behind Roosevelt. Four years later, after New Deal projects had begun to be implemented, even more of these voters joined the Democratic ranks. They delivered another smashing electoral victory for FDR, giving him a 61–36 percent win over the Republican Alf Landon. Landon won only two states, Vermont and Maine, as Roosevelt won the Electoral College by a record 523–8 margin. These voters would not abandon FDR's party again for decades.

Roosevelt used his victories to remake American government. The first national unemployment insurance system was passed. Federal insurance of bank deposits (via the FDIC) followed, as did a host of new regulations and programs. The government employed people in public works; it subsidized home ownership through the Federal Housing Administration (FHA); and it built publicly owned units for people too poor to purchase their homes. The Social Security Act established the first retirement pension program in America as well as the forerunner of the main welfare program, Aid to Families with Dependent Children (AFDC). Banks and Wall Street were federally regulated by the Glass-Steagall Act, the Securities Act, and the Securities Exchange Act. Finally, employers were forced to bargain with labor unions that had organized their workers, as a result of the Wagner Act. Federal spending and borrowing rose, and the top tax rate on the wealthy rose from 25 percent in 1930 to over 81 percent by 1939.

Throughout this period Roosevelt stressed that the New Deal was consistent with American individualism. His fifth fireside chat, for example, told Americans that the New Deal was merely "a fulfillment of old and tested American ideals. . . . All that we do is fulfill the historic traditions of the American people."[29] The 1936 Democratic National Convention was held in Philadelphia, "a fitting ground on which to reaffirm the faith of our fathers" according to the renominated president. He repeated this theme again in his second inaugural address and in fireside chat 12. He even compared the New Deal to "the frontier husking bee" in a 1938 speech commemorating the 150th anniversary of the Northwest Ordinance. He went on in that speech to say, "Our recent legislation is not a departure from but a return to the healthy practices of mutual self-help of the early settlers of the Northwest."

Indeed, we owe one of our nation's most beloved buildings, the Jefferson Memorial, to Roosevelt's interpretation of American history. Construction on that edifice to liberty was authorized in 1934, and FDR himself presided over its opening on Jefferson's two hundredth birthday.[30]

Republicans railed that America was being destroyed, but Americans disagreed. They rewarded Roosevelt with an unprecedented third term in 1940, giving him a 55–45 victory over the Republican Wendell Willkie. Again, formerly Republican working-class voters gave FDR the decisive margin; Roosevelt won narrow victories throughout the Midwest and Northeast on the strength of votes in industrial counties and cities.

The intervention of World War II halted further domestic policy changes, but FDR signaled his intention to press on. His 1944 State of the Union address declared that every American should have rights to things like "earn[ing] enough to provide adequate food and clothing and recreation . . . a decent home . . . adequate medical care . . . and a good education."[31] He called these and other government guarantees a "Second Bill of Rights"—the speech became known as the "Economic Bill of Rights" speech. The federal government also created the War Production Board to govern the American economy through the war and established wage and price controls through another agency.[32]

Both FDR's actions and his aspirations were unprecedented, but Americans rewarded him with a record fourth term in 1944. Yet again Roosevelt won narrow victories in industrial states with votes from working-class urban and industrial county voters.

It may seem strange to most readers, but Ronald Reagan supported these changes. The future president acknowledged that by "the end of World War II, I was a New Dealer to the core." He said that in late 1945:

I thought that government could solve all our postwar problems just as it had ended the Depression. I didn't trust big business. I thought government, not private companies, should own all our big public utilities; if there wasn't enough housing to shelter the

American people, I thought government should build it; if we needed better medical care, the answer was socialized medicine.[33]

Countless interviews with his friends and coworkers show that the war had not changed Reagan's belief: he was as passionately pro–New Deal and liberal before the war as he was in 1945.

Neither Reagan nor his friends and acquaintances go into much detail in these interviews about *why* he was so devoted to Roosevelt's New Deal. But upon close examination, we can see how FDR's support for the average American against the powerful and his invocation of traditional American values would have attracted the young Reagan.

Consistent with FDR's devotion to the average American, Reagan's strongest political principle was always that that person should be free to pursue a life of his or her own choosing. In his autobiography he wrote:

> Throughout my life, I guess there's been one thing that's troubled me more than any other: the abuse of people and the theft of their democratic rights, whether by a totalitarian government, an employer, or anyone else.[34]

This view pervaded his politics throughout his life, and those who knew him then noted how strongly he believed this. His high school science teacher, Bernard Frazer, remembered his young charge as someone who "bled for humanity."[35] Reagan noted that he changed his mind about being forced to join a union, the Screen Actors Guild (SAG), as a condition of being able to work in movies after he learned how extras and less famous actors were "exploited" by the studios.[36] He viewed the Democratic Party then as the "party of the people."[37] He desperately wanted to help "the dispossessed, the unemployed, and the homeless,"[38] and described himself as "passionately devoted to the working man."[39] As a child from a working poor background with personal experience of the Depression's ravages, he enthusiastically approved of FDR's calls to action.[40]

Roosevelt also extolled the average person's dreams rather than those of the economically successful or the inventive. His philosophy was most succinctly stated when he accepted the Democratic nomination in 1940:

Democracy can thrive only when it enlists the devotion of those whom Lincoln called the common people. Democracy can hold that devotion only when it adequately respects their dignity by so ordering society as to assure to the masses of men and women reasonable security and hope for themselves and their children.

Roosevelt's "national policy" was based "upon a decent respect for the rights and the dignity of all our fellow men";[41] the goal of his four terms was "to advance the lot of the average American citizen who had been so forgotten after the last war."[42]

Reagan's love of the average American knew no boundaries. Jack Reagan made a point of raising his children to see the good in every person regardless of his or her color or creed, a lesson Ronald Reagan took to heart. He stood up for his black teammates on the Eureka College football team when they encountered segregation;[43] he resigned from a prestigious Hollywood country club in 1937 when he learned they did not admit Jews;[44] he praised the combat sacrifices of Japanese American soldiers in World War II at a time when anti-Japanese prejudice was so rampant that over 100,000 American citizens of Japanese descent had been sent to internment camps by his political idol.[45] The young Reagan as much as the mature Reagan was always on the side of the common man from every background.

Reagan's devotion was not condescending. He always believed that almost everyone, regardless of circumstance or ability, could and should run his or her own life.[46] Reagan summarized this belief nicely in his autobiography:

Individuals determine their own destiny; that is, it's largely their own ambition and hard work that determine their fate in life. . . .

Every individual is unique, but we all want freedom and liberty, peace, love, and security, a good home, and a chance to worship God in our own way; we all want the chance to get ahead and make our children's lives better than our own. We all want the chance to work at a job of our own choosing and to be fairly rewarded for it and the opportunity to control our own destiny. . . .

Not everyone aspires to be a bank president or a nuclear scientist, but everyone wants to do something with one's life that will give him or her pride and a sense of accomplishment.[47]

FDR would have agreed. While Reagan would ultimately view government as the chief obstacle among those barriers, FDR identified monopoly and the control of government by the "moneyed few" to be the primary barriers to a self-chosen life. Once big businessmen were required to bargain fairly with their employees and could no longer pay them "starvation wages"; once public investment in roads, schools, parks, and access to health care were sufficient; then the average person could enjoy "true individual freedom."[48] That emphasis on self-government meant that Roosevelt believed in both a collective responsibility to prevent "undeserved poverty" and that the average person's work was an essential component of human happiness. Calling the New Deal "a great national crusade to destroy enforced idleness which is an enemy of the human spirit,"[49] Roosevelt proclaimed that "in a land of vast resources no one should be permitted to starve."[50] This was not intended to be a permanent handout for all. Instead, FDR's aim was to procure work for everyone who wanted a job and could hold one. "We prefer useful work to pauperism of the dole,"[51] he proclaimed, and said it should not be the "destiny of any American to remain permanently on relief roles."[52] One may "by sloth or by crime decline to exercise" his right to "make a comfortable living,"[53] "but it may not be denied him."

Reagan would echo these sentiments throughout his career even as he ultimately placed more faith in purely private enterprise to provide the opportunities and the comfort everyone craved. Even the phrase he used to explain who could legitimately call upon the government for permanent assistance—those who "through no fault of their own" could not support themselves—owes an unacknowledged debt to Roosevelt. FDR used the exact phrase when referring to people who deserved government help in a 1937 fireside chat.[54]

Thus Reagan could write in a 1947 newspaper article that "[America's] highest aim should be the cultivation of freedom of the individual for therein lies the highest dignity of man."[55] That sentence could easily fit into any of Reagan's most famous speeches, but he wrote it while he was a self-described New Deal Democrat.

Reagan's love of America also found its parallel in Roosevelt's thought. Later in life he would say that America was a unique nation in mankind's history, a place that "above all places, gives us the freedom to reach out and make our dreams come true."[56] He would call America a "shining city on a hill" and "the last best hope of man on earth." FDR was less poetic than Reagan, but no less emphatic, when he said in his third inaugural that "the democratic aspiration is no mere recent phase in human history. It is human history." He went on:

> In America [this aspiration's] impact has been irresistible. America has been the New World in all tongues, and to all peoples, not because this continent was a new-found land, but because all who came believed they could create upon this continent a new life—a life that should be new in freedom.

Reagan displayed this special patriotic love of America during his New Deal days too. In January 1940, he prevailed upon his fiancée, Jane Wyman, and the woman who got him his first break in show business, Jo Hodges, to go to Mount Vernon with him. His fascination with everything he saw there left a lasting impression on the women, so much so that Wyman arranged to have a replica of a writing desk of George Washington's that Reagan deeply admired made for his study.[57] By 1941 Reagan was studying the Constitution in his spare time between movies.[58]

Roosevelt also made other promises that an older Reagan would cite to explain his youthful enthusiasm. He rightly notes in his autobiography that "Roosevelt ran for president on a platform dedicated to reducing waste and fat in government."[59] Reagan also said that one of FDR's sons, FDR Jr., "often told me that his father said many times his welfare and relief programs during the Depression were meant only as emergency, stopgap measures, not the seeds of what others tried to turn into a permanent welfare state."[60] Reagan comforted himself by saying, "If he [FDR] had not been distracted by the war, I think he would have resisted the relentless expansion of the federal government that followed him."[61]

Reagan also argued that Democrats after Roosevelt had abandoned the true philosophy of the party's founder, Thomas Jefferson. Reagan's Jefferson was a man who advocated a small government that left as much power as possible in the people.[62] By demanding "the right to regulate and plan the social and economic life of the country and move into areas best left to private enterprise," the Democrats had left behind their founder's—and, purportedly, Reagan's—philosophy, thereby forfeiting Reagan's allegiance.[63]

Roosevelt's unexpected death in April 1945 forced the Democrats to decide how to carry out his legacy. Roosevelt's New Deal always had two main competing strains of thought. One was that America's promise could be restored by measures that gave average people a fairer shake in life through government regulation of the free market and guarantees of protection against undeserved poverty. The other was that America's promise was fundamentally compromised by the modern economy and that only top-down governmental planning could ensure individuals' freedom. The battle over which of these ideas would define the Democratic Party was fought in the election of 1948 between the incumbent, President Harry S. Truman, and the former vice president Henry Wallace.

Wallace and many other disgruntled New Dealers were upset that the War Production Board, which they viewed as a potential vehicle to introduce national peacetime economic planning, had been abolished by Truman in late 1945. Desiring a rapid transformation of American society, they formed a new political party, the Progressive Party, to carry on their battle.

The Progressive Party platform is among the most left-wing documents ever produced by a significant American political party. It proclaimed that "the national wealth and natural resources of our country belong to the people who inhabit it."[64] Because "every effort to give effect . . . to Franklin Roosevelt's Economic Bill of Rights . . . has failed because Big Business dominates the key sectors of the economy . . . the people, through their democratically elected representatives, must take control of the main levers of the economic system." Wallace's Progressives proposed public ownership of "the largest banks, the railroads, the merchant marine, the electric power and gas industry, and industries primarily dependent on government funds or government purchases such as the aircraft, the synthetic rubber and synthetic oil industries." The rest of the economy would be run indirectly by a council of economic planning that would "develop plans for assuring high production, full employment, and a rising standard of living."

Truman's Democratic Party platform presented an entirely different interpretation of the New Deal. The party did not endorse national economic planning or public ownership. Instead, it proposed extensions or the creation of popular public programs such as Social Security and the GI Bill.[65] It called for increasing the minimum wage, increasing old-age and survivors' Social Security benefits by at least 50 percent, and creating a new benefit for disabled people under the Social Security Act. Instead of an America run from the top, Truman's Democrats envisioned a more traditional America aided by the firm hand of government to ensure a broader distribution of wealth and opportunity than a fully free market ostensibly would bring.

The two parties also differed on foreign policy. Truman's Democrats were unabashedly anti-Communist and defended the president's Marshall Plan, aid to Greece and Turkey to combat Communist guerrillas, and other anti-Soviet policies. The Progressives rejected all of this, arguing instead for "negotiation and discussion with the Soviet Union to find areas of agreement to win the peace."

Reagan was staunchly behind Truman in this campaign. He co-chaired the organization Hollywood for Truman and campaigned actively for Truman and other Democratic candidates, such as the Senate nominee Hubert Humphrey.[66] Reagan's speeches focused on a major Democratic campaign theme, attacking "Republican inflation," but from time to time he also endorsed other aspects of the Democratic platform.[67] His attacks on inflation also stuck to the Democratic Party theme that it was the result of "big business" raising prices unnecessarily to fuel profits.[68] This did not mean he was against the private sector, though. He told the Los Angeles Rotary Club that he was "for the free-enterprise system" and "against statism."[69] Reagan's intense anti-communism, generated (as we shall see in the next chapter) because of his recent involvement in stopping the attempted Communist infiltration of the movie industry, did not preclude his support for Truman. Indeed, the Truman-inspired Democratic platform was itself a strongly anti-Communist document.

By choosing to back Truman and the Democrats in the intraliberal war with Wallace and the Progressives, Reagan showed how he understood what the New Deal meant. In his mind, the New Deal was meant to reshuffle the classic American deck, not create a new America from an entirely different set of cards.

Even long after his partisan switch, Reagan expressed fondness for Truman and his presidency. Calling him "an outstanding president," he credited Truman with common sense that allowed him to stand "up to the bureaucrats" and make tough decisions.[70] Revealingly, in 1989 Reagan said:

He wasn't a tax-and-spend Democrat; during the past sixty years there have been only eight scattered years when the federal budget was in balance and four of those years was under Truman. *I think he and I were in tune on a lot of things about govern-*

ment and I think if he had lived longer he might have come over to the other side like I did. [Emphasis added.][71]

While Reagan rarely crusaded for expanded government programs, this glowing endorsement of a man whose biggest domestic priority was expanding those programs offers an important indication that Reagan's conservatism was not as reflexively anti–New Deal as that of many other conservatives.

Reagan's later success in winning over loyal Democrats was presaged in these years. Reagan's love of Roosevelt and choice of Truman over Wallace and Dewey mirrored exactly the political movements of the working-class Catholic voters who became known during his own presidency as "Reagan Democrats." These voters had elected FDR four times, and they provided Truman's margin of victory in his come-from-behind win over the Republican Tom Dewey. Wallace generated virtually no enthusiasm in working-class Catholic neighborhoods—he received a mere 2.4 percent nationwide and ran best in urban, Jewish neighborhoods and rural Scandinavian counties in the Upper Midwest.[72] The intra–New Deal battle ended in a landslide victory for Truman's reformist interpretation of FDR's heritage.

The 1940s ended with Reagan firmly in the ascendant Truman Democratic camp. He had begun to encounter many of the things he would later cite as reasons for his political move: Communist subversion, high marginal tax rates, and intransigent bureaucracies. He also had formed lasting friendships with many conservative Republicans with whom he regularly had good-natured but intense political discussions; some, like the businessman Justin Dart and the actor and future US senator George Murphy, would become his biggest backers when he came over to their side in the 1950s. But none of these experiences had so far moved Dutch Reagan one iota. He entered the 1950s as loyal a Democrat as he was in the 1930s. The story of why he split from the Democrats in that later decade explains how he remained a child of the New Deal even when he became the Democrats' most potent adversary.

CHAPTER 2

RONALD REAGAN, ALL-AMERICAN

To this day, Ronald Reagan is known among his conservative acolytes as "the Gipper." This nickname comes from his portrayal of the Notre Dame football halfback George Gipp in the 1940 film *Knute Rockne, All-American*. Gipp, as portrayed by Reagan, is a talented, decent young man whose untimely death on the eve of a crucial game leads to Reagan's most-remembered line as an actor: "Someday when the team's up against it, breaks are beating the boys, ask them to go in there with all they've got, win just one for the Gipper." In conservative circles, "win one for the Gipper" has come to mean fighting even harder to show loyalty to Reagan's principles.

The 1950s are when most conservatives think Reagan's principles changed from those they abhor to those they love. Conservatives who genuinely want to win one for the Gipper, then, should be extremely interested in what Reagan said and did during this crucial period, as it is in these times that he formulated his ideas clearly and set the stage for his rapid emergence as conservatism's last, best hope after Barry Goldwater's electoral thrashing in 1964.

Reagan's wife Nancy echoed the idea that understanding this period is crucial if we want to understand Reagan. "All of his ideas or thoughts were formulated well before he became governor or certainly president," she said in 2000.[1] If we want to know what those ideas were, then, we must examine what he said while he was formulating them.

Others before me have argued that Reagan changed political allegiance more than he changed political ideals. The author of the most widely praised biographies of Reagan, Lou Cannon, a journalist from California, wrote that Reagan was "an undoctrinaire conservative. The conventional wisdom 'He had once been a Liberal. He now was a Conservative.' is wrong."[2] Another early biographer, Bill Boyarsky, goes further, saying, "In 1947, when he was a Democrat, his ideas didn't sound much different from his pronouncements as a conservative Republican twenty years later."[3]

Neither man, however, quite grasps what Reagan actually believed in either stage of his life. Boyarsky has a superficial understanding of Reagan's views and proclaims he was as antigovernment in 1947 as he presumes him to have been in 1967, a man as wedded to voluntarism and opposed to government programs earlier as later. Cannon sees a bit deeper, noting that Reagan never rejected the primary programmatic legacies of the New Deal. But he fails to find a principled thread tying Reagan's earlier and later selves into a complete whole, instead ascribing Reagan's undoctrinaire conservatism to a pragmatic, deal-making nature that allowed him to recognize what could be changed and what was not up for discussion. Cannon leaves open the possibility that in Reagan's heart of hearts, his transformation had been much more complete and thorough than Reagan himself ever said.

The Reagan biographer Stephen Hayward comes much closer to the mark when, in his *The Age of Reagan*, he slyly notes that Reagan's thought was much closer to Franklin Roosevelt's than is commonly believed.[4] That's also what I discovered when I dove into this period with gusto. Reagan's speeches, the ones that earned him conservative accolades, were always punctuated with clear endorsements of the public New Deal's aims and many of its means. Even when decrying the loss of freedom that he believed was occurring, Reagan continued to argue that the basic Roosevelt-Truman public philosophy was sound.

Instead of criticizing the programs the New Deal Democrats had enacted and that Dwight Eisenhower's Republicans were protecting and slowly expanding, Reagan attacked waste and bureaucratic control. Reagan's basic argument was that under the guise of helping people meet legitimate American aspirations, unelected men and women were slowly reducing the free republic of our inheritance to a planned, socialized state in which average people were no longer their own masters, and even their elected representatives were increasingly powerless to fight back. He never named Henry Wallace's Progressives by name, but the principles he attacked were exactly those that were present in the Progressive Party's platform: the drive for government planning, the end to large-scale, wholly private initiative, and the creation of an extensive redistributive state that was not premised on need or an inability to provide for oneself.

Conservatives who overlook these nuances tend to argue that Reagan came over to their side through some combination of his extensive reading of political and economic tracts during this period, especially those penned by free-market authors. Others cite his sudden postwar encounter with 94 percent marginal income tax rates as a decisive element in his shift to the right.[5] They also tend to say that Reagan's conservatism arose after a vicious battle with Communists trying to infiltrate Hollywood during the late 1940s when he was president of the Screen Actors Guild, and that his personal friendships with the Republican family of his second wife, Nancy Davis, and the conservative General Electric executives who employed him after 1954 led him to see business in a different light.[6] None of these was unimportant, but it's noteworthy that Reagan himself either remained a liberal after these supposedly searing experiences (as was the case after his battle with the Communists and his exposure to the top income tax rate) or that he failed to mention these influences as decisive.

Reagan's own description of his change shows how much continuity remained in his views. In his personal experiences with governmental bureaucrats and in those he heard about traveling about the country, he came to realize that his core values were being threatened. Average, decent people were being told what to do; his own movie industry was being broken up because of governmental lawsuits. He also saw that business need not be exploitative of its workers, as too many businesses had been throughout his youth. None of these experiences shook him from his belief that government could be used for good; they merely convinced him that government in the wrong hands, and motivated by a faith in government power as good unto itself, could be a dangerous force for ill, or even evil.

Reagan's argument, as it congealed in the talks that became known as "the speech," was that Americans could have the economic and physical security they craved and the freedom they deserved. Liberals would overlook his support of economic security as much as conservatives would in their appreciation (or deprecation) of his views, but the voters who would end up championing his cause were wiser. "He really isn't like a Republican," his biographer Lou Cannon quotes one worker as saying. "He's more like an American, which is what we really need."[7] By the eve of his nationally televised coming-out party in 1964, he had become what he would remain for the rest of his life: Ronald Reagan, all-American.

Reagan started the 1950s as much of a New Deal Democrat as he had always been. Actively supportive of the Democratic nominee for US Senate in California in 1950, he remained loyal to his party for many years thereafter. It's true that he supported the Republican Dwight Eisenhower for president in 1952, but he had been part of a group that had asked the World War II hero to run as a Democrat in the campaign's early stages. Eisenhower had encouraged such a call by not stating which party he supported throughout the early postwar period. When he told America that he was a Republican, Reagan— like millions of average, working-class Democrats across the country— stayed loyal to the general. As Reagan wrote in his autobiography, "I decided: If I considered him the best man for the job as a Democrat, he still ought to be my choice."[8]

Reagan's support for Ike wasn't blind. He said in a letter shortly after the election that he thought Eisenhower impressed less, and his Democratic opponent, Adlai Stevenson, impressed more, as the campaign went on.[9] And he had nothing but contempt for Ike's running mate, California senator Richard M. Nixon:

> Pray as I am praying for the health and long life of Eisenhower because the thought of Nixon in the White House is almost as bad as that of "Uncle Joe." Let me as a Californian tell you that Nixon is a hand-picked errand boy with a pleasing facade and naught but emptiness behind. He has been subsidized by a small clique of oil and real estate pirates, he is *less than honest* and he is an ambitious opportunist completely undeserving of the high honor paid him.[10]

But even if he wasn't yet a Republican, Reagan did back Ike twice as a "Democrat for Eisenhower."

Ike's own views show why a New Dealer like Reagan could back him. Unlike many Republicans, Eisenhower was not opposed to the core principles of the public New Deal. His views, which in his later autobiography, *Mandate for Change*, he would label as "Modern Republicanism," acknowledged that the social peace and the sense of economic security the New Deal had provided were crucial elements of a modern state.[11] Eisenhower would not merely preserve what had been enacted under Democratic presidents; he expanded Social Security benefits and coverage, created the first national disability insurance program, started the Interstate Highway System, and extended the first federal aid to K–12 education in the form of the National Defense Education Act. In effect, Eisenhower offered a conservative interpretation of New Deal principles.

Liberal Democrats wanted more, but Americans were satisfied: they reelected Ike in 1956 with a landslide 57–42 percent victory over Adlai Stevenson, an improvement over his already hefty 55–44 percent defeat of Stevenson in 1952. To this day, Ike is one of only four presidents (Andrew Jackson, Lincoln, and FDR are the others) who won the popular vote by 10 percent or more in two consecutive elections.

Eisenhower's two victories were fueled by strong support from

Democrats like Reagan. In the Northeast, Ike increased the Republican share of the vote in Catholic areas by as much as 30 percent in 1952, and he increased his share of the northeastern Catholic vote even more in 1956.[12] Similar trends were found in Catholic areas in the midwestern industrial states bordering the Great Lakes and in French Catholic southern Louisiana. According to Kevin Phillips, a political analyst, "once Eisenhower had proved that a Republican administration did not jeopardize the economic gains of the middle class—most of whom had risen under the auspices of the New Deal and World War II—the party was able to profit enormously from Catholic preference for Republican anti-communism abroad and social conservatism at home."[13]

Eisenhower made even greater gains throughout the South, but the cause for that was more complex. White southern political loyalties had been set in stone for the most part since the Civil War. Areas that had wanted their states to remain in the Union supported Republicans while the rest of the old Confederacy backed Democrats. The latter trend increased after blacks, who had supported Republicans because of their role in ending slavery, were largely disenfranchised (along with many poor whites in some states) after 1890 because of Jim Crow laws. By the early 1930s, the southern states with the largest share of African Americans in their populations gave Roosevelt between 75 and 98 percent of the vote. Democratic support in other southern states was only slightly less strong, averaging between 65 and 69 percent.

This changed, however, after the Democratic Party endorsed a strong platform plank in favor of a federal civil rights act at its 1948 convention. Many southern Democrats were conservatives who favored a more restrictive interpretation of the New Deal. They had remained Democrats primarily because of the party's opposition to using federal power to repeal Jim Crow and improve living conditions for African Americans. The passage of this plank meant they no longer felt they had a home in the Democratic Party.

These Democrats chose to fight. They followed South Carolina Democratic governor Strom Thurmond, who ran for president on the States' Rights Party ticket. He was on the ballot in fifteen states, including all eleven states from the former Confederacy. Thurmond won only four states in the Deep South with heavy black populations, but he pulled votes away from Harry Truman throughout the region.

Eisenhower was no racist, but it was clear that he was less enthusiastic about moving quickly on civil rights legislation than the Democrats' 1952 nominee, Illinois governor Adlai Stevenson. Democratic strength dropped significantly throughout the South, allowing Ike to carry four southern states outside the Deep South, the first time any southern state had backed a Republican nominee since 1928. Ike improved his performance throughout the South in his 1956 rematch with Stevenson, adding another two southern states to his column, including Deep Southern Louisiana.

It is difficult to know how much of Eisenhower's support was due to his embrace of the New Deal consensus and how much was a negative expression of opposition to Democratic civil rights policies. Intense debate still rages as to what the shift of southern white loyalties to the GOP means. Liberals and progressives tend to argue that race was behind much if not all of the shift, while conservatives and Republicans tend to argue that race had been the only glue that held southern conservatives to the Democrats for decades. Once that glue was dissolved, this argument runs, ideology reasserted itself and conservatives stopped being a house divided between two parties.

The truth probably lies somewhere in between both views, but it is hard to argue that Ike's lack of opposition to the FDR legacy wasn't a significant part of his appeal. Barry Goldwater twelve years later would be much more opposed to federal civil rights legislation than Ike, but he was also much more opposed to FDR's legacy. Outside the five Deep Southern states where blacks were most numerous, Goldwater received well less than Eisenhower's 1952 share of the vote.

Ike's conservative-tinged New Deal sympathies may have thrilled a popular majority, but they angered a small but intellectually rigorous minority. Disaffected anti–New Dealers began to coalesce in Ike's first term around a small, seemingly quixotic magazine founded by a young, pugnacious Yalie whose prior claims to fame had been authoring books

attacking his alma mater and defending the Communist-baiting senator Joseph McCarthy. *National Review* would become Ronald Reagan's
favorite periodical, and its founder, William F. Buckley Jr., one of his
best friends, but the man and his magazine started as loud critics of
Eisenhower's "dime store New Deal."

Buckley's view then, and that of the many anti–New Dealers who
called themselves conservatives, was that the very edifice of the New
Deal was contrary to constitutional and traditional principles. His famous mission statement for *National Review* identified conservatives as
opponents of the New Deal and said:

> It is the job of centralized government (in peacetime) to pro-
> tect its citizens' lives, liberty and property. All other activities
> of government tend to diminish freedom and hamper progress.
> The growth of government (the dominant social feature of this
> century) must be fought relentlessly. In this great social conflict
> of the era, *we are, without reservations, on the libertarian side.*[14]
> [Emphasis added.]

The New Deal's acceptance of state power was intrinsically threatening, and cooperation with it meant following the rest of the world
down the long, dark road to a centralized planned society.

At the end of this road lay not the New Jerusalem of a socialist utopia but the hell on earth of a Communist state. "A boot stamping on a
human face—forever" was how the author of *1984*, George Orwell, described communism;[15] Buckley in *National Review*'s mission statement
called it "the most blatant force of satanic utopianism."[16] Buckley and
his followers often felt they were fighting a doomed battle to save humanity from this scourge, but believed it was their obligation to "stand
athwart the tide of history, yelling 'Stop!'"[17] This stand included fighting the extremely popular president and war hero. The "Eisenhower
program," Buckley wrote, is "an attitude, which goes by the name of
a program, undirected by principle, unchained to any coherent idea as
to the nature of man and society."[18] *National Review* refused to endorse

Ike for reelection in 1956 even though there was never any thought he might lose.

Barry Goldwater followed Buckley in this critique of Ike. He starts his bestselling 1960 book, *The Conscience of a Conservative*, with explicit attacks on Eisenhower and Nixon for their acceptance of the New Deal.[19] He marks the Eisenhower-sponsored National Defense Education Act for extensive and specific criticism, arguing that it was unconstitutional despite the apparent need for improved science education after the Soviet launch of the first human-built earth satellite, Sputnik, in 1957.[20] Conservatism in the mid-to late 1950s was defined by a staunch to expanding federal power at home, regardless of the justification, the need, or popular support. Backing Eisenhower may have been a sign Reagan wasn't fully of the Left, but it was no early indication that he had fully embraced the Right.

There is little indication Reagan was embracing much of anything in the mid-1950s. His political involvement dropped off markedly after 1952. He headed the campaign for the reelection of Fletcher Bowron as the mayor of Los Angeles in 1953, but otherwise didn't do much politically until he emerged in the later part of the decade as a speaker before conservative groups.[21] This may be attributable to his marriage to Nancy Davis in March 1952 and the birth of their daughter, Patricia, later that year. His movie career was also in terminal decline during this period, and he had to take to the road to support his new family, first as emcee of a stage show in Las Vegas in 1953, and more permanently when he joined General Electric in 1954 as the host of a television drama anthology, *General Electric Theatre*. Part of his GE responsibilities involved traveling across the country to GE's many plants to talk about his Hollywood experiences and to represent the company. Since Reagan was afraid to fly, this meant he spent long stretches of the year away from home on trains. He would have had little time to be active in politics even if he had been so inclined.

More important, however, this is the time when he stopped thinking of himself as a Democrat and started to entertain the notion that he was a conservative and a Republican. Since he reappeared at the end of the decade as an active conservative commentator, even though Nancy had given birth to a son, Ron Jr., in 1958 and he had two young children at home, we should presume that Reagan's lack of political involvement had more to do with his ongoing change of heart and less to do with constraints on his time. What he thought during the time between 1953 and 1958, then, is of crucial import to understanding him.

Despite this, there is virtually no contemporaneous information about his thinking and what changed his mind. He gave a speech in 1952 and another in 1957 that show portions of what would become his worldview, but for the most part there are no letters, no speeches, and no newspaper or magazine articles from this time by him or anyone who knew him that touch on his change of heart. Thus, we must rely on after-the-fact explanations, his two extant speeches, and the speeches and interviews he gave after 1956 to understand the essence of Reagan's conservatism.

Writing decades later, Reagan took great pains in his autobiography to paint his 1950s conversion in as rosy as terms as possible. He wrote that he first started having doubts about liberalism in the early 1950s, citing his experiences with wartime bureaucrats, a four-month stay filming a movie in Labor-governed London, and his exposure to Communist infiltration of Hollywood as forces that started to wean him from his belief in government intervention.[22] Since these experiences loom so large in the Reagan transformation story, it's worth exploring a bit what actually happened in each.

The first experience supposedly happened during Reagan's service as an officer in World War II. Despite his age—he was nearly thirty-one years old when the Japanese attacked Pearl Harbor in December 1941—Reagan was called up to active duty because he had enrolled in the army reserves in the mid-1930s while working in Iowa as a sportscaster. He had avoided having his poor eyesight detected upon signing up, but now that there was a shooting war going on, the army would take no chances on someone so nearsighted that he had to wear thick glasses when not filming. Reagan was therefore assigned to stateside duty and eventually assigned to a Los Angeles–based unit that spent the war making films to boost morale for the home front. As he tells it, late in the war he felt he needed to dismiss a less-than-competent secretary. Bureaucrats from the War Department, however, told him it would be easier to promote and reassign her than to fire her because of civil service protection.[23]

This was the second time Reagan says he experienced what he interpreted as bureaucrats protecting their own turf. His father, Jack, had found work running Lee County's relief programs in 1932, and then had moved on to running the county's new, New Deal–funded Works Progress Administration office in 1933. His job was to try to find temporary work for the unemployed. But the men themselves started to decline the offers, as taking part-time work made them ineligible for other relief programs that provided a more steady income. Reagan later interpreted this as proof that "the first rule of a bureaucracy is to protect the bureaucracy."[24]

Neither experience, however, seemed to move Reagan at the time. He was, as we have seen, relentless and passionate in his defense of the New Deal during the 1930s despite his father's experience. And he came out of the army dedicated to such a strong brand of liberalism that he knew he was "still being called a Red in certain Hollywood circles."[25] In hindsight he might have recalled these incidents and seen how they confirmed his new perspective, but at the time they did not alter his political views.

His stay in England (from November 1948 through March 1949) also does not seem to have moved his contemporaneous political views. There's no denying that Reagan did not like the England he found. Wartime rationing and price controls were still in effect, leading to widespread shortages of food and a lack of the sort of creature comforts most Americans took for granted. The air was sooty with the famous London coal-streaked fog, which would disappear for good only in later years. There was no central heating, and fuel rationing meant the cold, damp English winter affected every facet of his stay from the movie set (many actors got colds from working in the poorly heated soundstage) to his hotel.[26] He even took the extreme step of writing the head of the studio, Jack Warner, humorously but pointedly detailing the many difficult, uncomfortable moments that were relieved only by the generous distribution of "YOUR cash."[27]

Reagan would later say this brush with "womb-to-tomb utopian benevolence" had shown him how the welfare state sapped the will to work.[28] But at the time this trip seems to have had little effect on his views. He campaigned actively for the Democrat Helen Gahagan Douglas in 1950, was considered as a Democrat for Congress in 1952, and argued in favor of New Deal liberalism with friends and acquaintances alike for years thereafter. Again, while his time in London clearly bothered Reagan, it is quite a stretch to say it changed his politics.

The final experience he mentioned was quite important and thus bears extensive examination. After his discharge, Reagan joined a host of liberal organizations because "he was 'hell-bent' on saving the world from Neo-Fascism."[29] Among them were the American Veterans Committee and the Hollywood Independent Citizens Committee of Arts, Sciences, and Professions (HICCASP). In the course of his involvement with these and other groups, Reagan expressed the then-common belief among liberals that Nazism and fascism had arisen in Europe in large part because of unemployment and economic discontent. Large expansions of government power and programs were, in his view, necessary to prevent "home-grown fascists" from "realiz[ing] their dreams of a strongman government in America."[30]

Unlike some in these groups, however, Reagan was always consistent in attacking "the menace of the complete left."[31]

They, too, want to force something unwanted on the American people, and the fact that many of them go along with those of us who are liberal means nothing because they are only hitching a ride as far as we go, hoping they can use us as a vehicle for their own programs.[32]

The solution to this, for Reagan, was simple: liberals needed to affirm their belief in the American form of government and private enterprise. His political coming of age began when he discovered just how many people in the organizations he had joined could and would not permit those groups from making such mom-and-apple-pie affirmations.

The most important of these episodes came in the summer of 1946 at an HICCASP meeting. FDR's eldest son, Jimmy, was a member and aware of Communist involvement in the group. He proposed that the Executive Committee issue a resolution in favor of private enterprise and the American Constitution. To Reagan's shock, many members vociferously opposed this, with some shouting that they would prefer Russia or the Soviet Constitution to America.[33] While Reagan was part of a small group to try to work out a compromise resolution, the effort ultimately failed in large part because of the refusal to explicitly condemn communism. Saddened and wiser, Reagan followed Roosevelt, the Oscar-winning actress Olivia de Havilland, and others and resigned from HICCASP.[34]

Shortly thereafter, Reagan played a leading role in turning back a more serious attempt by Communists to infiltrate Hollywood. An organization called the Conference of Studio Unions (CSU), a group consisting of nine smaller and distinct unions, started to try to break other studio unions away from the larger, more powerful International Alliance of Theatrical Stage Employees (IATSE).[35] One such effort was the CSU's attempt to attract the small, 350-member union of set decorators. IATSE refused to recognize this move, and the resultant battle over union jurisdiction threatened to break out into an industry-wide strike by all unions, a move that would shut Hollywood down.

While the specifics regarding Communist involvement in the CSU effort remains disputed to this day, there is significant evidence that many leaders in the CSU were either Communists or were working in league with Communists. Reagan increasingly spoke out in meetings of the Screen Actors Guild against supporting a strike in support of the CSU. As a result, he was appointed to a special committee to address this dispute. His leadership in opposition to what he saw as a Communist-inspired attempt to take over the movie industry's labor unions led to a threatening phone call. The caller told him that if he re-sisted the CSU's efforts, a group would come and "fix his face"—throw acid in it—so that he would never act again.[36] Reagan was licensed by the police for months thereafter to carry a loaded pistol in a shoulder holster for self-protection.

Reagan successfully kept SAG and other unions out of the CSU plan, helping to lead to its demise. A grateful union rewarded him by electing him in March 1947 to the first of many terms as its president.

While crucial to understanding Reagan's future path, this experi-ence did not swing Reagan from left to right as is often claimed. Its pri-mary immediate importance was to awaken Reagan to the tactics and determination Communists employed. The searing fight confirmed him in an intense, lifelong opposition to communism and the Soviet Union, but at the time intense anti-Communist sentiments were com-mon in the Democratic Party. Indeed, the question of whether com-munism was an inherent and implacable foe of the United States was a primary factor in the division between Truman and Wallace in 1948. The Democratic Party remained open to fierce anti-Communists for many years thereafter. It was only with the rise and increasing domina-tion of the party by the neo-Wallaceite New Left—which the nomina-tion of George McGovern in 1972 symbolized—that anti-communism of Reagan's variety became unwelcome in Democratic ranks. Had the intensification of his opposition to communism been the only or even the major item he changed his mind on, Reagan could have joined the many future members of his administration, such as UN Ambassador Jeane Kirkpatrick, and fought the battle against communism within the Democratic Party until well into the Carter administration in the late 1970s.

Reagan's activities in 1948 show how little his encounters with communism changed his views on domestic policy. His public stance against communism in America's most visible industry immediately made him a national public figure. Important newspapers like the *Chi-cago Tribune* asked for his views on how to fight communism. The House Un-American Activities Committee, then at the height of its influence, even subpoenaed him to testify in an investigation into the Communist infiltration of Hollywood. Despite these high-profile opportunities, nothing Reagan said or did demonstrated any change in the opinions he had expressed before these events.

In both cases, Reagan gave a strong defense of civil liberties, opposing efforts to ban the Communist Party ("Tomorrow it may be the Democratic or the Republican Party that gets the ax").[37] His *Tribune* interview also reiterated his previous views regarding the importance of liberalism to America's future, saying "the only logical way to save our country from all extremists is to remove conditions that supply fuel for the totalitarian fire."[38] Later that year, Reagan made a national radio address on behalf of the International Ladies' Garment Workers' Union supporting Truman's election and decrying "Republican inflation" and excessive corporate profits.[39] Reagan would never again be accused of being a Red, but his move to the political right remained many years in the future.

Something did happen then, though, that would start to push Reagan away from the Democratic Party: the government's 1948 victory in an antitrust suit against the movie industry. In *United States v. Paramount Pictures, Inc.*, the Supreme Court held that the movie industry's ownership of movie theaters, and the requirement that only those theaters could show their first-run films, violated the Sherman Antitrust Act of 1890.[40] These practices had meant that studios could ensure their films would be aired before the public; it also allowed them to pay less in theater-rental charges than if they had to compete to rent screen space. This gave studios increased profitability and economic security, which gave in turn allowed them to place actors, writers, and directors under contracts, thereby guaranteeing their ability to produce films quickly and at relatively low cost.

Reagan had been the direct beneficiary of what was called the "studio system." He had been signed to a contract by Warner Bros. in 1937 on the basis of one screen test, and was then given dozens of B-level films to act in within his first couple of years in California.[41] Thousands of actors were in Reagan's position, given some measure of economic security by the contracts, even if many of those agreements were tilted heavily in favor of the studios. Similar levels of security were given to others employed by the industry.

These contracts came at a price, however. The studio controlled the ability of an actor to make a film—the studio could both deny the actor the right to work for another studio and control which films the actor appeared in. The same multiyear contracts that gave aspiring actors security prevented stars from fully benefitting from their fame if they did hit it big. As one might expect, stars came to resent this system, at it both lowered their wages and gave them less freedom to work as they saw fit.[42]

Unlike his first wife, Jane Wyman, Reagan never hit it big enough to experience the downsides of this system. His career, on the rise in late 1941 from well-reviewed roles in *Knute Rockne* and *Kings Row*, was seriously damaged by his wartime military service.[43] He had been surpassed in the acting pecking order by the time he was discharged in late 1945, and his career went into a slow and steady decline as both the quality and the quantity of his parts shrunk.

The government's antitrust victory came at a poor time for the studios. Television became a significant competitor by the early 1950s; combined with the reduced profits and increased risks associated with dismantling the proscribed practices, studios began cutting the number of films they made and reducing the number of contracts they gave. Reagan's was one of the contracts reduced in scale and remuneration.

By 1953 Reagan was financially on the ropes. He had been divorced by his first wife in part because of his heavy political involvement, and his second wife was an actress even lower on the totem pole than he.[44] With a newborn in the house and heavy debt from land purchases he had made during more fruitful economic times, Reagan needed to make a living. The answer to his financial problems, becoming the host of a television show sponsored by General Electric, also gave him the exposure to life outside Hollywood that changed his politics.

Part of Reagan's deal was that he would also travel the country in the company of a GE executive, Earl Dunckel, and give speeches to

GE plants. Starting in August 1954, Reagan was on the road almost a third of the year giving talks.[45] Initially they were about only his life in Hollywood, but by 1956 Reagan started to include references to the industry's travails with the antitrust suit and with local efforts to censor movie content as "a kind of warning to others."[46] Let's allow Reagan to take it from here:

> Well, after I began to include these remarks in the speeches, an interesting thing happened: No matter where I was, I'd find people from the audience waiting to talk to me after a speech and they'd all say, "Hey, if you think things are bad in your business, let me tell what is happening in my business. . . ."
>
> I'd listen and they'd cite examples of government interference and snafus and complain how bureaucrats, through overregulation, were telling them how to run their businesses. . . .
>
> From hundreds of people in every part of the country, I heard complaints about how the ever-expanding federal government was encroaching on liberties we'd always taken for granted. I heard it so often that I became convinced that some of our fundamental freedoms were in jeopardy because of the emergence of a *permanent government* never envisioned by the framers of the Constitution: a federal bureaucracy that was becoming so powerful it was able to set policy and thwart the desires not only of ordinary citizens, but their elected representatives in Congress.[47]

Reagan's life had taken a dramatic and fateful turn.

His GE experience influenced his political outlook in another crucial way: it disabused him of the notion that large businesses were usually in the wrong. Uniquely for companies in that time, GE's chairman, Ralph Cordiner, ran a decentralized business that gave individual plant directors significant power and authority.[48] Cordiner, with the assistance of his vice president for labor, Lemuel Boulware, also tried to treat workers well enough that they wouldn't want to follow confrontational unions.[49] That doesn't mean GE's plants weren't unionized or were free from conflict, but it did mean that workers were treated as human beings rather than parts no less disposable than the machines they operated. Reagan saw both of these approaches in practice and began to think that business could be humane and that labor could work in a genuine partnership with management.

Something else was going on that likely was noticed by Reagan: Democrats started to campaign on a softer line toward the Soviet Union. The 1956 Democratic presidential nominee, Adlai Stevenson, proposed eliminating the peacetime draft and negotiating with the Soviet Union to end nuclear weapons testing and lower defense spending. Other liberals denied the existence or the extent of Communist spying within the United States, going so far as to question whether the events Reagan had experienced were examples of Communist subversion as he believed. Reagan never questioned these people's motives or sincerity, but he did increasingly come to think that mainstream liberalism was hopelessly naive when it came to Communist tactics and intentions.

Most observers agree that by 1956, Reagan had stopped privately defending New Deal liberalism.[50] For a number of reasons Reagan remained a registered Democrat for another six years, but in his mind he was turning away from the Democratic Party. His public speeches increasingly focused on politics, the threat to freedom, and the need for ordinary Americans to retake their government and recommit it to the promises of the founding. What most observers consider his conservative conversion was nearly complete.

It is here when the public trail begins to pick up in earnest. No copies of Reagan's speeches from the mid-1950s seem to have survived in print or audio form, but a number of his talks from after 1956 do. Biographers and analysts uniformly cite Reagan's invocations in this period against the power of government and the bureaucracy, his increasing criticism of the progressive income tax, and his cries that freedom was at risk at home and abroad if people did not mobilize to retake their government. These broad themes were spoken primarily by the political right at this time. But one should never take what someone else says at face value when access to the original source is available. Curious as to what I would find, I traveled to the Reagan Presidential Library to listen and to watch the newly minted "right-winger" when he was only beginning to emerge into the public eye.

The Reagan Library is a beautiful, California-mission-style building set on a hilltop in the suburban Simi Valley. The setting is serene and the research library is even quieter. As I entered and was set up for my encounter with Reagan's formative period, the archivist in charge of the audiovisual collection warned me to be prepared for a different Reagan than I was used to. He was specifically referring to his rapid, energetic speaking style, so much quicker and passionate than the warmer, grandfatherly tones many associate with his presidential utterances. But he may as well have been referring to his ideas.

Reagan's post-1956 speeches are a fascinating blend of conservative warnings about the dangers of increased governmental power and communism and explicit acceptance of most of the procedural and programmatic legacy of the New Deal. In talk after talk, he both inveighed against a government that regulated and taxed too much *and* endorsed the post–New Deal expansion of federal power that helped the poor and the common person live more comfortable lives. The result was a compelling, spellbinding, and wholly original approach to the problems of 1950s and early 1960s America.

Reagan made this work by making the bureaucracy, not the New Deal, the focus of his assault. He paraded example after example of bureaucrats issuing or enforcing regulations that appeared to defy common sense but forced honest Americans to do something harmful or objectionable.[51] He chronicled the government's attempts to compete with private enterprises and detailed the high salaries many government officials made. The result was a government that was taking 31 percent of the national income in taxes but was primarily serving its own interests, not those of people on whose behalf it claimed to govern.[52]

The progressive income tax was a particular focal point for criticism. Contending that it was the invention of Karl Marx, Reagan argued that high marginal tax rates constituted "avowedly confiscatory discrimination against incentive and initiative."[53] He assailed the 91 percent top rate of tax, but spent more time detailing the high marginal tax rates levied on those with middle or slightly higher than middle incomes. At a time when the average family made slightly more than $6,000 a year, he attacked the fact that a family making $8,000 a year was in the 34 percent bracket and one earning $12,000 faced a 43 percent marginal rate.[54] Even then, the average individual, not the most successful one, was the person Reagan primarily addressed.

The result was a threat to American freedom itself. Time and again Reagan would argue that history shows that "any time the tax burden of a country is 25 percent or more" the free enterprise system is in danger.[55] Even Congress seemed powerless to stop this bureaucratic power grab. Reagan told his audiences of his visits to Congress, in which congressmen would freely tell him they had little power to control the bureaucracy or question its budget priorities. Unless the American people woke up and mobilized to retake power soon, the last, best hope of man on earth might pass from history.

It is easy to see from these passages how liberals and conservatives alike could view Reagan as a threat or a hero. The liberal who believed that increasing federal spending and power were essential would see an implacable foe, while the conservative who opposed the same proposals would see an invaluable ally. Liberals in particular could hear echoes of FDR's nemesis, Herbert Hoover, in Reagan's warning. Hoover's 1932 speeches in opposition to Roosevelt struck many of the same themes about how larger government power threatened the loss of American freedom. Hoover even advanced the argument that free enterprise would be threatened if overall taxation rose above a particular level (Hoover placed the danger point at 16 percent of national income).[56] Both sides in the dispute that would come to shape American politics for the next half century could reasonably come to their own version of the same conclusion: if Reagan opposed the expansion of federal power and high levels of taxation with such passion and vigor, he must be on or opposed to my side.

Those views ignore, however, how intricate Reagan's argument actually was. By making unelected bureaucrats the enemy, Reagan left open the possibility that elected officials could exercise power responsibly. By making governmental control and planning the primary evils to be feared, he left open the possibility that government—even the federal government—could do some things well that would help rather than hinder traditional American values.

Reagan's failure to attack most specific government programs begged this question even more. By making popular control of government rather than strict adherence to the Constitution's doctrine of enumerated powers the solution, he left open the possibility that the government that would result would continue to do many of the things promised by Roosevelt, Truman, and Eisenhower. In short, the attention-getting critiques that most observers then and now paid attention to were only half of the story. The real issue was how far Reagan would extend those critiques.

Reagan's speeches always included a long section after the critiques that addressed these questions. They would always include sentences that made clear that his argument did not extend to programs that sought to alleviate poverty, give people economic security, or provide educational opportunity. In short, he was not attacking the principal achievements of the New Deal; he was attacking only the sort of excesses that characterized the state-centric interpretation of the New Deal made by followers of Henry Wallace.

His 1958 speech to the California Fertilizer Association makes this crystal clear.[57] In the speech, after launching his broadsides against high taxation and bureaucratic control, Reagan took on the Veterans Administration and the proposal to establish Medicare. In each case he distinguished what was on offer from what would be legitimate programs to help people in need. His criticism of the VA was against giving $100-a-month pensions to World War I vets "whether they need it or not." His critique of Medicare was that it would be an unnecessary "free lunch" that gave everyone the same plan despite the fact that increased coverage of private health insurance and pensions were giving millions of seniors access to medical care. "How many [Medicare proponents] are really concerned with taking care of a need," he said, "or are simply doing it because they believe in government doing all these things?"

Reagan then turned to a staple of his talk, the blanket assertion of a principle of what would constitute legitimate government action. When I heard this iteration of it, I was so taken by its scope and its precision that I played back the tape repeatedly for fifteen minutes so I could transcribe every word. Here is what Reagan said:

> Certainly no thinking American would dispute the idea that there should be an economic floor below which no American should be allowed to live. In the last few decades we have indulged in a great program of social progress with many welfare programs. I'm sure that most of us in spite of the cost wouldn't buy back many of these projects at any price. They represented forward thinking on our part.

The New Dealer or the Modern Republican would find these statements uncontroversial. Indeed, FDR had said something similar in fireside chat 5: "In a land of vast resources no one should be permitted to starve." But there were, in fact, many thinking Americans who did dispute that idea and were willing to buy back these projects at any price. They called themselves conservatives.

Reagan's lines were not simply throwaways that he ignored when evaluating specific policies. Consider public universities. The large, multicampus systems we know today were in fact the brainchild of state-level New Dealers and Modern Republicans. The 1950s were when the modern, giant systems were beginning to be built. They were then often, as in Reagan's California, tuition free, funded wholly by the taxpayer. Conservatives who were primarily interested in limiting taxation and public power might have been expected to resist or oppose the significant expansion of public higher education then under way. Not Reagan.

Reagan specifically endorsed this expansion in his 1957 commencement address to his alma mater, Eureka College. "We have a vast system of public education in this country, a network of great state universities and colleges and none of us would have it otherwise," he told the graduates.[58] Reagan's fear was not that these institutions would drive the taxpayer into penury; it was that some people would "urge expansion of this system until all education is by way of tax-supported institutions." "No one advocates the elimination of our tax-supported universities," he said, but eliminating private education would threaten academic freedom "for when politics control the purse strings, they also control the policy."

This passage demonstrates what is clear throughout his speeches, that Reagan aimed to preserve freedom and not simply to oppose government. High taxation was a problem, but government control that threatened to replace self-government with imposed conformity was the biggest problem. He told the graduates what he often said to his audience:

> There are many well-meaning people today who work at placing an economic floor beneath all of us so that no one shall exist below a certain level or standard of living, and certainly we don't quarrel with this. But look more closely and you may find that all too often these well-meaning people are building a ceiling above which no one shall be permitted to climb and between the two are pressing us into conformity, into a mold of standardized mediocrity.

Conservatives of that era often believed that the very programs that "placed a floor" under people were the ones that built the ceiling of taxation that pressed people into conformity. Reagan disagreed, arguing that taxes could be significantly reduced by cutting useless programs and budgetary fat.[59]

Reagan separated from conservatives in another important policy area, the role and power of organized labor. America's politics and economy were much different then. Large-scale manufacturing was the economy's lynchpin. Outside of the conservative South, the US workforce was heavily unionized. These private-sector unions (public employees had not yet won the right to join unions) formed the Democratic Party's political backbone. They provided the financing for its campaigns and the organizational muscle behind its efforts. Union members also provided the bulk of Democratic Party voters in non-southern states, much as management and nonunionized employees formed the bulk of Republican voters.

These facts made labor policy a key matter of partisan political combat. Democrats had used their power in the 1930s to pass the Wagner Act, a bill that forced management to collectively bargain with unions that had been supported by a majority of the firm's employees. The act also required all employees of a unionized firm to join the union whether they wanted to or not. While battles between unions and management covered a host of other issues, this requirement was a focal point of intense debate between the two sides. Since union members were required to pay dues to belong, anything that affected how many people paid those dues was hotly disputed.

Republicans moved quickly to undo some of the prounion elements of the Wagner Act when they regained control of Congress after the 1946 elections. With the support of conservative southern Democrats, they passed the Taft-Hartley Act over President Truman's veto. Among other things, Taft-Hartley permitted states to opt out of the requirement that all employees join a union in an organized company. Subsequently, passing these state-level laws—which conservatives called "right-to-work" bills—became a top priority.

Reagan had been a staunch union man in his New Deal days, heading SAG for six years between 1947 and 1952. Despite his movement away from loyalty to the Democratic Party, Reagan never abandoned his support for labor's right to organize. This extended to right-to-work laws: Reagan opposed these as governor even though they "include . . . a certain amount of compulsion as regards to union membership."[60]

This belief became highly relevant in 1958 as conservatives and employers successfully placed initiatives that authorized right-to-work laws on the ballots in four states, including California. The battle was particularly intense there, as Senator William Knowland, a favorite of Buckley's *National Review*, made Proposition 18 a primary issue in his effort to become governor. Knowland wanted to run for president and indeed had been encouraged by Buckley to do so in 1955 when it looked as though Eisenhower would not run for reelection because of his health.[61]

Despite Reagan's fear of government power and the support of his supposed ideological allies and employer, Reagan opposed Proposition 18. He explained why in a November 1958 radio interview.[62] His experience with SAG led him to think a union shop (the term for an arrangement in which employees are required to join a union as a condition for employment) was fair. Reagan opposed a closed shop, which is a system that forces employers to hire new employees only from the ranks of the unions, saying that established a monopoly and that "monopoly is wrong in all its forms." But union shops did not infringe on management's right to hire whom it chose and hence were fair.

Reagan's view again prevailed. All four initiatives went down to defeat, three (including California's) with over 60 percent voting no.[63] Knowland's presidential ambitions also were dashed as he lost by a 60–40 margin to the man Reagan would go on to defeat in 1966, the Democrat Pat Brown.

This seemingly minor election would prove to have major consequences for Reagan. National conservatives were left leaderless by Knowland's defeat. They cast about for a new leader, and soon found one: Barry Goldwater. But for Knowland's defeat to Brown, Reagan's rocket to stardom in support of Goldwater's 1964 presidential bid might never have happened.

Reagan's opposition to right-to-work did not mean he unquestioningly backed the union agenda. In his November 1958 interview, he noted that GE had "enlightened management-labor relations" that "[treated] employees as customers."[64] The company used the phrase "corporate citizenship" to describe its approach, an idea Reagan said had not existed among management before the 1930s. Quoting the legendary labor head Samuel Gompers, he contended that "labor and management must be partners" and that there was no longer any room for purely confrontational labor tactics. He also argued that too many union decisions were being made solely by the leaders without directly consulting the members. Reagan's views on labor policy, as on so many other things, did not fit neatly into the "left versus right" paradigm that was beginning to take shape.

Reagan's philosophy also differed from the conservative right's in what he did not say. Conservatives of the time often spoke of how the Constitution was being violated by the federal government. Indeed, the leading conservative grassroots organization of that day was called Americans for Constitutional Action.[65] They contended that the Constitution was intended primarily to limit congressional power and that Congress could legitimately legislate only over matters that had been expressly delegated to it in Article I. Labor relations, farm aid, welfare programs, aid to education, urban renewal, and a host of other post-1932 federal programs were not expressly included in Congress's Article I powers, and therefore could not be legitimately be addressed by Congress without a constitutional amendment.

Reagan never made this argument the center, or even a significant portion, of his creed. His argument was not that the people were, through their representatives, doing things they were not permitted to do. Instead, he contended that the people themselves were being ignored by the unelected, and that the proper remedy to big government was the restoration of popular control. His view of the Founders' philosophy was simple: "Government should only do those things that the people can't do for themselves."[66] In this he followed his idol FDR, who often cited or quoted Abraham Lincoln for the same proposition.[67] Following this principle meant that he could enthusiastically support "forward-thinking" social programs that most conservatives thought were unconstitutional usurpations of states' or individuals' rights.

Reagan's philosophy was pretty much set by the late 1950s. He would increasingly identify as a Republican and never again campaigned for a Democrat, but he did not change the basic core of his politics. He would be on the right in the context of the debates of his time, but he always presented himself as what he was: a disappointed former Democrat who still believed that government could give people a hand up without placing its hands too firmly on them.

This was clearly on display in the 1960 election. Ike's vice president, Richard Nixon, was preparing his own run for the White House and in doing so wrote a letter to Reagan after receiving a copy of a speech Reagan had given in New York City in May 1959.[68] Reagan had never been a fan of Nixon's, but he responded graciously in a note dated June 27.[69] Within a month Nixon had made international news when he engaged in an impromptu debate with Soviet premier Nikita Khrushchev on the virtues of their two systems. Reagan never discussed this episode publicly, but it must have been music to his anti-Communist ears. He wrote Nixon in early September congratulating him on his performance, a note that started a lifetime connection between the two that was sometimes warm, always respectful, and in which Reagan was usually supportive of Nixon's political ambitions.[70]

Reagan jumped into the 1960 campaign with enthusiasm. He wrote Nixon again in July 1960, stating how he was appalled at the convention acceptance speech of Nixon's Democratic opponent, John F. Kennedy.[71] Reagan wrote that Kennedy's speech was a "frightening call to arms" for the expansion of federal government power. He offered his services to Nixon as a surrogate speaker, noting that he had been giving versions of the talk Nixon had approved of the year before "in more than 38 states to audiences of Democrats and Republicans." Nixon took him up on the offer, leading Reagan to give hundreds of speeches on his behalf. According to his autobiography, he even told Nixon he was going to register as a Republican but remained a Democrat at Nixon's request because his efforts would "be more effective" that way.[72]

What seemed obvious to Reagan—that Nixon would make a good president and Kennedy a bad one—was not to Buckley and other conservatives. Richard Nixon had been a model "Modern Republican," a man whose voting record in Congress had been squarely middle of the road and who offered anti–New Deal conservatives little if any hope that the federal behemoth would be tamed. Their fears had been only exacerbated by an agreement Nixon made right before the GOP convention with the liberal Republican governor of New York, Nelson Rockefeller. Meeting in secret in Rocky's lavish Fifth Avenue apartment, Nixon defused a potential Rockefeller challenge for the nomination by hammering out a compromise on the platform. The compromise, labeled the "Compact of Fifth Avenue," moved the GOP significantly to the left, calling for expanded federal programs for civil rights, medical care for the elderly, expanded farm programs, and federal aid to education.[73]

The Right erupted in horror. Barry Goldwater denounced the agreement as a "surrender" and "the Munich of the Republican Party."[74] Conservatives on the GOP Platform Committee tried to derail the proposals. In the end, with all the power of the establishment and the vice presidency behind him, Nixon could secure the committee's passage of the compromise by only a 50–35 margin.[75] In the general election, many conservatives refused to back Nixon even at the expense of electing Kennedy. Buckley said Nixon would be "an unreliable auxiliary of the right" and *National Review* refused to endorse him.[76] Other conservatives heeded Barry Goldwater's call to reluctantly back Nixon while preparing to make the GOP more reliably conservative. "Let's grow up, conservatives," Goldwater told delegates after the Platform Committee had backed the compact. "We want to take this party back, and I think some day we can. Let's go to work."[77] Reagan, however, shared neither this dismay nor this reluctance.

Reagan continued to support Nixon after his defeat even though many conservatives continued to oppose him. He told his longtime pen pal, Lorraine Wagner, in July 1961 that he had declined an offer to run for California governor, an office that Nixon was seeking, because "I don't think I'm right for the part."[78] We don't know who asked him, but in the Republican primary, most conservatives backed Assemblyman Joe Shell rather than the former vice president. Shell waged a bitter battle against Nixon for the GOP nomination. Nixon won 2–1, but many angry conservatives refused to back him in the general election because he had denounced the John Birch Society and refused to pledge to cut the state budget.[79] Reagan, however, was not one of them. Even though Reagan actively participated in a conservative-backed primary challenge to the very liberal Republican incumbent, Thomas Kuchel, he was not involved in Shell's more serious challenge to Nixon.[80] Reagan spoke on Nixon's behalf in the general election, even giving an election-eve televised speech on Nixon's behalf.[81]

Reagan backed someone else in 1962: John Rousselot, a staff member of the John Birch Society, and a candidate for Congress. He also finally made the full leap over to the Republican Party, reregistering as a Republican in the spring, and increased his national speaking efforts, spreading his gospel farther and farther afield.

His speeches in the early 1960s maintained the same form as those from the late 1950s, albeit with a new focus on foreign policy. He often started his 1960s talk by condemning communism, telling the Phoenix Chamber of Commerce, for example, that "the number one problem in the world today is the ideological struggle with Russia."[82] He then went on to identify a shared characteristic between liberalism, socialism, and communism. This core connection, which Reagan identified as a belief in government as a solution to social problems, led liberals to be unable to see Communist tactics for what they were and hence made them unreliable leaders in the fight for world freedom.[83] He told the Conservative League of Minneapolis that liberals were naive in rejecting the existence of the internal threat from communism simply because there were actually few American Communists.[84]

The increasing drive among liberals to find accommodation with the Soviet Union also bothered Reagan. He thought it would give up on the billion people "enslaved behind the Iron Curtain."[85] Opposing "peace without victory," Reagan urged Americans to stand fast in the struggle against communism.

The 1960s Reagan reprised his earlier critique of progressive taxation and high tax burdens. At the time, federal marginal tax rates ranged from a low of 20 percent to a high of 91 percent. Contending there "is no moral right" to rates above 50 percent,[86] Reagan backed the Herlong-Baker tax bill, which would have reduced rates for all individuals and corporations, leading after a five-year period to federal marginal rates between 15 and 47 percent.[87]

Many see his steadfast, if not strident, anti-communism and his critique of high federal tax rates as proof of Reagan's belief in pure conservatism. It's true that in these matters he was firmly allied with the conservative movement. But the remainder of his talk dealt with domestic policy issues, and here we see that Reagan maintained his firm commitment to the governing principles of the public New Deal even while he was criticizing its excesses and the way the principles of the 1948 Progressive Party were increasingly becoming Democratic Party dogma.

Reagan approached domestic policy in the 1960s through the same lens he had previously: "need." If someone needed federal help to live a dignified life outside poverty, then Reagan was for the program in question. If, however, government help or control was extended to people who did not need it, he was not only opposed to it, but he questioned the motives of those who supported such efforts. The fact they would use "humanitarian" arguments to propose mandatory programs for people who did not need it, Reagan contended, was proof that the programs themselves were intended to introduce regimented socialism rather than to address genuine social ills.

He extended this analysis to a host of federal programs, existing or proposed.[88] The Veterans Administration filled three-quarters of its hospital beds with non-service-related injuries. Farm policy forced farmers to plant or not to plant according to government dictate while farmers outside government programs were doing just fine. Proposed federal aid to K–12 education was unneeded, he said, because there was no proof local districts and states were unable to meet the need for more schools and higher teacher salaries. Public housing was fine in theory, but in practice people who weren't poor were increasingly permitted to live in taxpayer-subsidized dwellings. In each case, Reagan accepted that some government action to help people in need was OK, but programs that did not meet legitimate needs went too far.

Reagan made this case most forcefully in regards to federally subsidized health care. He acknowledged that the poor would need the government's financial help to get the care they needed. Indeed, his statement in this regard was characteristically bold and comprehensive: "As one conservative let me say any person in the United States who requires medical attention and cannot provide for himself should have it provided for him."[89]

To that end, he enthusiastically backed a recently enacted bill called the Kerr-Mills Act. That bill provided federal funds to states to set up programs to pay for medical care for poor senior citizens. That, plus efforts by the American Medical Association and Blue Cross and Blue Shield to develop more comprehensive proposals to use public funds to help poor people pay for health insurance premiums, covered the genuine need. To continue to push for a compulsory government insurance program for all senior citizens whether they already had private insurance or not—the program we know as Medicare—without even waiting to see if Kerr-Mills and private efforts succeeded in making health care affordable for all, was proof for Reagan that health care policy was merely an excuse to socialize medicine and America.[90]

Reagan remained firmly against government planning. Many of the specific lines he would utter in his famous October 27, 1964, televised address on behalf of Goldwater began to make their appearance in his regular talks. He told a convention of California Realtors in late 1963, for example, that a planned economy was a liberal goal, and quoted the Democratic senator William Fulbright as saying that our "president is a moral teacher."[91] Reagan excoriated the idea of a planned economy, saying you "cannot control things; you can only control people."[92] Echoing themes he would act on as president, he called for deregulation, tax simplification, ending bracket creep in the tax code because of inflation, and imposing a spending limit that would bar running perennial deficits.

Looking at his views at this time, one can easily see why Reagan would always argue he had not changed. He remained sympathetic to the common American with a firm belief in that person's innate dignity and ability to advance himself if able. He did not waver in his support for government assistance to provide for that person if he was not able to avoid poverty on his own, and to provide publicly financed ways to improve himself by pursuing further education. Reagan still believed that America was a special, unique place that was divinely inspired to give people around the world freedom, dignity, and hope. And he still believed that America needed to be internationally active to protect and extend freedom even if the enemy had changed from fascism to communism. Reagan's politics were much different by 1964, but his core principles had remained intact.

The Democratic Party of 1964 was different, however. While Reagan always underplayed the degree to which Truman Democrats favored larger federal programs than he later endorsed, orthodox Democrats of his youth favored regulation of private-sector excesses rather than government planning. As we saw in the last chapter, this was one of the primary differences between the Progressive Party, which did support planning, and mainstream Democrats. But by the early 1960s even mainstream Democrats endorsed and practiced some degree of social and economic planning.

John F. Kennedy was by no means the most liberal Democratic politician, but his inauguration brought many of these new ideas to power. His economic advisers believed the economy could be managed, heated up and cooled down on command through the adroit application of fiscal policy.[93] Industries could be cajoled, or "jawboned" as the saying went then, by direct presidential intervention into forgoing price increases that they otherwise felt were necessary to their businesses.[94] In the heady optimism of the 1960s, it appeared to some on the left that America's problems could be solved simply by an application of will and knowledge, leading the country toward what Kennedy's adviser Arthur Schlesinger labeled "a not undemocratic socialism."[95]

The Democratic liberal mind-set was described well by the leading political journalist of the age, Theodore H. White. In his landmark book *The Making of the President, 1960*, White described the Democratic view of American prosperity as "a torrent of self-indulgence," a torrent that proper national leadership would dry up and direct to publicly directed ends.[96] The debate between Democrats and Republicans of this era was simple, according to White:

> How were American energies to be used? That was the question. By private enterprise or by public plan? . . . What price good schools, good medicine, good roads, new bridges—at what sacrifice of good meats, louvered windows, new cars, new appliances?[97]

Against this backdrop, Reagan's frequent quote from the man who would become vice president in 1964, Minnesota Democratic senator Hubert Humphrey, that "we don't want a planned society, we want society planning," was merely a sad punch line to a joke many Americans didn't want told.[98]

Republicans and conservatives had tried to hold back this tide to no avail. Eisenhower had thought his brand of Modern Republicanism could gain popular support, but after he left office in 1961 Republicans held only 175 seats in the House and 36 in the Senate. Conservatives argued the Republican defeats were due to accommodation with the New Deal; they would seek to capture the 1964 GOP presidential nomination and mobilize people who had not voted in decades with "a choice, not an echo."[99] The struggle between these factions would consume the Grand Old Party throughout most of 1964, culminating in a fractious and vicious convention fight that saw the conservative favorite, Barry Goldwater, prevail and tell Americans in his convention speech that "moderation in the pursuit of justice is no virtue; extremism in the defense of liberty is no vice."[100]

Reagan would burst upon American politics toward the end of that tumultuous year. He would do so by endorsing the most controversial major-party nominee in almost a century, yet his endorsement would be couched in terms that even those frightened of Goldwater could find comforting. His televised address on Goldwater's behalf was simply a revised version of the talk he had been giving since the mid-1950s. He would endorse Goldwater the candidate, but more important, he would present his own interpretation of the New Deal's promises to Americans for their consideration.

Coaches for both teams in the ideological fight between right and left would from that point forward seek to put a "C" for conservative on the Gipper's helmet. But he would always run on the label he had devised for himself over decades of thinking about politics: "A" for all-American.

CHAPTER 3

"A TIME FOR CHOOSING": A STAR IS BORN

The classic showbiz rags-to-riches story is when an actor goes out on stage an understudy and comes back a star. On October 27, 1964, that happened to Ronald Reagan.

Reagan gave a nationally televised address on behalf of Barry Goldwater that evening. Millions of Americans watched him for the first time. By the end of the half hour, they had a new hero. By the end of the week the nearly broke Goldwater campaign was flush with cash sent by Reagan's viewers. By the end of the year, Goldwater's financial backers were asking Reagan to run for governor of California—and many were already thinking of the next step up.

They had heard Reagan give a version of the talk he had given for the prior seven years on what he called "the mashed potato circuit." As we saw in the last chapter, this talk in all its versions drove home a few simple themes: American freedom was under assault by Communists abroad and by liberals at home. The federal government was taxing, regulating, and commanding away traditional American virtues in violation of the Constitution and beyond all control of the public. The solution to this was for the people to take back control of their government through vocal, political action in both political parties. If the people failed to do this, freedom itself was at risk.

These messages were red meat to a conservative audience that had believed them for a very long time. But, as we have seen, Reagan's message also included many themes inspired by his youthful faith in the public New Deal, which other leading conservatives lacked, ignored, or outright opposed. Reagan's newfound fame was due to his standard, mid-1950s conservative themes combined with his forceful charisma on camera. But it was also due in part—and his ability in later years to succeed where Goldwater and others had failed was due largely—to these unorthodox elements.

A careful review of what became known as "the speech" shows it contained all the standard features of Reagan's regular talk. Tellingly, it also included some original elements that were intended to appeal overtly and covertly to Democrats who still loved Franklin Roosevelt. In this vein, "the speech" contained briefer invocations of the same unorthodox features that made Reagan's conservatism unique. In short, everyone watching that night heard the full Reagan philosophy.

One can understand how unorthodox Reagan's conservatism was only by comparing it with that of conservatism's reigning king, Barry Goldwater. The publication of his bestselling book, *The Conscience of a Conservative*, in 1960 had made Goldwater an overnight conservative hero in much the same way that Reagan's speech made him Goldwater's overnight heir. But in many crucial elements, the philosophy Reagan was selling was not the same one Goldwater was hawking. In its tolerance of federal and state governmental power to advance the ability of the average person to live with comfort, respect, and dignity, Reagan's conservatism was far more activist—and far less opposed to the principles of the public New Deal—than was the Arizona senator's.

Reagan's ideas were different from his mentor's in another, less obvious way. Reagan proclaimed that America was special because it enabled everyone to live according to his or her own choices, but Goldwater's conservatism bore the stamp of a more traditional conservative belief that America was great because it enabled the naturally great to rise. This difference is indeed subtle, but it made all the difference in the world. A person following Goldwater's ideas would be naturally inclined to think people deserved everything they got in life, and that the government's attempt to place a floor under people's standard of living was itself morally suspect. A person following Reagan's ideas, on the other hand, could distinguish, as Reagan did, between government efforts designed to lift up and those intended to pull down.

Goldwater's landslide defeat sent conservatives scurrying back home to determine how they had lost. Could Americans really want what Reagan called "the soup kitchen of the welfare state"? Reagan took an active part in that autopsy, although he said in one postelection speech it couldn't rightly be called an autopsy because the patient, conservatism, wasn't dead.[1] His analysis, though, again demonstrated that his conservatism was different in both its focus and its relationship to the New Deal. He would end 1964 as conservatism's last, best hope, but he would also end the year poised to begin to transform conservatism itself.

Reagan started his speech by stating that he had "been permitted to choose [his] own words and discuss [his] own ideas" in the talk.[2] Reagan is in fact understating his authorship, as he both wrote all of his own speeches and continued to do so throughout most of his public life until he became president.[3] The initial statement also had another, less obvious purpose. It placed the audience's attention on Reagan, not on the man whom he was endorsing. Indeed, Goldwater wasn't even mentioned until the twelfth paragraph and then only in passing. Reagan, who often played supporting roles in his movie career, was clearly going to be the leading man in his own, self-authored show.

With this in mind, it's important to note what came next: Reagan told his audience that he was a former Democrat.[4] This was not a standard feature of his regular speech. Introducing Reagan's prior partisan allegiance into the script early served two purposes. It allowed those Democrats who were watching to see someone like them espouse conservative ideas, and, as important, it gave him legitimacy when he claimed later in his speech that he, and all conservatives, endorsed key philosophical elements from the public New Deal.

After these two innovative elements, "the speech" settled into familiar territory for a mid-1960s conservative. Reagan decried the high tax burden Americans faced. He assaulted deficit spending and low but steady inflation. He argued that America was "at war with the most dangerous enemy that has ever faced mankind in his long climb from the swamp to the stars," communism.[5] And he praised the Founding Fathers for instituting a novel idea, "that government is beholden to the people,"[6] and thereby giving everyone "man's age-old dream, the ultimate in individual freedom consistent with law and order."[7]

These conventional arguments had an unconventional twist, however, in the hands of the former Democrat. As we saw in the last chapter, Reagan's argument was not that the New Deal programs were themselves wrongheaded or unconstitutional. Rather, he contended that since their stated humanitarian goals could be accomplished with less sweeping and expensive programs, their authors must have another goal. They must intend to use these programs as bait to attract Americans to adopt the government-planned society long sought by socialists worldwide.

Thus, Reagan could tell his audience that what others said was the key choice in the election, "between a left or a right," was wrong. "There is no such thing as a left or right," he said, "there's only an up or down."[8] The real issue in the election, the real options that Americans had to choose between, was "whether we believe in our capacity for self-government or whether we abandon the American Revolution and confess that a little intellectual elite in a far-distant capital can plan our lives for us better than we can plan them ourselves."[9] Here again we see echoes of Reagan's liberal period. This is exactly what he said was the main issue for the world and for America during his "hemophiliac liberal" days of 1947 and 1951 as he condemned communism, fascism, and Nazism for believing that only a few were better fit to rule the people rather than the people themselves.[10] It was also how Roosevelt defined the challenge facing America in 1932, the reason Americans needed a new deal.

If the problem was government planning and not government action per se, then some government actions on humanitarian grounds could be legitimate. And it is to these things Reagan turned after a lengthy critique of how the government's farm, public housing, and welfare policies cost too much and delivered too little.

Reagan starts this, the most important part of his speech, by attacking liberal bias.

> Anytime you and I question the schemes of the do-gooders, we're denounced as being against their humanitarian goals. They say we're always "against" things—we're never "for" anything. Well, the trouble with our liberal friends is not that they're ignorant; it's just that they know so much that isn't so.[11]

Reagan then delves into Social Security, saying, "We're for a provision that destitution should not follow unemployment by reason of old age, and to that end we've accepted Social Security as a step toward meeting the problem."[12] After arguing that Social Security should be run as the insurance program it was promised to be, with decent rates of return and the ability to name one's beneficiaries, he turns to the proposed Medicare program. Before criticizing that, he says, "We're for telling our senior citizens that no one in this country should be denied medical care for lack of funds."[13] In two short lines, Reagan incorporated into conservatism the main popular element of the public New Deal: the willingness to use government power to prevent people from experiencing undeserved poverty.

His appeal even included a subliminal echo of Franklin Roosevelt. His line about liberals "knowing so much that isn't so" is funny, witty— and plagiarized. It had been uttered by FDR, quoting Woodrow Wilson using that identical phrase, in his fireside chat 7 nearly thirty years before. We don't know whether Reagan intended this homage to Roosevelt or whether his photographic memory simply recalled the line.

But the implicit message is clear: the problem isn't that the New Deal's aims were wrong, it's that the Democratic Party is no longer pursuing those aims at all.

Reagan's specific attack on Medicare shows this clearly. His complaint was against the compulsory, one-size-fits-all model that "forc[es] all citizens, regardless of need" into the same program.[14] This, according to Reagan, was evidence that the Democrats who proposed these things were really using Harry Truman's party to advance Henry Wallace's agenda.

He was much more specific about this in his regular talk, as we saw in the last chapter. There Reagan argued that the continued efforts to pass Medicare after the passage of the Kerr-Mills Act, which gave federal financial aid to the states to set up programs allowing the poorest 10 percent of seniors to pay their medical bills, "without even giving it time to see if it worked," was proof that Medicare's proponents were primarily interested in extending government control instead of helping people in need.[15]

The next two items Reagan said conservatives were for continued in this vein. He said conservatives were for the United Nations, but opposed to its structure, which let small nations outvote larger ones like the United States and its allies.[16] He said conservatives were for foreign aid, which was initiated by FDR during the war and extended to peacetime by Truman in the Marshall Plan, but against the waste, extravagance, and bureaucracy-creating results the current program had created.[17] Again, it was not the principles of the public New Deal that Reagan objected to; he opposed the manner in which those principles were either ineptly implemented or intentionally subverted.

Reagan followed this with another appeal to Democrats who supported the New Deal but opposed socialism. He raised the example of the 1928 Democratic presidential nominee, Al Smith, who left the Democratic Party in 1936 charging that the "Party of Jefferson, Jackson, and Cleveland" was being led down the path of "Marx, Lenin, and Stalin." "To this day," Reagan argued, "the leadership of that Party, *that honorable Party*" (emphasis added) has continued to pursue socialism rather than American ideals.[18] Any Democrat listening to these words would hear a clear message: If the battle in this election were really between Roosevelt and Hoover, I'd be with you— and with FDR.

It is here, three-quarters into the speech, that Reagan launches into his only significant defense of Barry Goldwater. What he says is telling. In essence, he defends Goldwater against the charge that he is merely a modern-day Hoover. For Reagan, Goldwater was a man who practiced New Deal principles voluntarily by establishing profit-sharing and medical insurance plans for his employees. "He took 50 percent of the profits before taxes and set up a retirement program, a pension plan for all his employees."[19] Reagan said Goldwater set up a child care center for the children of mothers who were his employees. He told stories of how Goldwater had supported the sick, flown medicine to Mexico to help flood victims, and interrupted his campaign—to his aides' displeasure—to "sit beside an old friend who was dying of cancer."[20] In Reagan's telling, Goldwater's most important attribute was his compassion, not his defense of liberty.

Reagan ended his defense of his old friend by saying "this is not a man who could carelessly send other people's sons to war."[21] This line was important, as the Democrats were effectively attacking Goldwater's intense anti-communism as an erratic willingness to engage in unnecessary wars. In response to Goldwater's backers, who had coined the phrase "In Your Heart, You Know He's Right" to encourage closeted backers to cast the vote they allegedly wanted to, Democrats said "In Your Guts, You Know He's Nuts."[22] They had even resorted to dramatic fearmongering.

In early September the Johnson campaign had aired perhaps the most famous campaign ad in history, the "Daisy" spot. In it a small girl picks the petals off of a daisy while counting. When she reaches nine, her image freezes and a male voice takes over, saying "ten." The male then counts down to zero, at which point three nuclear explosions are shown. The commercial ends with another voice saying, "Vote for President Johnson on November third. The stakes are too high for you to stay home."[23] Without mentioning Goldwater's name, the Johnson campaign had made its point. One man might start a nuclear war, the other will not.

Reagan used this defense to launch into his final section of the speech, an appeal for a vociferous anti-communism. He argued that the Democrats' approach amounted to appeasement, a fear of riling an adversary that was already bent on America's defeat. Such a road would guarantee war, Reagan argued, because ultimately America would have to fight or surrender.

Here Reagan delivered some of his most stirring lines, lines that more than anything else probably sealed his future fate as conservatism's savior. They bear repeating in full:

> You and I know and do not believe that life is so dear and peace so sweet as to be purchased at the price of chains and slavery. If nothing in life is worth dying for, when did this begin—just in the face of this enemy? Or should Moses have told the children of Israel to live in slavery under the pharaohs? Should Christ have refused the cross? Should the patriots at Concord Bridge have thrown down their guns and refused to fire the shot heard 'round the world? The martyrs of history were not fools, and our honored dead who gave their lives to stop the advance of the Nazis didn't die in vain. Where, then, is the road to peace? Well it's a simple answer after all.
>
> You and I have the courage to say to our enemies, "There is a price we will not pay." "There is a point beyond which they must not advance." And this—this is the meaning in the phrase of Barry Goldwater's "peace through strength."[24]

Fifty years later, even after Reagan's resolute courage brought the free world to that peaceful victory over communism that those of us who followed him only dreamed of, those words still move me beyond compare. How they must have sounded to the adults who heard them in my infancy I can only imagine.

Reagan then launched into his famous conclusion, one that both included phrases he had uttered many times before and one new one. Again, in full:

You and I have a rendezvous with destiny. We'll preserve for our children this, the last best hope of man on earth, or we'll sentence them to take the last step into a thousand years of darkness.[25]

Reagan had uttered variants of the last sentence many times before, but the first sentence was new. It was quoting Franklin Roosevelt's call from his 1936 renomination acceptance speech that the New Deal generation had "a rendezvous with destiny." Reagan's appropriation of one of the Great Communicator's most famous phrases could not have been an accident. The entire speech had been directed at one audience, the men and women who, like Reagan, had once believed the Democratic Party was their vehicle but now had to face the truth that it had become wedded to another cause. The phrase "you and I" makes this appeal personal: he is addressing each Democrat who loves America to join him in the crusade, not to leave what he or she had believed behind but to have the courage to fight for what he or she believed. Over the next sixteen years, in speech after speech, Reagan would renew this personal appeal to his kinsmen—and they would respond.

For decades commentators have presumed that this speech on behalf of Barry Goldwater in fact was simply a restatement of the senator's craggy conservatism. George F. Will even wrote that Reagan's victory in 1980 showed Goldwater had won, "it just took 16 years to count the votes."[26] But Will also wrote later that Americans were indeed conservatives; with Reagan's win, they had voted to conserve the New Deal.[27] This latter statement is closer to the truth, as a close comparison between Goldwater's and Reagan's conservatisms shows.

The two men agreed on a lot. They both valued freedom. They were both fervent anti-Communists. They both believed the government, especially the federal government, taxed and regulated too much. Despite this, they disagreed on three very important matters.

Reagan and Goldwater disagreed fundamentally on what was wrong with the federal government. For Reagan, the problem was that a permanent bureaucracy had wrenched control of the people's government from their hands. This had led to a steady expansion of governmental power, as bureaucrats concerned more with their livelihoods than with the well-being of their fellow citizens pushed to do more and more. For Goldwater, the people's government itself was at fault. Goldwater's critique was that the Constitution had established narrow powers for the new Congress. The people's representatives could only legitimately deliberate, tax, and spend in the execution of these powers. Anything else was, without a constitutional amendment, an improper and illegal usurpation of power from the people and from the states.

Goldwater believed these powers were extremely narrow. "The *legitimate* functions of government are . . . maintaining internal order, keeping foreign foes at bay, administering justice, [and] removing obstacles to the free interchange of goods."[28] (Emphasis in the original.) The Tenth Amendment to the Constitution reinforces this limitation of the federal government's power by recognizing, in Goldwater's words, "the States' *jurisdiction* in certain areas. States' Rights means that the States have a right to act or *not to act*, as they see fit, in the areas reserved for them."[29] (Again, the emphasis is Goldwater's, not mine.) Accordingly, in this view, the federal government has no right, regardless of what the people and their representatives want, to legislate, tax, or spend in relation to a host of matters that had by 1960 become commonplace for it to act: welfare, health, education, labor relation, agriculture, and housing, to name only a few.

Reagan's regular statements that some degree of federal action to place a floor underneath Americans' standard of living were entirely inconsistent with Goldwater's view of the Constitution. For Reagan, the problem with federal government programs was that they cost too much and had expanded beyond their legitimate, humanitarian goals. For Goldwater, those programs were inherently illegitimate. Goldwater had even started *Conscience* with an explicit criticism of former president Eisenhower and former vice president Nixon because they were willing to use the government to solve human problems.[30] These programs were to Goldwater illegal no matter how well they were run or how legitimately needy their recipients were.

This sharp difference on the problem's cause necessarily resulted in a sharp disagreement on the actions that should follow. Reagan urged citizens to lobby their congressmen, get involved, and try to take back control of their government by pruning the programs back to their proper scope and size. Goldwater urged immediate action to repeal as many of these programs as possible as soon as possible, and for such efforts to continue until the entire constitutional violation was mended. This led to his famous statement that

> I have little interest in streamlining government or in making it more efficient, for I mean to reduce its size. I do not undertake to promote welfare, for I propose to extend freedom. My aim is not to pass laws, but to repeal them. It is not to inaugurate new programs, but to cancel old ones that do violence to the Constitution, or that have failed in their purpose, or that impose on the people an unwarranted financial burden.[31]

Reagan's standard speech regularly focused on waste and inefficiency rather than the heart of a program itself. He always called for ways to run something more cheaply, to use the knowledge of businesspeople instead of bureaucrats to ensure that legitimate recipients got what they needed and taxpayers got what they deserved. For Goldwater, this was simply wasted effort focusing on a symptom rather than the disease itself.

Their third important difference is subtle but crucial. It has to do with the fundamental nature of America's promise. As we have seen, for Reagan that promise was one made to every man and woman regardless of talent or disposition. To be sure, he valued those with ambition and initiative. His standard speech in the late 1950s said that America could place a floor under every American's standard of living without placing a ceiling above those who sought more. But he judged America by its ability to let the common person thrive.

Goldwater scoffed at such notions: "We have heard much in our time about 'the common man.' It is a concept that pays little attention to the history of a nation that grew great through the initiative and ambition of uncommon men."[32] And again: "A society progresses only to the extent that it produces leaders that are capable of guiding and inspiring progress."[33] Given these presumptions, it is only natural that Goldwater could write that "we are equal in the eyes of God but we are equal *in no other respect*."[34] (Emphasis in the original.) America was great for him because it enabled the exceptional to climb mountains, not because it enabled the average to live their lives according to their wishes, no matter how humble their aims or deep the valley in which they chose to dwell.

Contrast Goldwater's views with the words Reagan chose as his epitaph. You can see them yourself, etched on the headstone above the grave he and Nancy share behind his presidential library in the stark, dry beauty of the California he so dearly loved. "I know in my heart that man is good, that what is right will eventually triumph, and there is purpose and worth in each and every life."[35]

I was surprised, as perhaps many of you are, when I first saw those words on his gravestone. I had eagerly awaited my visit to his graveside, wondering which of his incredible accomplishments were immortalized for all to recall. Thomas Jefferson had chosen his authorship of the Virginia Bill of Rights and the creation of the University of Virginia, for example, to color eternity's view of his life. But Reagan chose something less selfish, but more important.

In a way, this is his interpretation of the Apostle Paul's famous line from 1 Corinthians 13:13: "And now these three things remain, faith, hope, and love. But the greatest of these is love." "I know in my heart that man is good" (faith). "That what is right will always eventually triumph" (hope). "And there is purpose and worth to each and every life" (love). I left the gravesite shocked, amazed, impressed, and even more dedicated to discovering who Reagan really was.

These three differences in principle and outlook meant Reagan and Goldwater differed on many important issues. Perhaps the most obvious one regards the role of labor unions. Reagan, a former union head and the only president to date who was a lifetime member of the AFL-CIO, always supported labor's right to organize. He supported this even when it required curbs on the employer's liberty to bargain with unions, as was done in the Wagner Act. As we have seen, he even supported the union shop, an arrangement that forces employees to join a union that is legally empowered to bargain with an employer on their behalf.

Goldwater, on the other hand, strenuously opposed the union shop. In *Conscience* he wrote, "Union shop agreements deny to those laboring men the right to decide for themselves what union they will join, or indeed, whether they will join at all."[36] He "strongly favor[ed] enactment of State right-to-work laws which forbid contracts that make union membership a condition of employment."[37] As we saw in the last chapter, Reagan opposed the California effort even as he was giving speeches nationally decrying the loss of freedom.

They also differed on the manner in which government spending and taxes should be reduced. Reagan always called for cutting taxes first, presenting the government with a set amount to spend and forcing it to cut what it otherwise would not.[38] Goldwater believed the opposite. "I believe as a practical matter spending cuts must come before tax cuts," he wrote in *Conscience*.[39] He feared that cutting taxes "before firm, principled decisions are made about expenditures" would court deficit spending and inflation.[40]

Crucially for our story, the two men differed sharply on government's role in providing support for the needy. Reagan always said that doing so was a legitimate function of government, even as he might have preferred such needs to be taken care of first through private charity and initiative. As his support of the Kerr-Mills Act and public housing shows, he was even supportive of federal government involvement where necessary. Goldwater, on the other hand, was not. Here's what he had to say about "welfare" in *Conscience*:

Let us, by all means, encourage, those who are fortunate and able to care for the needs of those who are unfortunate and unable. But let us do this in a way that is conducive to the spiritual as well as the material well-being of our citizens—and in a way that will preserve their freedom. *Let welfare be a private concern.* Let it be promoted by individuals and families, by churches, private hospitals, religious service organizations, community charities and other institutions that have been established for this practice. . . . Finally, if we deem public intervention necessary, let the job be done by local and state authorities that are incapable of accumulating the vast political power so inimitable to our liberties. [Emphasis added.][41]

Goldwater left no doubt as to how seriously he took this principle. Elsewhere in *Conscience* he wrote:

The only way to curtail spending substantially, is to eliminate the programs on which excess spending is consumed. The government must begin to *withdraw* from a whole series of programs that are outside its constitutional mandate—from social welfare programs, education, public power, agriculture, public housing, urban renewal and all the other activities that can be better performed by lower levels of government or by private institutions or by individuals. [Emphasis in original.][42]

WHY AMERICA WILL CONTINUE TO SPIRAL DOWNWARD

The programs Goldwater identified were in essence everything that had been established since Franklin Roosevelt had been elected with the greatest landslide in American history. Goldwater was, therefore, essentially running to repeal the results of the 1932 election. Decades of prosperity had not changed the American people's minds. He lost by an even greater margin in terms of the popular vote than did Herbert Hoover in the depths of the Great Depression.

Compare these words, and sentiment, dismissive at best of public involvement and inimical to any federal government involvement in

WE HAVE BEEN SPOILED SINCE 1932, AND WILL NEVER GIVE UP 'OUR PROGRAMS' CASE IN POINT, OBAMACARE, SO WE WILL COLLAPSE!

alleviating the plight of the poor, with Reagan's words from 1965 in a talk entitled "The Myth of the Great Society."

> We [Republicans] too want to solve to the best of our ability the problems of poverty, and hunger, health and old age and unemployment. We can put a floor below which no American will be asked to live in degradation without erecting a ceiling over which no citizen can fly without being penalized for his initiative and his effort.[43]

Lest anyone think this was a postelection shift, recall that Reagan had said much the same thing many times in his standard pre-1964 speech. The contrast between conservatism's two heroes on this point cannot be starker. Reagan and Goldwater agreed on much, but they differed a lot on what each knew in his heart was right.

Goldwater's defeat hit the young conservative movement hard. Its hero had been creamed by 22.5 percent in the popular vote and by over 430 electoral votes. Lyndon Johnson's 61 percent of the vote remains to this day the highest percentage of the popular vote a presidential candidate has ever received. Goldwater had carried only his home state of Arizona, by a narrow margin, and five states in the Deep South whose opposition to the Civil Rights Act of 1964 led them to abandon a century of Democratic Party loyalty.

The debacle also hurt Republicans at all levels of government, but it was particularly damaging in Congress. The GOP lost 36 House seats, reducing its share to a mere 140, less than one-third of the total and the smallest the party had held since after FDR's 1936 Depression-era landslide. It lost only two seats in the Senate, but it had held only 34 seats before the election. That puny 32-seat total was also the smallest Republican share of the Senate since 1936. The Grand Old Party was now powerless to affect the course of national policy.

What had happened? Did conservatism have a future?

Reagan played his part in the postelection analysis, offering a characteristically optimistic take. But his words were as unconventional as they were reassuring. They again showed to those who had eyes to see that his conservatism was different.

Reagan's handwritten thoughts were published in a December 1964 issue of *National Review* magazine, then at its height of influence among conservatives.[44] He argued that Goldwater lost only because people "were scared of what they thought we represented."[45] Liberals, Reagan argued, had both "portray[ed] us as advancing a kind of radical departure from the status quo" as well as taking "for themselves a costume of comfortable conservatism." "Unfortunately," Reagan noted, "human nature resists change and goes over backward to avoid radical change."

Of course, Barry Goldwater's own words showed that he *did* advocate radical change. Goldwater had tried to back away from some of his words during the campaign, but there was no mistaking who thought the programs passed since 1932 were suspect and who thought they were just fine. Reagan here passes over Goldwater's genuine extremism in the defense of liberty.

But if Reagan understandably soft-pedaled his differences with Goldwater and other conservatives, he was absolutely right about what would come next. He said that liberals would change from being defenders of the status quo to advocates for a radical expansion of government. "Our job beginning now is not so much to sell conservatism as to prove that our conservatism is in truth what a lot of people were voting for when they fell for the cornpone come-on."

Reagan then ended with a paragraph crucial to understanding both his philosophy and his approach:

In short—time now for the soft sell to prove our radicalism was an optical illusion. We represent the forgotten American—that simple soul who goes to work, bucks for a raise, takes out insurance, pays for his kids' schooling, contributes to his church and charity and knows there just "ain't no such thing as a free lunch."

That last line says more than it lets on. Barry Goldwater had mocked the focus on "the common man" in his magnum opus. In contrast, "the forgotten American" is who FDR had said he sought to represent in 1932. Reagan here is making his intent clear: by not contesting the basic philosophical insights of the public New Deal, conservatives can win back the forgotten Americans who now had been forgotten by the leadership of the very party that had remembered them in the first place.

This approach can work only if conservatism is comfortable with at least the basic philosophy of the public New Deal. Conservatives may differ strenuously with liberals over the scope and size of major government programs, and often differ over the existence of some programs less essential to keeping Roosevelt's and Truman's promises that all Americans should have a respected place at America's economic table. Certainly Reagan viewed the programs that had implemented the New Deal's promises to be too large in either scope or in cost. But make no mistake about it: Reagan was not advocating a return to the Herbert Hoover's GOP or the pugnacious conservatism of Goldwater's *Conscience*. A victorious conservatism had to be of Reagan's, not Goldwater's, flavor.

Conservatism would begin to change in Reagan's direction over the next few years. William F. Buckley, the founder and editor of *National Review*, had famously refused to endorse Dwight Eisenhower's reelection because he was too committed to the existence of the New Deal. After 1964, however, Buckley began to advocate incrementalism in politics. It was only then that he adopted the mantra for which he is still known, that conservatives should support the most conservative electable candidate. His *NR* colleague Frank Meyer also began to move conservatism away from its staunch neolibertarianism into what became known as fusionism. This philosophy held that conservatives of all stripes could disagree about many things so long as they agreed on two: opposition to the rapid expansion of federal government power and staunch anti-communism. The early conservative emphasis on libertarianism was waning.

These changes within conservatism had an important unintended effect. Those who took Buckley's early libertarianism most seriously began to leave the conservative movement, no longer satisfied by what they found there. In 1968 they founded their own magazine intended to compete with *National Review* for thought leadership on the right. *Reason* was inalterably committed to "free minds and free markets," and many of those active in its founding were also instrumental in the founding of a new political party, which would be dedicated to freedom above all else. Thus was born the Libertarian Party and the libertarian movement.

All that was in the future, set into motion by the events of 1964. Of more pressing import for Reagan was a meeting only a few days after his postmortem had appeared in print. In December, a few wealthy, largely self-made conservative businessmen went to Reagan's home in Pacific Palisades. There they asked him to run for governor of California in the upcoming 1966 election. Reagan had been invited to run for public office many times before, both as a Democrat and as a Republican. He had always turned the offers down.[46] But this time he did not, his head perhaps turned by the "heady wine" he had drunk from the excitement generated by his televised address.[47] While it took him over a year to formally enter the race, his willingness to entertain his own candidacy was a turning point. The Reagan Era had begun.

CHAPTER 4

THE CREATIVE SOCIETY, STARRING RONALD REAGAN

R eagan's old movie boss, Jack Warner, had a memorable response
when he heard Reagan was running for governor. "Ronald Reagan
for Governor? No. Jimmy Stewart for Governor, Ronald Reagan
for best friend."[1]

By 1965, however, Reagan's career was no longer restrained by his
former boss's opinion. Like Sylvester Stallone, who vaulted himself to
movie stardom with a self-authored script, the movie *Rocky*, Reagan
had written his own leading role and had found producers willing to
finance the venture. The object of his affection may have spurned his
advances in his film career, but he was finally going to have a shot to
get the girl.

The script, however, had to change as the show went into production. As an after-dinner speaker, Reagan had the luxury of being able to
simply critique what was wrong. In his new role as a candidate, he had
an obligation to answer the questions he had raised. Thus, the period
between 1965 and early 1967 is crucial to understanding Reagan's phi-

losophy. He had the luxury to say anything he wanted. What he chose to say revealed what those who had been watching closely would have expected: his conservatism was less antigovernment and more accommodating to the public New Deal than anything Goldwater or other early 1960s conservatives had ever presented.

In both his campaign and precampaign speeches, Reagan emphasized popular control *of* government, not opposition *to* government, as his primary theme. The problem he attacked was not government per se but how government had grown remote by empowering bureaucrats and how it had started, through the Great Society, disconnecting income from work. None of the major innovations of the New Deal would be repealed or even verbally critiqued; indeed, Reagan always made clear that legitimate humanitarian goals would be honored and maintained.

These themes eventually coalesced into what he called the Creative Society. That society was one in which government had an important role in providing leadership, creating opportunity for its citizens, and taking care of those unable to care for themselves. It would unleash the creativity and compassion of its members, however, by giving individuals and nongovernmental entities the power to create and innovate and by looking outside the bureaucracy for answers when it faced a social problem that required some governmental action. One can see this as a conservative interpretation of the public New Deal or as a fleshing out of Dwight Eisenhower's Modern Republicanism, which Ike had described as one that is "conservative when it comes to economic problems but liberal when it comes to human problems."[2] The fact that Barry Goldwater explicitly attacked Ike's statement in *Conscience* seemed not to matter to either Reagan or his adoring audience.

Reagan's Creative Society was also neither ideological nor partisan. Throughout this period, Reagan argued that differences among Republicans were unimportant compared with the challenge they all faced from the liberals. His words and deeds in this, the dawn of the conservative takeover of the Republican Party, were the antithesis of divisive or confrontational. Moderates and different shades of conservative all had a place at his table.

He also argued that Democrats and independents were welcome. One did not need to check one's party affiliation at the door to enter Reagan's house. Once inside, of course, the host wouldn't object if you wanted to try on another suit of partisan clothes. But it was also OK if one did not. Reagan was seeking to lead a popular revolt, not a partisan one.

This philosophy was on display as early as November 1964. In an election postmortem speech delivered to the Los Angeles County Young Republicans, Reagan made many of the points he raised in his short *National Review* piece. But he also noted that a recent Gallup poll had found four ideas were popular across party lines: prayer should be allowed in public schools, the federal government's power was too great, welfare programs had a demoralizing effect on their recipients, and government corruption was too extensive.[3] These themes, especially the middle two, would feature prominently in his 1966 campaign.

Reagan's broader philosophy of government was more clearly enunciated in a speech he gave in 1965 entitled "The Myth of the Great Society." The speech was given after the massive output of congressional legislation in the wake of the Democratic Party's 1964 landslide. In what would become the largest expansion of federal government power for nearly fifty years, Congress passed bills authorizing a multitude of new programs including Medicare, Medicaid, and a host of antipoverty initiatives that would become known was the War on Poverty. The Voting Rights Act of 1965 was part of this landmark effort, and what would become the food stamps program would pass shortly thereafter. If there was ever a time to make the sort of criticisms Goldwater levied in *Conscience*, this was that time.

Reagan's criticism was much more muted than Goldwater's even as it was quite sharp. Despite opposing Medicare just a year earlier in his televised address, Reagan does not mention its passage directly or indirectly in this speech. There was no call to repeal and replace Medicare. Neither did he attack or even name Medicaid in the wide-ranging address.

Instead, Reagan attacked the War on Poverty. His specific criticism had nothing to do with that war's "humanitarian aims"; with these he had "no quarrel."[4] Instead, he argued that it amounted to a "vast federalization of public life," disconnected income from work, empowered social planners, and enriched an army of highly paid federal government employees whose interest it then became to perpetuate their programs regardless of their necessity. Indicative of this middle-ground approach was Reagan's discussion of public housing. We "should provide adequate shelter for those, who through no fault of their own, cannot provide for themselves," Reagan said. The problem with the Great Society was that it was too broad in its scope, and this failed to induce people to improve themselves.

Reagan continued this approach when discussing urban renewal. While eliminating slums was "a worthy goal," he opposed the liberals' use of eminent domain to take property from one private owner only to resell it to a private developer to build a government-favored project.

Toward the end of his speech he made one of his clearest statements ever regarding his philosophy of government. After arguing that Republicans could not let their enemies divide them into moderate, liberal, and conservative camps in the face of the common foe, he said the united party must run "by standing on principle." The principle he then articulated (which we examined earlier) was not what many of his modern-day defenders would expect:

> We too want to solve to the best of our ability the problems of poverty and hunger, health and old age and unemployment. We can put a floor below which no American will be asked to live in degradation without erecting a ceiling over which no citizen can fly without being penalized for his initiative and his effort.

There is nothing about that statement with which Franklin Roosevelt or Harry Truman would have disagreed, even as they likely would have interpreted it differently than Reagan. Libertarians and staunch constitutionalists, however, could not have agreed with it. Of greater political import, the modern-day followers of Henry Wallace would have vehemently opposed it as being insufficiently critical of the systemic inequities of modern American capitalism. Once again, Reagan's conservatism was inherently grounded in an interpretation of the principles of the public New Deal and focused its criticisms on those who opposed the New Deal from the left.

Reagan spent much of 1965 preparing for his candidacy. Although he did not officially declare it until January 1966, he was interviewing potential campaign consultants much earlier in the year.[5] His choice might have surprised and unsettled some of his more ideological supporters had they noticed: he chose the same firm that had run Nelson Rockefeller's California Republican presidential primary effort just a year before, Spencer-Roberts.

Stu Spencer and Bill Roberts were the deans of the then-nascent field of political consulting in California. They worked only for Republicans in partisan races, but tended both personally and professionally toward the moderate side.[6] They met and interviewed Reagan with trepidation, fearful that he would be a stereotypical conservative, angry and uninterested in pragmatic politics.[7] They instead found an intensely earnest and intelligent man who knew his weaknesses, was willing to learn, and didn't care at all that they had savaged Barry Goldwater in the prior year's race. By their third meeting in the spring of 1965, they were hooked and signed on for the duration.

Reagan knew he lacked knowledge of what state government did, so he agreed to be tutored by two academics hired by Spencer and Roberts. In between his tours of the nation attacking liberalism he also traveled California in what would today be called an exploratory candidacy. He also delved into briefing books the academics and their team put together.[8] Reagan would never become a master of the details of government, but he learned enough that he would understand the basic issues he had to address.

Reagan's campaign stressed the same themes he had previewed in his 1964 and 1965 addresses, starting with his formal entry into the race. His platform was relatively moderate: in a half-hour televised talk he called for a better business climate, a law that would give cities and counties more power to combat crime, and lower property taxes.[9] Reporters at his initial press conference tried to paint him as an extremist, a John Birch Society sympathizer or at least an antigovernment zealot. But Reagan presented the same measured replies he had given previously, refusing to endorse the Birchers and keeping his specific critique of government to a minimum. When asked if he was a right-wing Republican, Reagan demurred, saying, "No, and I don't believe in hyphenating Republicans any more than I believe in hyphenating Americans."[10] He emphasized his campaign could appeal to the "millions of fine, patriotic and sincere Democrats who are concerned about fiscal irresponsibility, excessive taxation, [and] the growth of government" simply by presenting his thoughts and proposed solutions.[11]

His most illuminating answer was to a question about the difference between the Republican and the Great Society approach to handling social problems. Citing "the Jewish book, the Talmud," Reagan said the least desirable way to help people was "the handout, the dole; the most desirable and the most effective is to help people to help themselves."[12] That latter approach, he said, represented "the Republican approach." It might have, although he would learn as governor that some of the most conservative state legislators had a much narrower view of who deserved help and what sort of help government should provide. But it definitely represented the approach Reagan had learned as a teen when he first read the book that led him to become a baptized Christian, Harold Bell Wright's *That Printer of Udell's*.[13]

Reagan first had to win the Republican primary before he could face the Democratic nominee. His opponent was the former San Francisco mayor George Christopher, a man firmly on the moderate side of the GOP. Christopher regularly attacked Reagan for his alleged extremism, arguing that a conservative Republican simply couldn't win.[14] Standing firm on his argument that dividing Republicans was counterproductive, however, Reagan refused to debate Christopher and did not lob similar charges at his foe. The contrast was telling: the moderate was negative and angry, the conservative positive and temperate.

Republican voters, who had only narrowly supported Barry Goldwater in the 1964 GOP presidential primary over the liberal New York governor Nelson Rockefeller by a 51–49 margin, gave the sunny Southern Californian a whopping 65–31 percent landslide in his first race.[15]

Christopher did, however, strike blood once in a very telling moment before the National Negro Republican Assembly's California Convention. While Reagan still refused to debate, Christopher made a presentation to the group directly after one by Reagan and while the first-time candidate was still there. Reagan had told the group that he had opposed the Civil Rights Act of 1964 as a "bad piece of legislation," a statement that Christopher predictably used in his talk to imply Reagan might be prejudiced.[16] This understandably infuriated a man who had been raised to see every person as a child of God. When a delegate stated he was "grieved" by Reagan's position, the political rookie exploded in anger. "I resent the implication that there is any bigotry in my nature," he shouted as he stormed out of the room.[17]

While he calmed nerves that evening by returning to the meeting and apologizing for his outburst, Reagan's positions on welfare, crime, and other issues often left him at odds with the African American community and gave room for the Left to argue he was antiblack. This impression was compounded in 1966 by his views on the Civil Rights Act and his support of a 1964 voter referendum overturning California's newly passed law banning discrimination in housing, the Rumford Act. While civil rights was not a Roosevelt priority in 1932, it certainly was a liberal priority by the end of his four terms. As we have seen, Harry Truman's support for a strong platform plank endorsing civil rights led to Strom Thurmond's anti–civil rights presidential campaign. Was Reagan's opposition to these laws motivated by bigotry, political calculation, or something else? If it was a matter of principle for him, how did he square that with his otherwise very consistent belief that government had a moral duty to act to support the dignity of even the poorest of Americans?

There is no evidence Reagan's stances were motivated by bigotry. Two reporters who covered him from the beginning of the 1966 campaign, Lou Cannon and Bill Boyarsky, defended Reagan against that charge even while disagreeing with his views on the Civil Rights Act and the Rumford Act.[18] Reagan had not only stood up for Eureka College's black football players in the incident noted in chapter 1; he had maintained a lifetime friendship with one of them, William Burghardt.[19] In all of his long years in the public eye, no political opponent, reporter, or biographer ever dug up even a single quote or incident in which Reagan had displayed animosity or prejudice toward blacks. Reagan's blowup was probably motivated by exactly what he said at the time caused it. "Bigotry," he said, "is something I feel so strongly about that I get a lump in my throat when I'm accused falsely."[20]

Nor is there any evidence he took his positions out of political calculation designed to covertly stoke racist support. California had long had less strained race relations than in other states, as the first African American major-league baseball player, Jackie Robinson, discovered when he left UCLA and Southern California in the 1940s. California whites still were often prejudiced, but this fact had not previously been enough on its own to sway voters to support a candidate with whom they otherwise disagreed. This was on display in the 1964 election, in which Goldwater—whose opposition to the Civil Rights of 1964 was a large issue in the race—received over 9 percent less of the popular vote than had Richard Nixon four years before. In the deeply prejudiced Deep South, in contrast, Goldwater ran between 10 and 62 percent ahead of the Nixon—the only states in the nation where Goldwater received a higher share of the vote than Nixon.

Reagan's stances were more likely the result of principle and a startling naïveté regarding the actual lives of African Americans. Reagan had told the Los Angeles County Young Republicans in 1964 that government should protect the rights of all regardless of race or creed, but that "human hearts" could bring this about better than legislation. "We cannot legislate love," he told the crowd.[21]

Reagan was also concerned about the loss of freedom when government, federal or state, dictates the immediate abolition of prejudice. This principle was in evidence in his opposition to the state's Rumford

Act. His concern was that it violated "the right of a man to dispose of his property or not to dispose of it as he sees fit."[22] This "infringement on one of our basic individual rights sets a precedent which threatens individual liberty."[23] Californians overwhelmingly agreed, as they had approved a referendum repealing the Rumford Act by a two to one margin. Nevertheless, the issue was again before the people in 1966 as the state's Supreme Court had invalidated that vote, making the Rumford Act again state law.

It is noteworthy that Reagan always expressed sympathy with African Americans and did not make some of the legalistic or insensitive comments often made on the right in those days. Goldwater had insisted that the Constitution gave the federal government no power to enact laws banning segregation or overturning a state's decision to whom to grant the franchise. Even William F. Buckley Jr., normally considered the epitome of the intelligent conservative, strenuously opposed federal laws designed to empower southern blacks, such as the Civil Rights Act of 1964, on grounds that on occasion veered into racial generalities.[24]

Reagan was able to reconcile his general love of all people with his early civil rights positions because of his lack of personal familiarity with black communities. He had lived in only three states, Illinois, Iowa, and California, none of which had legal segregation at the time he lived there. The first two had only tiny African American populations in the cities in which he had lived, and his life in California was centered on Hollywood and the Westside of Los Angeles, neighborhoods that were then almost entirely white. He had encountered anti-Catholic prejudice in his youth and anti-Jewish prejudice in the movie industry. In both cases he firmly stood with the minority group. But he had never lived in close proximity to black neighborhoods or socialized with groups with a significant black contingent.

As late as 1980, Reagan could look back on his youth as one in which he was completely unaware of racial animosity. During the 1980 debate with Jimmy Carter, he angered his lifelong friend Burghardt, when, in answering a question about civil rights, he declared that in the

1920s most Americans didn't even know they had racial problems.[25] While America certainly did have racial problems then; he probably represented the view of many white Americans in that era who, secure in their racial dominance, faced no significant public outcry to the status quo. Against such a cloistered background, Reagan could easily have believed centuries of racial prejudice could be overcome as easily as his parents had taught him it could.

This accidental isolation led Reagan to be genuinely surprised when he learned as governor how African Americans perceived public matters. As we shall see in the next chapter, Reagan met frequently in his first years as governor with African American leaders and learned how what he perceived as a matter of freedom was perceived by them as a matter of oppression. He quickly muted his support for the repeal or amendment of the Rumford Act, and Reagan never again raised the issue after an attempt to limit the act's scope initially failed in the legislature. Christopher's in-person attack, however, started the perception that Reagan was hostile to blacks.

Racial prejudice may not have been a vote winner in 1966 California, but that does not mean racial tensions were not an issue. Los Angeles had been victimized in the summer of 1965 by horrific riots in the black neighborhood of Watts. The incumbent Democratic governor, Pat Brown, had been out of the country when they started, and in that day before frequent air travel and the Internet he was unable to return or show he was in control of events as the city burned. His lieutenant governor, Glenn Anderson, dealt feebly with the tumult, failing to call out the National Guard to keep order until after most of the looting and mayhem had occurred. Voter anger at this, as well as at rising crime, increasing property taxes, and student demonstrations against the campus administration and the Vietnam War at the University of California at Berkeley put Governor Brown in a tough place as he sought his third term.

Keeping with his mantra that fights between Republicans helped the enemy, Reagan took aim at Brown over these issues even before his primary was over. Staying on message, Reagan drew a sharp contrast between a governor and government that failed to listen to the people and a citizen-politician who would.

Reagan's kickoff speech raised what would in years hence become conservative staples: crime, taxes, and morality. Saying that California's streets "became jungle paths after dark"—another line opponents seized on to allege he was stoking racial prejudice—he called for more power for cities and counties to fight crime.[26] The student demonstrations had begun to spin out of control, sometimes leading to violence and disruption of classes. He criticized the demonstrations and attempts to stop classes at UC Berkeley, arguing that everyone had the right to free speech, including the students who wanted to take classes but were prevented by the campus disruptions from doing so. He later supported a voter initiative that would have restricted pornography sales.[27] The relatively large state budget and correspondingly high tax burden was criticized; notably absent was any mention of specific budget cuts or programs that would be repealed.

Reagan continued to stress these themes throughout the spring, adding a couple as the campaign progressed. He argued against political corruption and the power of special interests, telling Californians that he would take politics out of judicial selection by handing the power to appoint judges to a nonpolitical commission.[28] He attacked the then-common practice of requiring government employees to contribute to the party in power, and also, perhaps surprisingly, supported making California's part-time legislature into a full-time body—with commensurately higher full-time salaries and levels of staff support.[29] After a state senate report accused the UC system of turning a blind eye to Communist infiltration of its ranks, Reagan pledged to create a commission to investigate the charges.[30]

Governor Brown's weak political status had encouraged a significant primary challenger, Los Angeles mayor Sam Yorty. Yorty attacked Brown from his right, making many of the same points on crime and big government as Reagan. While ultimately unsuccessful, the mayor's challenge diverted Brown's attention from Reagan at a time when Reagan was only beginning to become known to the average California voter. Ominously for Brown, Yorty also attracted a large degree of support in white working-class communities in Southern and Central California. He received nearly one million votes—one million people whose general-election votes would decide who won.

Reagan made his aims clear to all immediately after the primary. He told a press conference the following day that "the Yorty people are a target for our attention."[31] He had a witty reply to reporters who said Yorty's vote represented a "white backlash"; it instead had demonstrated a strong "Brown backlash."[32] In this film, Yorty voters were the girl and the leading man would ardently pursue her until he had won her favor.

A more doctrinaire antigovernment conservative would have found this difficult. Such a person, like Goldwater, would have had to live down, distinguish, or reject a host of statements opposing things these voters liked or promoting ideas they scorned. Reagan, as we have seen, was different. He had always maintained even in his most angry, pre-1964 speeches that the goals of the public New Deal were morally sound and worthy. He had always made clear declarations that programs and policies that efficiently promoted those goals were the proper province of government, even in some cases the federal government. His "New Deal conservatism" was fresh, novel, and very appealing.

Governor Brown, like many liberals and conservatives before and after, missed these cues. He tried desperately to use Reagan's support of Goldwater against him and charged that his opponent was just as conventionally conservative. These efforts took two primary forms: tying Reagan to the extreme John Birch Society and charging that Reagan opposed or intended to restrict many popular government programs.

Neither effort was successful, because they had no basis in fact. Reagan had never been a member of the society and had never endorsed its aims. He made clear in a statement that he repeated throughout the campaign that he would not reject the support of individuals associated with the society because their votes would represent their agreement with his philosophy, not his endorsement of theirs.[33] The second attempt failed both because specific charges contrary to Reagan's speeches could be easily denied, but also because Reagan took pains to inoculate himself against the charges by preemptively rejecting some well-known conservative positions.

This approach was clearly on display in his September 9 speech kicking off the fall general election campaign. Reagan reminded Californians he had opposed the 1958 right-to-work initiative and continued to do so.[34] He specifically rejected cuts to the state's unemployment insurance program.[35] He called for strengthening Social Security and restated his long-held belief that those "in need" deserved state-financed welfare.[36] Expenses could be lowered primarily by removing those not in need from the welfare rolls and by employing the talents of businesspeople and other private-sector experts to find ways to reduce the cost of delivering needed services.

All these ideas were fleshed out in a speech that laid out his vision for government, "The Creative Society." Intended to draw a contrast with President Lyndon Johnson's government-expanding Great Society, the Creative Society could have been a paean to private enterprise and charity, a positive and ingenious way to market a Goldwater-inspired conservatism. It certainly lauded individual initiative and action, but what is striking is how little its vision of the government's role differed from that of the public New Deal.

Reagan makes this clear at the outset. His major critique of liberalism had always been, as we saw in the prior chapters, its tendency to place rule by government-selected experts at the heart of American life. These bureaucrats, in Reagan's view, had a tendency to acquire power for its own sake and to mistake their interests for those of the people they purported to serve. Thus, Reagan's speeches always strained to prove that genuine humanitarian interests could be met with much less intrusion, and a much lower cost in terms of both money and relinquished freedom, than the statist methods liberals advocated.

Nowhere in Reagan's long catalog of speeches did he make these points so clearly and so sharply than in the opening paragraphs of the "Creative Society" speech. Let's read those sections in full before analyzing them in detail:

I think it's time now for dreamers—practical dreamers—willing to re-implement the original dream which became this nation— the idea that had never been fully tried before in the world—that you and I have the capacity for self-government—the dignity and the ability and the God-given freedom to make our own decisions, to plan our own lives and to control our own destiny.

Now it has been said that nothing is more powerful than an idea whose time had come. This took place some 200 years ago in this country. But there is another such idea abroad in the land today. Americans, divided in so many ways, are united in their determination that no area of human need should be ignored. A people that can reach out to the stars has decided that the problem of human misery can be solved and they'll settle for nothing less.

The big question is not whether—but how, and at what price. We can't accept the negative philosophy of those who close their eyes, hoping the problems will disappear, or that the questions of unemployment, inequality of opportunity, or the needs of the elderly and the sick will take care of themselves. But, neither should we unquestioningly follow those others who pass the problem along to the Federal government, abdicating their personal and local responsibility.

The trouble with that solution is that for every ounce of federal help we get, we surrender an ounce of personal freedom. The Great Society grows greater every day—greater in cost, greater in inefficiency and greater in waste. Now this is not to quarrel with its humanitarian goals or to deny that it can achieve these goals. But, I do deny that it offers the only—or even the best—method of achieving these goals.[37]

Reagan's words are clear: he plans to interpret Franklin Roosevelt's legacy, not reject it.

Reagan's thought had three central concepts, each of which is on display here. The first was "self-government"; the second, "need"; the third, "dignity." Let's examine each in turn in the context of this passage.

Self-government has a clear but wide meaning for Reagan. It certainly applies to the ability of the people to set the course of their government through elections. We have seen how that idea led him to reject the bureaucratic liberalism that led to social planning. Self-government also had a narrower, personal meaning for Reagan—the capacity of an individual to set his or her individual course through choice and initiative. Certainly no conservative would object to either of these notions.

Reagan's sense of self-government, however, had two other implications to which mid-1960s conservatives did often object. Reagan rarely speaks of limits to the people's power as expressed through elections. Unlike Goldwater and other strict constitutionalists, Reagan did not believe the New Deal was illegitimate because no constitutional amendments had been passed to grant Congress the power to make the decisions it did. For Reagan, it was sufficient that Congress *had* decided—and once it had decided, the only questions were whether it had decided wisely and whether its will was truly being carried out.

Reagan also rarely spoke of individual rights even as he championed individual freedom, and he never made their defense the centerpiece of his public philosophy. Freedom, yes; that he believed was crucial to a person's pursuit of happiness. But the idea of a right that could never be infringed for any reason and under any circumstance even by the wisest and the most transparently democratic election—that concept was alien to Reagan's way of thinking. Accordingly, Reagan was always willing to entertain a host of governmental actions to achieve humanitarian goals, provided that the people and not the self-anointed few were doing the choosing.

Self-government also involved a notion of obligation for Reagan. To govern one's self did not mean, as it often does for libertarians and some conservatives, that one's own choices have moral weight simply because one makes them. A self-governing individual *should* care for his or her community and all of those in it, even—perhaps especially—

those who "through no fault of their own" cannot take care of themselves.

This was what attracted Reagan to Barry Goldwater, the fact that Goldwater did personally undertake his obligations to his employees, his neighborhood, and his community of his own volition. On the level of abstract thought, the two men had important, if subtle, disagreements. Indeed, Reagan once called Goldwater a "fascist SOB" to his face when they were just getting to know one another in the mid-1950s.[38] But on the human level, Reagan could see that Goldwater cared about people and sacrificed money and time to help them. For Reagan, this was true self-government in action.

Of course, not everyone is as noble as Barry Goldwater. As James Madison said in the *Federalist* number 51, "If men were angels, no government would be necessary."[39] Thus, Reagan always recognized that government could and should legitimately act to ensure that every American had sufficient material goods and opportunity such that his or her ability to engage in self-government was real and not simply an empty promise.

Hence his easy acceptance of the second idea "whose time had come," that "no area of human need should be ignored." This was the public New Deal's central teaching, that neither tradition nor constitutional text prevented America's governments, federal or state, from acting to pay attention to those needs. Rejection of this concept formed the heart of Hoover's critique and pre-Reaganite conservatism, and forms the heart of libertarianism today.

Most conservatives and libertarians read those words and see no limitation on governmental power. Reagan, however, disagreed. For him, "need" was an objective, not a subjective, concept. Much as we can know the weight of a block of iron or the height of a man, Reagan believed we could know whether a person "needed" help to live a life of dignity, comfort, and freedom.

This idea was at the heart of his argument in the 1950s and 1960s that so-called liberals must really be socialists. Time and again he showed how their purported aims could be met through less prescriptive, less expensive, and less mandatory approaches. We saw this clearly in prior chapters in his discussion of why he opposed Medicare: since only 10 percent of seniors "needed" help and the Kerr-Mills Act gave them that, the continued pressure for Medicare must mean that Medicare's advocates were using humanitarian ends to justify a massive power grab. They must, Reagan logically deduced, be more interested in the power of the state than in the happiness of the individual. And this belief that the state ought to hold and wield power for its own purposes, he contended, was the central concept that united American liberalism, socialism, and communism, a belief that made the liberal—against his or her own intent—unable to clearly see the Communist threat.

Reagan never defined "need" in his speeches or his private writings. We can, however, get a sense of what he meant by looking at those instances in which he approved of governmental action.

Sometimes those instances were rather narrow. Take, for instance, his oft-repeated statement that society had an obligation to take care of those "who through no fault of their own" could not care for themselves. This phrase always meant at least people who were disabled or physically or mentally unable to work. It also was used to refer to the elderly or the sick. In practice, it also referred to single mothers with minor children, as they were the primary beneficiaries of the AFDC program that was the major "welfare" program in the mid-1960s.

Reagan often, however, made much broader claims for legitimate government action. In the area of medical care, he told an audience in 1962 that "any person in the United States who requires medical attention and cannot provide it for himself should have it provided for him."[40] Lest one think this statement was inspired by the political need to react to the heady liberalism of the 1960s, Reagan repeated and expanded on this sentiment in a private letter in 1979.[41]

We can infer from his discussion of the governmental provision of medical care for the poor that Reagan thought financial need—poverty and near poverty—justified governmental action. This inference starts to get at the heart of Reagan's thinking, as he expressed an identical thought in the context of other programs.

Social Security, for example, was needed to solve the problem of "unemployment caused by old age." He rarely discussed Social Security in detail publicly after 1964, but when he did he always maintained that people who needed it would get it. In private letters he was more direct. He often wrote, for example, that Social Security should always have had a means test.[42] Those who needed it to live on should get it, but those who did not should not.

Reagan also applied the concept of financial need to public education at all levels. He told the libertarian magazine *Reason* in 1975 that "tuition should never be a block to anyone getting an education who could not afford to go the university."[43] Earlier in the same interview he implicitly backed universal public K–12 education. He also noted without argument that society "then extended [public education financing] to higher education because there was a segment of our society that could not get education." His only question with respect to this decision was "why government didn't think in terms of saying, 'We will provide an education for the individual that can't provide for himself, but we'll do it by way of the private sector universities.'"

One could argue that higher education is more of a want than a need. Food to live on, housing to live in, and the money to buy either: those things most people could agree are needs rather than wants. But one can live, and often quite nicely, without going to college. How can that constitute a need that government can legitimately provide to all?

Here we get to the most obscure but most important of Reagan's core principles: human dignity. For Reagan, it was not enough that a person have the legal right to be free, or that he or she have the physical sustenance to survive. He or she must also have the means to live with dignity, a state that involved possessing both the ability to choose for one's self and sufficient material goods to enable those choices to become a reality.

The first point is clear from Reagan's frequent invocation of freedom to choose one's life destiny as America's cardinal virtue. As early as 1957, for example, he told the graduates of Eureka College that the Cold War was "a simple struggle between those of us who believe that man has the dignity and sacred right and the ability to choose and shape his own destiny and those who do not so believe."[44] He told the Los Angeles County Young Republicans in 1964 that conservatives were for "freedom, self-reliance, and dignity."[45] Dignity extended to the destitute too. Reagan had a problem with welfare only when it "substitute[ed] a permanent dole for a paycheck,"[46] thereby "destroy[ing] self-reliance, dignity, and self-respect." His welfare reform program was intended, he said, to "maximize human dignity."[47] If people could not choose how they wanted to live their life, if they relied on another's beck and call for their livelihood, then those people could not live with dignity.

He stressed the second point more obliquely, but no less clearly, in a host of speeches. He told the Conservative League of Minneapolis in 1962 that he believed "comfort, and even a few luxuries, should be provided" for people who could not earn enough in their working life to support themselves in old age.[48] He often spoke about his support for public housing by saying no American should be "forced to live in degradation." Indeed, he said in the "Creative Society" speech that for those who must depend on society, "our goal should be not only to provide the necessities of life, but those comforts such as we can afford that will make their life worth living."

Contrast this expansive view with the more crabbed one of his good friend William F. Buckley Jr. In an August 1983 column, Buckley discussed how government programs to fight hunger cost more than they should. Citing a 1969 study that showed "99 percent of our biological requirements" could come from "four basic foods . . . bulgur wheat, dried skimmed milk, dried beans, and lard," Buckley said that hunger in America could be eradicated if "every grocery store in the United States would be furnished with as much of these four foods as there was any call for."[49] This program would eliminate "biological hunger, as distinguished from, say, gourmet hunger" at less than 25 percent of the cost of the food stamps program.[50] Such a program would give "society a perfectly defensible sense of moral composure," according to Buckley.[51]

Like most conservatives of that generation, I idolized Buckley. He was responsible for the only time in my life I seriously came to oppose a position Reagan held. I watched, enraptured, as a sixteen-year-old when Buckley debated Reagan on his PBS show, *Firing Line*, over whether the United States should give up control over the Panama Canal. I went into the debate agreeing with Reagan, but came out agreeing with Buckley. Like many, I was enthralled by his charm, his wit, his eloquence. One brief exchange between the two, one I've remembered vividly for forty years, showed how the erudite editor could win friends instantly. After about an hour of formal debate, Reagan was allowed to question his close friend directly. He started by humorously asking, "Why haven't you already rushed across the room here to tell me that you've seen the light?" Buckley sat calmly and replied drolly, "I'm afraid that if I came any closer to you the force of my illumination would blind you."[52]

Buckley and Reagan had more to do than anyone else with making American conservatism a viable creed and a political force. Yet when it came to the matter of the quality of life for the poor, Buckley had more in common with Goldwater than with Reagan. The idea that compassion requires more than simply keeping the poor alive, but instead insists that one recognize "the purpose and worth in each and every human life," seems to have been difficult to grasp for two of conservatism's three most important figures.

The rest of Reagan's "Creative Society" speech follows from these three premises. If it is legitimate for popular government to decree that "the problems of human misery can be solved," then it follows that "the big question is not whether—but how and at what price." If self-government and dignity are essential to human happiness and freedom, then it follows that attempts to meet those needs and solve those problems must maximize the ability of all citizens to choose their own paths and solve their own problems to the greatest degree possible. And if one believes human need is objective rather than subjective, then limiting governmental assistance to need solves the problem of cost.

This Creative Society was not to be a wholly private, decentralized one. Proclaiming that "there is no major problem that cannot be resolved by a vigorous and imaginative state administration willing to utilize the tremendous potential of our people," Reagan called for a vast, government-led initiative to "call . . . on the best in every field to review and revise our governmental structure and present plans for streamlining it and making it more efficient and more effective."[53] Under his leadership, California's government would "coordinate the creative energies of the people for the good of the whole." One can almost hear in Reagan's call the echoes of FDR's earlier call for "bold and persistent experimentation" as the hallmark of his New Deal. Reagan's government might be smaller, but it would be no less active or energetic.

Some might read this as perilously close to Henry Wallace's planned society. Not so, said Reagan. Echoing the essential insights from the Nobel laureate Friedrich Hayek's classic book, *The Road to Serfdom*, Reagan said that "the idea of an economy planned or controlled by government just doesn't make sense. No matter how talented the government is, it is incapable of making the multitudinous decisions that must be made every day in the market place and in our community living."[54] Thus, his government would push decentralization—local communities should govern more of their own affairs and people should have more control over theirs. But it would not remain aloof and indifferent to solving problems the people wanted addressed.

Reagan then offered a few specific proposals to flesh out these ideas. Local governments should be able to pass ordinances that make it easier to control "skyrocketing crime." Business and community leaders should be consulted as to how best to "make California once again attractive to industry." "Campus researchers and others experienced in philanthropy" would be convened to determine how to address the welfare caseload, which had doubled in the prior five years, such that those who needed permanent or temporary help received it and those who could support themselves would be helped to do so. Control over education should also be passed from Sacramento to local school boards and individual state colleges and universities.

Reagan emphasized that these efforts need not result in new government programs. He approvingly cited a number of examples of private-led efforts that rehabilitated the sick and assisted the poor. They, however, were to be only the preferred, but not the sole, approach. The Creative Society wasn't "some glorified program for passing the buck and telling people to play Samaritan and solve the problems on their own while government stands by to hand out Good Conduct ribbons."

He ended his speech by reprising the essential choice facing Americans that he posed in his speech on behalf of Goldwater. Decrying government planning and control, he said people who called for that "in reality are taking us back in time to the acceptance of rule of the many by the few"—exactly the evil he decried in 1947 when he was an ardent New Dealer. He called talk "in America of left and right" to be "disruptive talk, dividing us down the center." The choice between left and right was a false one. "The only choice we have is up or down—up, to the ultimate in individual freedom consistent with law and order, or down to the deadly dullness of totalitarianism."

This self-avowedly centrist approach left Brown little room to effectively attack Reagan. As Reagan refused to make the sort of wild, bombastic claims that often got conservatives into trouble, Brown was increasingly left with nowhere to go to revive his flagging poll numbers. He resorted to a tactic that would be reprised by Reagan's later foes, one that would fail as badly in this first attempt as it would in later campaigns. Brown tried to scare California voters, especially African Americans, into thinking Reagan was both too wild and inexperienced to be trusted with high office and prejudiced against minorities.

Brown targeted Reagan's acting career. Claiming that as an actor Reagan had no knowledge of or experience with state government, Brown ran a series of television commercials focusing on Reagan's lack of direct knowledge. The spot ended with Brown telling a group of African American schoolchildren that Reagan was an actor, "and you know who shot Lincoln, don't you?"[55]

Subtle innuendo in the Daisy ad had worked for LBJ against Goldwater, but this ham-handed effort fell flat. Much as Jimmy Carter would attack Reagan on the issue of race so viciously in 1980 that liberal editorial pages called him to stop engaging in a campaign of meanness, Brown's unfounded insinuation turned voters off. A small but persistent lead for Reagan turned into a large one, and it became clear the only thing left up for grabs was Reagan's victory margin.

Reagan's campaign did what it could to maximize that margin. My first political memory is as a five-year-old boy seeing a Reagan for Governor sign in front of Ricky Gutierrez's house on Burbank Boulevard in the Woodland Hills portion of Los Angeles, a neighborhood of small, three-bedroom, 1950s-built homes. In researching this book, I discovered why I saw that sign. From the start Reagan had showered attention on the state's large Mexican American population. In speeches, signs, and ads, Reagan asked Latinos "*Ya Basta?*" or "Had Enough?"[56] Shrewd Democratic Party poll watchers saw early on that Reagan would do better than most Republicans among these voters, and indeed he did, Ricky's parents' among them.[57]

Reagan also showed that no one understood working-class, New Deal–friendly Democrats better. He won statewide by nearly one million votes out of six and one-half million cast, a 58–42 percent landslide. His strongest base of support, and the places where he increased support over traditional Republican levels, was in those working-class neighborhoods where Republicans had traditionally struggled. These areas were places like the San Fernando Valley, the part of Los Angeles where I lived, and in countless faceless suburbs unknown to most but home to millions of people. Places like Norwalk, Lakewood, and Hawthorne, places settled by southern and plains Democrats fleeing the Dust Bowl or northern and midwestern ethnics looking for a better climate and a better life. So long as the Republican Party fought elections on themes like business versus labor, or liberty versus the New Deal, they voted strongly for Democrats. But when the question was, as Reagan put it, not between left or right but between up or down, they enthusiastically favored "up," even when it carried a Republican label.

One can see this most clearly by comparing Reagan's share of the vote with that of the 1962 Republican gubernatorial nominee, Richard

Nixon. Nixon lost Norwalk by a 65–35 percent margin in 1962, but Reagan carried it four years later by a 57–43 margin, a stunning 22 percent improvement that was more than twice his statewide gain.[58] Other working-class white suburbs saw similar gains. San Leandro, a suburb of Oakland, went for Brown over Nixon in 1962 by a 60–40 percent margin, but in 1966 it favored Reagan over Brown by 58–42. South Gate, another Los Angeles white working-class town, switched from being 54 percent Democratic in 1962 to 66 percent in favor of Reagan in 1966, while nearby Lakewood went from 58–42 Brown to 62–38 Reagan.

These trends applied in rural areas as well. In more highly educated counties populated by traditional Republicans, Reagan ran only slightly ahead of Nixon's 1962 performance.[59] The San Francisco Peninsula, for example, was then largely Republican. Reagan ran between 4 and 7 percent ahead of Nixon in the four counties that comprise the peninsula. But in the then-traditionally Democratic rural counties inland from the coasts, Reagan ran unprecedentedly far ahead of Nixon. He ran between 12 and 28 percent ahead of Nixon in each of the nineteen rural counties north of the state capital of Sacramento, many of which had been carried by John F. Kennedy in the 1960 presidential election. Reagan did only slightly worse in the rural counties to Sacramento's south, running between 9 and 17 percent better than Nixon in all but one of those fifteen noncoastal, rural counties. Rural, working-class Democrats found as much to like about Reagan's new politics as did their suburban counterparts.

Reagan's victory meant his ideas would now be put to the test. California had been running a budget deficit during the campaign, a fact that would require whomever won to decide how to bring it into balance. Reagan had often proclaimed that the government spent and taxed too much. Would he challenge the bigger government consensus and try to dramatically cut state spending or accommodate spending by hiking taxes?

Those who heard only the antigovernment rhetoric in his speeches would have had reason to think he would try to undo many of the programs that at that time were relatively new. Medical assistance to the poor, known in California as Medi-Cal, had been passed by Congress only in 1965. The federal government's expansion of the nation's main welfare program, Aid to Families with Dependent Children (AFDC), was also relatively recent, a product of the Great Society. The state had only recently expanded its three state-financed higher education systems, the University of California, the California State University system, and the two-year California Community Colleges. Goldwater-style conservatism would clearly have favored attacking these programs before raising a dime in tax hikes.

Those who listened more closely could have found clues to what they would later explain as Reagan's "pragmatism." His speeches, as we have noted, always included segments that clearly stated a philosophical support for the aims of many, if not most, of the programs whose survival the liberals so dearly loved. Reagan thought these aims could be accomplished in other, less expensive ways, but he never expressed the Goldwateresque view that their existence itself was an imposition on liberty.

One could also have seen glimpses of the real Reagan in an exchange he had with the prominent NBC journalist Sander Vanocur on that network's premier Sunday political talk show, *Meet the Press*.[60] On that show, Reagan was asked whether he opposed the legacy of Supreme Court Chief Justice Earl Warren, who had been a moderate-to-liberal Republican governor of California until his appointment to the court by President Eisenhower.[61] As a justice, Warren led the court into its most aggressively liberal phase, expanding the reach of the Bill of Rights into many areas that had hitherto been considered the province of politics, especially at the state level. In this role, he had come to be strongly disliked on the right as someone who was trampling the Constitution. Reagan's answer to Vanocur's question spoke volumes as to his character and philosophy.

Reagan started by asking Vanocur whether he was asking about "the Earl Warren of the Supreme Court or the Earl Warren as Governor of California." While Vanocur later said this astute reply showed "he was in the presence of a real political pro," Reagan's follow-on was more revealing of the man.[62] When the journalist clarified he was referring only to the gubernatorial Warren, Reagan expressed strong approval of his predecessor. He told viewers that most Californians would want to return to the days of Earl Warren, ones that included significant expansions of government spending and the state's higher education system.

He also praised the former California governor and senator Hiram Johnson, whose Progressive Party had controlled state government for four crucial years in the early twentieth century. Johnson, who was Teddy Roosevelt's running mate when the former president tried to regain his old job in 1912 as the Progressive nominee, had sought, in Reagan's words, "to return power and authority to the individual" when governor.[63] The fact that he did so by severely restricting the power of political parties to control who they nominated and by creating the state's first workman's compensation insurance system—both significant expansions of government power opposed by conservatives of that era—seemingly paled in importance for Reagan compared with the aim of increasing the ability of the average citizen to influence his or her government and to live with greater economic security.

None of this was inconsistent with what he had told Californians he would do during the campaign. Indeed, in a record his campaign sent to California voters entitled "Year of Decision," he specifically said they would "get the services their taxes pay for without breaking their backs to pay for them."[64] He promised only to halt rising crime and the increasing cost of welfare, to give union members the right to a secret ballot on matters of union strikes, and to give more control to local governments. Nothing in this platform implied that he would back sharp cutbacks to services voters valued in the face of a rising deficit.

Nor, as we have seen, was this platform opposed to what he had been telling Americans he favored in the prior decade. To borrow a phrase from President Bill Clinton, Reagan's view of the New Deal and its state counterpart was to "mend it, not end it."

Both archconservatives and hyperliberals would find this out by the end of his first year in office. The former would find they had less to hope, and the latter would discover they had less to fear, than a superficial reading of Reagan would have led them to believe. But all that was in the future. Right now, Reagan could bask in the glory of a lightning-fast rise to national prominence and an even greater stage on which to shine. His first turn as leading man had produced great box office. He had finally kissed the girl, and she had kissed him back. Despite the inevitable twists and turns of political life, Reagan had found the rest of him, and he would keep finding it for the rest of his life.

CHAPTER 5

CALIFORNIA POLITICAL THEATER: RONALD REAGAN PRESENTS

The scene: California's ornate State Capitol rotunda. The date: January 2, 1967. The time: a few minutes after midnight. The space under the dome is filled with people, among them governor elect Reagan, his wife, Nancy, California Supreme Court Justice Marshall McComb, and a host of supporters and reporters. The purpose: to take the oath of inauguration.

After reciting the oath of office, his right hand firmly placed on a four-hundred-year-old Bible, Reagan turned to his old friend from the movie business, the Republican US senator George Murphy. "Well Murph," he quipped, "looks like we're back on the late show."[1] The laughter soon faded, but the challenge Reagan faced did not.

Rarely in American political history had someone done what Reagan had achieved, obtain political power almost exclusively because of his own ideas. Those ideas, presented in speeches to audiences both national and local, had encouraged the powerful few and the anxious many to seek him out, asking and even begging him to make those ideas real. Now as governor he would have both the opportunity to deliver and the necessity of fleshing out those ideas through the actions he took. Before he completed his oath, Reagan had been solely a man of speech. Now he would forevermore be one of words and of deeds.

The specific challenges he would face changed frequently over the eight years he was governor. But meeting those challenges always involved applying the same, sometimes contradictory ideas he had presented for decades. Would Reagan's desire to reduce government's cost and size lead him to try to undo many of the New Deal–inspired programs that had made government big? When public sentiment seemed to support increased government regulation, as it did by the end of his first term in regards to environmental protection, would Reagan side with those who wanted to expand government? In short, was liberty threatened so much by larger government that the beast needed to be starved, now, and not simply tamed?

Reagan's record in office revealed what people should have seen all along. In what he did and in what he did not do, Reagan showed that his view of the proper role of government involved much of what had been done in the post-Roosevelt era. He would raise taxes rather than seek to repeal the programs that made taxes high. In many cases, he would expand spending on popular items like K–12 education much faster than his liberal predecessor had. He would expand regulation when he thought doing so would help protect the environment. In short, he would interpret rather than oppose the New Deal legacy.

This did not mean he was a liberal. Democrats, who controlled the state legislature for most of his tenure, always wanted to spend and tax more and cut less than he wished. They would often characterize his economies or reforms as heartless cuts that endangered the welfare of the poor and middle class. They would continue to try to cast him in the role they wanted him to play, that of the conservative antigovernment extremist.

Most conservatives never wavered in their support for him. Taxes and spending went up, but the legions of California conservatives whose devotion had made him governor loved him as much on his last day in office as they did on his first.

Most, but not all. Some conservatives were firmly committed to Goldwaterite principles and thought their leader was too. By the end of his first year in office, they had become disillusioned with him and sought to warn conservatives in the rest of the country that Reagan wasn't who they thought he was. But these warnings went unheeded, suggesting they were irrelevant to the real concerns most conservatives had. Reagan's popularity among the average rank-and-file conservative voter in the nation grew throughout his time in Sacramento. By the time he left office voluntarily in early 1975, these voters wanted to see more of their hero. Later that year, they would get their wish.

In January 1967, however, all that was in the future. Reagan may have already had his eye on the Oval Office, and it is certain that some of his staff and backers did. But first, he had to show he could govern. The challenges he faced were daunting.

California's looming budget crisis was well known during the 1966 campaign. Reagan's opponent, the incumbent governor, Pat Brown, and the Democratic-controlled legislature had hiked state spending quickly without increasing taxes. The state had met its constitutional obligation to run a balanced budget only by using time-honored "one-shot" techniques such as delaying payments and accelerating when taxes were due. All observers knew that those shots had all been fired: whoever won would have to put the state budget on course to be structurally balanced by midyear 1967.

Reagan was expected to try to do this by cutting spending, and his first budget cut spending a lot. Submitted in late January, the document was sparse on details—most budget items had notations of "last year's spending minus 10 percent"[2]—but was long on cuts. The $4.6 billion budget was smaller than Brown's budget from the prior year. Even this budget, considered radical and draconian, would not have balanced the budget. From the beginning, all parties involved recognized that some tax increases were necessary.

The new governor had alluded to this in his first inaugural address. Despite the deep budget crisis, he told Californians that he would "turn to additional sources of revenues only if it becomes clear that economies alone cannot balance the budget."[3] He detailed no program for elimination; even when it came to welfare he emphasized that the state would help the aged, the disabled, and those who must depend on others. "The goal," he said, "will be investment in, and salvage of, human beings."

Reagan's first budget was widely considered to be unrealistic because of its lack of detail. The state was legally bound to protect state grants to local school districts, community colleges, and welfare programs that were shared with federal government such as Medi-Cal (the Golden State's version of Medicaid, the federal-state program to pay for health insurance for the poor and medically needy) and Aid to Families with Dependent Children (cash grants to mothers, mainly unmarried, with children). Balancing the budget without increasing taxes would have required the Democratic-controlled legislature to change these laws, something that clearly would have required a great deal of political effort from the newly elected governor. Reagan did not indicate he was willing to do that in either the budget or in any of his public pronouncements. Indeed, all Reagan told Californians he would do was "cut, squeeze, and trim" to reduce "the cost of government"; he never indicated he wanted citizens to tighten their belts and expect less from the state.[4]

He seemed to be relying on a commission of businessmen that he had convened to review state management practices to find inefficiencies in management and service delivery that could reduce spending significantly without cutting the services themselves. Reagan had long championed the belief that "economies"—what we now call "waste, fraud, and abuse"—were responsible for much of government's cost.[5] The commission did find changes in management practices that could save a significant amount of money. But by the end of March, it was clear that these changes would come nowhere near to balancing the budget on their own.

This discovery forced Reagan to submit a second budget in late March, one that offered significantly higher spending levels than those he had proposed just two months before. This $5.06 billion budget replaced the "10 percent reduction" rule with specific recommendations.[6] It also scaled back proposed cuts to spending not protected by law, such as state grants to the University of California and the state university system. The remaining cuts included eliminating 3,700 jobs in the state's Department of Mental Hygiene—the department in charge of state mental hospitals and community treatment centers—and continued trims in the higher education budget. It also required the University of California and the state university systems to adopt formal tuition charges for the first time, a highly controversial move in a state that had long prided itself on funding top quality, tuition-free public universities. But most important, Reagan's second budget was deeply out of balance.

Reagan followed this new budget with a proposal for what was at that time the largest state tax hike of any state in history. The $946 million proposed hike increased all sorts of taxes: sales taxes, personal income taxes, corporate taxes, and a host of other, smaller taxes all went up.[7] The effect was quite progressive: most of the increased burden would fall on businesses and the well to do.[8]

Today such a proposal would be decried by the Republican right, primarily on what would be called Reaganite grounds. "No new taxes" is a mantra for the modern conservative. But back then the proposal met with very little resistance. Democrats shrewdly insisted that all Republicans vote for the tax hike before any of their members supported it, and Reagan gamely rounded up the few GOP votes that weren't on board. In the end, every Republican member of the lower house, the state assembly, and all but one Republican state senator—Orange County freshman John Schmitz, the legislature's only avowed member of the John Birch Society—went along. Reagan's cuts, efficiencies, and tax hikes became law.

Throughout his life Reagan would present this as a victory, a small step in reining in the size of government. He championed the small property-tax-relief component of the tax bill (effectively, he increased taxes on the well off to fund property tax cuts for middle-and working-class homeowners) and the slower rate of government spending growth as the beginnings of the "prairie fire" revolt of average people who wanted government "to be fair, not waste their money, and intrude as little as possible in their lives."[9] He castigated Schmitz as the sort of person who "jumps off the cliff with the flags flying" while saying that he, on the other hand, was "willing to take what he could get."[10] In short, he characterized his differences with Schmitz as tactical rather than principled in nature.

There is some truth to this explanation. Reagan was a skilled nego-tiator from his years as president of the Screen Actors Guild. He would refer to those days frequently during his political career, often describ-ing a negotiation over this or that as being not as difficult as dealing with studio bosses. Schmitz, in contrast, was a flamboyant showboat who loved media attention and never pulled his punches. He went on to become a congressman in 1970, but lost renomination in 1972 after spending two years attacking President Nixon for being a liberal. He then ran for president himself that year on the American Independent Party ticket, the party founded in 1968 as a vehicle for the segrega-tionist governor George Wallace. Political realities never affected John Schmitz's thinking.

Reagan's tactical explanation for his budget behavior, however, ob-scures the degree to which he was being consistent with the principles he had long laid out for public consideration. His fiery speeches in the late 1950s and early 1960s, for example, had always included statements expressing agreement with most of the programs that had been enacted in the post–New Deal era. As we saw in chapter 2, Reagan supported public housing, medical aid for the needy, public universities, and a host of other programs opposed by the intellectual conservatives of that day. He had even said that these programs represented "social progress" and that he would choose not to repeal them "at any cost." He had argued that reducing waste and inefficiency could make big changes in the level of taxation. Reagan's budget challenge put to the test his thesis that waste, not the programs themselves, gave rise to expensive government. It forced him to confront the conflict between attacking high taxes and supporting many then-new programs. In the end, when the "waste and inefficiency" argument was shown to be wanting, he chose to hike taxes rather than cut or eliminate programs he by and large supported.

Reagan could have argued that he would have had to fight the legislature tooth and nail to change the laws that placed most spending out of bounds, and that such a fight was bound to fail. He never made that argument, however. In hindsight that is not surprising, because Reagan often was willing to fight tooth and nail for things he really cared about. The battle over imposing tuition in the University of California system was a contemporaneous example of how he could fight cleverly and tenaciously to get what he wanted.

The UC system is and was governed by a board of regents. The regents were appointed by different entities at different times, so in early 1967 Governor Reagan—who was automatically a regent by virtue of his office—did not control a majority of the appointments on board. To get tuition adopted, he would need to persuade many people appointed by his liberal predecessor or who had no ties to him.

Reagan took on this challenge with relish. Over and over he tried to get the regents to adopt a charge and call it tuition so that some of the people who used the UC system paid for some of its costs. Finally, the issue came to a head at a regents meeting in August 1967. Reagan had insisted that the charge be labeled as tuition as a matter of principle, but lost a vote on his proposal early in the meeting. As the meeting broke for lunch, he was heard to mutter to one of his staffers that "you never leave the stadium at the half."[11] During the break, Reagan found that he could get the charge approved if he simply dropped his demand that it be labeled "tuition." When the regents reconvened, Reagan indicated he was willing to drop his demand. In return the regents backed a $200 annual charge for attending the university.[12] Liberals like Assembly Speaker Jesse "Big Daddy" Unruh, who was also a regent, were outraged. They knew that a rose by any other name would smell as sweet: tuition was tuition no matter what it was called. So did Reagan. Once the charge was approved, it was only a matter of time before the name was changed. By 1970, the UC system was formally charging tuition. In 2016–7, the amount for tuition and mandatory fees had risen to nearly $13,500 a year for California residents.[13]

This battle, seemingly over how to balance the state budget, was actually a statement about Reagan's principles of government. Reagan had said that there is no such thing as free college, there's only the question of who will pay for it.[14] Many UC students came from families earning well above the average income for that time.[15] Reagan had long argued that government should help people who needed help, but not financially help those who didn't. The UC tuition debate was an excellent place to make his point: average taxpayers should not have to bear the full cost of educating a person whose families could afford to pay part of the cost themselves.

Indeed, Reagan's tuition proposal was tied to an increase in state scholarships for students whose families could not afford it. He also rejected his budget chief's recommendation to adopt tuition for the state's community college students, as those people came largely from families with average or below-average incomes.[16] Reagan's lifetime commitment to helping people in need, but only people in need, was on full display here.

Reagan's philosophy of government was also on display in how he sought to address the state's Medi-Cal program. This program had been created only in 1965 as part of Lyndon Johnson's Great Society. The program established the government as the insurer for welfare recipients and other categories of medically needy people the state chose to insure. If hard-core opposition to government social programs had been part of Reagan's agenda, the budget shortfall and the relatively recent adoption of this program would have provided perfect cover for a push to return to California's pre-1965 reliance on county-financed public hospitals to pay for medical care for the poor.

Despite Democratic charges to the contrary, Reagan never even contemplated doing that. In minutes from an early cabinet meeting,

Reagan approvingly cited Medi-Cal as "help" for people who otherwise could not afford their medical bills.[17] Before that help, he said, hospitals charged clients who could afford to pay more to cover the costs for those who could not.[18] Now, the state would ensure that poor people would have a predictable source of funds to cover the care they needed.

As we saw in the previous chapters, Reagan had long said he supported government provision of medical care for those who couldn't afford it themselves. He reiterated that commitment in a 1968 letter to his longtime pen pal, Lorraine Wagner. "My philosophy about medical care for the poor can be stated very simply," he wrote. "No one in this country should be denied medical care because of a lack of funds, and no one will be denied such help in California."[19]

Reagan did try to cut back Medi-Cal's coverage of certain procedures and populations, but his principle for doing so was consistent with his longstanding philosophy. He argued that Medi-Cal coverage was more generous than that available in the private sector for many workers. It struck him as unfair that people could do better on the public dime than they could by working, so he attempted to pare back the program by executive order. This effort was blocked by the courts, which said such changes could be made only by legislation.[20] Reagan dropped the issue in 1967 only to revisit it in his second term, when he made welfare reform his top priority. That later effort would again show that when Reagan wanted something, he would fight tooth and nail to get it.

He faced another time for choosing with regards to efforts to repeal the state's open housing law, the Rumford Act. That act had outlawed a property owner from discriminating against a potential buyer on the basis of race. It had been repealed by popular vote in 1964 only to be reinstated by the California Supreme Court. Reagan had called for its repeal during his campaign, and advocates of repeal in the legislature took up the challenge when it convened.

Despite his call, Reagan never exerted political capital on behalf of the repeal efforts. Instead, at a key moment in the legislative battle, Reagan let it be known he was satisfied with a compromise reform measure that would simply have exempted owners of single-family homes from the act's requirements.[21] This compromise satisfied neither those who wanted full repeal nor those who backed the law to begin with. The center did not hold, and the legislature adjourned without changing the act at all.

Meanwhile Reagan was meeting with leaders of African American groups and communities. Perhaps for the first time in his life, Reagan had to confront the realities stemming from centuries of formal and informal racial prejudice. He began to see what he had missed when he opposed the Civil Rights Act of 1964, that blacks had been excluded from full participation in American life by the direct and indirect effects of prejudice. He pledged later that year that he would work to give blacks an "equal place on the starting line" so they could fulfill the American dream that anyone can become what he or she wants.[22] By 1968, Reagan had completely abandoned his prior stance. He told the California Association of Realtors, the prime financial backer of the initiative that had tried to repeal the Rumford Act, that he now opposed full repeal. After meeting with minority group leaders, he said, he had learned that the act was an important "symbol" of the principle of non-discrimination, and as such it should be retained.[23]

The Rumford Act debate again showed how Reagan dealt with the conflict between two competing principles. On the one hand, Reagan had always believed that the government should stand with average people in their quest to live full lives of their own choosing. From his earliest days he had included members of any race, ethnicity, or sex in that group; nondiscrimination was a deeply held ideal for him. On the other hand, he cherished liberty. A law that circumscribed one person's liberty could be justified only if it gave another person a chance at living a self-chosen life that he or she would otherwise not have. Once Reagan learned the full measure of feeling in the black community, his strong instinct in favor of nondiscrimination took hold. In the end, he took the same position on civil rights measures in 1968 that he had believed in as a New Deal liberal in 1948.

Some politicians might have tried to hide their views from their backers. Not Reagan. He defended his tax hike and his budget to all comers, even his conservative supporters. Two nearly identical speeches given in April 1967 before the premier conservative grassroots groups in California, the California Republican Assembly (CRA) and the United Republicans of California, bear this out.

Those speeches emphasized that the tax hikes were necessary not only to balance the budget, but also to pay for new necessary spending. He told the groups that half of the record tax hike, which had at that point not yet been approved, was needed to pay off accumulated debt and to set the state budget on course to being regularly balanced.[24] Another quarter was needed to maintain services after population growth and inflation, and the final quarter would finance needed property tax relief.

His defense of his budget was also instructive. He proclaimed that he was seeking only to economize government, not eliminate "needed services or programs." His aim was cutting "fat and waste," and he had gone as far with that as he could. He noted that he had promised to cut government "without hurting the truly needy and truly deserving." To that end, he supported the inclusions in his budget of salary increases for state employees, more funding for disabled children, and other new spending that had not been proposed by his liberal predecessor.

Most conservatives gladly backed him. There is no indication that conservative activists tried to lobby against his proposals. His poll ratings did not slip; no rumors of conservative revolt reached reporters' ears. Conservatives were not yet in a mood to hunt "RINOs" who strayed from the purist orthodoxy. The same California conservatives who had backed a man in 1964 who had pledged to repeal most of modern government eagerly backed a man in 1967 who was raising their taxes to keep most of it.

Most, but not all. Some conservatives, people whom Reagan would label in his autobiography as "radical" or "ultra" conservatives, did turn against him.[25] They clearly saw that he was not going to lead the fight to value liberty ahead of government programs that arguably helped people lead better lives. They wanted someone who thought the drive for civil rights legislation was ultimately a drive for government power, and thus must be stopped at all costs. They were people who believed deeply in the vision Barry Goldwater had set forth in *The Conscience of a Conservative*, and by the end of 1967 they knew in their hearts that Ronald Reagan was not right.

CBS news discovered this when it went to California to film a documentary on the rising star. Airing on December 12, 1967, "What about Ronald Reagan?" introduced the nation to a man who political elites were already saying could be the next Republican nominee for president. Far from castigating him as a loony right-winger, the hour-long documentary explained the roots of Reagan's appeal in evenhanded terms while also giving his critics a chance to present their views. Some of those critics, it turned out, were on the right.

John Schmitz was the most prominent anti-Reagan conservative. Asked to explain why he thought "the deeds did not match the words," Schmitz quickly named four items: the tax hike, the failure to cut spending, the failure to repeal the Rumford Act, and the backtracking on a promise to create a commission to investigate reported Communist infiltration of the University of California.[26] Another conservative summed up the "ultra's" feelings: they had been "betrayed."

One disappointed conservative went so far as to write a short book detailing Reagan's conservative apostasies. *Here's the Rest of Him*, written in cooperation with Schmitz by a conservative activist, Kent Steffgen, is a difficult read. Its combination of lurid polemics and over-the-top characterization with a degree of inside baseball analysis of personnel moves involving long-forgotten politicians can leave one thinking it is something best left to the fever swamps of the Right. But one should look beyond that, for beneath the off-putting tone and in-the-weeds focus Steffgen was absolutely right. Ronald Reagan was not, and never had been, the sort of conservative that Steffgen and other activists wanted.

Steffgen's essential complaint was that Reagan was reconciled to the structure of modern government that he had inherited from the Democrats. Reagan's second budget, which significantly increased spending and included some of the new spending items Reagan had defended before the CRA, showed that he was "committed to the liberal or socialist premise that a large population demands a large government to rule over it."[27] Steffgen argued that Reagan should have eliminated a host of programs that primarily benefitted blacks, eliminated state subsidies for special education and community colleges, cut university spending by forcing tenured professors to increase their teaching loads, eliminated the portion of Medi-Cal that went for medically needy (as opposed to poverty-stricken) individuals, and dramatically cut back on AFDC spending.[28] In short, Steffgen thought Reagan should have governed like Goldwater.

We can see the vast difference between these two views in how Steffgen described Medi-Cal and the importance he ascribed to opposition to civil rights measures. The former he repeatedly described as "socialized medicine."[29] As such, the "only logical solution" for a conservative was "to advocate outright repeal" of Medi-Cal. Reagan's approach of simply trying to cut waste and place the program on sound fiscal footing missed the point.

Even on that basis, however, the problem would still remain. In Steffgen's view, medical care, the cost of which under Medi-Cal was raised through state taxes, should be financed precisely the other way around: first, from one's relatives; second, from one's club, organization, or fraternal order; if still more money were needed, then third, from the city in which one lived; fourth, from the county; and fifth, and last, from the state.[30]

The state and the federal government should be "the very last public agenc[ies]" to levy taxes to pay for medical spending on the poor, Steffgen argued, because they are "the farthest removed from the level of collection and, therefore, the most liable to irresponsibility."[31] Of course, Reagan had always rejected those ideas, as demonstrated through his support for the Kerr-Mills Act, his characterization of Medi-Cal as "help," and his clear statements even in his televised address on behalf of Goldwater that he believed conservatives were for telling Americans that no one should be denied medical care because of a lack of funds.

Steffgen's emphasis on opposition to civil rights is even more revealing. Reagan's change of heart on the Rumford Act placed him behind
"the minority view—the 15% minority—at a time when the American
majority is mad enough about civil rights pressures to bring on a second
U.S. Civil War."[32] Reagan's statement that he had backed the goals of
the Civil Rights Act of 1964 all of his life met with Steffgen's scorn,
as did Reagan's statement that he would never patronize a business
that practiced discrimination.[33] Reagan's oft-repeated statement that
he would back the enforcement of civil rights principles "at the point
of a bayonet if necessary," as Ike had done at Little Rock and Kennedy
at Oxford to enforce mandated integration of public schools and universities, was considered by Steffgen to be both contrary to the Constitution's guarantee of property rights and political suicide.[34] In light
of this, Steffgen's recommendation that conservatives consider backing
the segregationist governor of Alabama, George Wallace, for president
in 1968 because he "had the only stand on the all-important civil rights
issue which is known to reflect the true majority interests" makes all
too much sense.[35]

It is tempting to ignore Steffgen's analysis because of the dripping
racism that pervades his book. To do so ignores how ingrained opposition to civil rights was in some precincts of the Right at that time.
In *Conscience*, Goldwater—who was no racist—addressed his constitutional objection to civil rights legislation before he addressed any single
economic or foreign policy issue, thereby ascribing a central importance to that issue. With regards to the Rumford Act, a full repeal bill
passed the California State Senate with support from *every* Republican
member. The 1964 initiative repealing the Rumford Act had passed
with 65 percent of the vote, an even higher share than Reagan had received in the much more pro-Republican election of 1966. Supporting
full repeal would have been the politically easy thing to do. The fact
Reagan chose not to do so after meeting with black leaders suggests he
acted on principle, not calculation.

Steffgen continued his crusade against Reagan for years, and in
1978 Reagan wrote a short letter responding to his charges.[36] He re-

jected Steffgen's claims that he had supported "back door socialism," citing the tax rebates he had returned to California taxpayers and his opposition to forced busing and the Equal Rights Amendment. Reagan also said he had opposed abortion on demand and socialized medicine. Steffgen, he wrote, was "an unmitigated liar."

Reagan may have wished that were so, but the real issue between them was a difference in principle over what conservatism was. Reagan always backed Medi-Cal and never considered it to be "socialized medicine"; Steffgen did. Reagan opposed abortion on demand but did sign—after considerable mental anguish—a bill that significantly liberalized California's abortion laws in a way that made abortion available in almost all circumstances.[37] Reagan defended himself against Steffgen's later charge that he had surreptitiously backed Nelson Rockefeller over Goldwater in 1964, but never responded to the charge that he had appointed Rockefeller backers to high positions in his government. He couldn't respond to that charge because he had, intentionally. It was part of Reagan's desire to unify a badly fractured party, a desire he had repeatedly told Republicans and conservatives he supported. Indeed, he even told the CRA in 1967 that he believed in party unity and that conservative primary challengers should not attack their more liberal opponents by name.[38] Reagan had always been clear that his vision of government did not involve a significant repeal of many post–New Deal, liberal-enacted programs; Steffgen's brand of conservatism believed that was the whole point.

The difference between the two men can be summed up with one Reagan quote. For Steffgen, Reagan's statement that "my views haven't changed much since I was a Democrat" was proof that he was a conservative in name only.[39] For Reagan, it was a badge of honor.

Reagan's ongoing political success, both in California and nationally, demonstrates that conservative voters were not as committed to repealing the New Deal or opposing civil rights as many of their leaders had supposed. In practice, they supported many of the same ideals that the working-class Democrats who backed Reagan wanted: support for traditional American values, economy in government, services that helped them get ahead in life, and opposition to communism at home and abroad. Reagan's budgetary record showed his commitment to two of these ideals; his actions in regard to university unrest and the Vietnam War demonstrated his commitment to the other two.

Modern campus unrest began at the University of California, Berkeley, in 1964. The so-called free speech movement ushered in an ongoing series of student protests about civil rights, the Vietnam War, and other concerns of the Left. By 1966 the protests had grown to the point that the campus was embroiled in conflict, sometimes leading to the cancellation of classes. Reagan decried this, arguing that students' right to protest did not mean they could do so in violation of university rules that harmed the right of other students to attend class without interruption. His audiences cheered, and Reagan had his first genuinely original populist issue.

Reagan never wavered in his policy that campus order should be maintained no matter what the cause the students were protesting. He supported university presidents who maintained order and even showed physical courage on some occasions, walking through or addressing groups of hostile students without the cordon of security agents we have now come to expect surround public officials.[40] He made clear that he would not hesitate to call out the National Guard when necessary to maintain order, on campuses or in the face of urban riots. Critics on the left denounced him for these actions, but Californians loved them.

Reagan also delighted conservative audiences with his vocal support for American involvement in the Vietnam War. He followed the private advice of the former World War II hero and president Dwight Eisenhower and argued that America needed to fight the war more aggressively. Like Ike, he favored more extensive bombing of North Vietnam and pursuit of Vietcong and North Vietnamese troops into neighboring countries and into North Vietnam itself, tactics the Johnson administration refused to employ on the grounds they could "expand" the war.[41]

Reagan's support of the Vietnam War was on full display in an hour-long televised appearance with Robert F. Kennedy, a US senator and potential Democratic presidential candidate. The CBS news pro-gram, *Town Meeting of the World*, aired May 15, 1967, and featured stu-dents from numerous countries attending university in England posing questions to the two men on live television.[42] Reagan looked assured, ruggedly handsome, and—speaking without cue cards or notes—in command of his facts and his opinions. He stoutly defended American involvement and aims in Vietnam in the face of consistently hostile questioning. At one point he even corrected one of the questioners' facts, proceeding to run through the entire history of the fight between North and South Vietnam with pinpoint accuracy. RFK privately fumed to his staff afterward that he had been soundly defeated by Rea-gan; millions of conservatives and working-class Americans found yet another reason to see Reagan's career progress onward.[43]

Reagan's support for South Vietnam was no surprise. He had long been a consistent and vocal anti-Communist. Indeed, anything short of a vehement endorsement of the war would have been cause for alarm on the right. But Reagan also offered a short clue as to his uncon-ventional conservatism during the broadcast. At the end of his long correction of the errant student, he said, "You might be surprised to learn that I support Diem's land reforms."[44] Those reforms, initiated during the Eisenhower administration by the first South Vietnamese president, Ngo Dinh Diem, involved the government's confiscation of land owned by wealthy Vietnamese, with compensation, and turning it over to formerly landless peasants to own and farm. American advisers had urged Diem to embark on this program so as to give the poor an economic stake in South Vietnam and thus reduce their potential sup-port for Communist infiltrators and agents.

Reagan had argued for the New Deal after World War II in part to prevent economic misery from causing people to consider supporting fascists or Communists. Twenty years later, his support for Vietnamese land reform showed he had not changed his views. For Reagan, gov-ernment action in violation of established property rights was always acceptable if doing so gave average people a chance to live lives of their own choosing and made democracies more stable.

Hard-line conservatives, however, would always hold a contrary view. During Reagan's first term, North Carolina senator Jesse Helms, initially a staunch ally of the president's, openly opposed administration policy with regards to fighting a Communist insurgency in El Salvador. The reason: Reagan backed a Christian Democrat, Jose Napoleon Duarte, who had initiated land reform. Saying Duarte was "far to the left of George McGovern," the ultraliberal Democratic presidential nominee in 1972, Helms chastised Reagan for refusing to point out "that land reform is a vast failure" and continuing to support Duarte.[45] Helms opposed Duarte for years, supporting Duarte's right-wing rival, Roberto d'Aubuisson.[46] D'Aubuisson and his ARENA party would frequently say Duarte was a watermelon: green (the Christian Democrats' party color) on the outside and Communist red on the inside.[47] Reagan had endured similar taunts from his brother and other Republicans during his liberal period; calling New Deal backers socialists or Communists was standard Republican rhetoric back then. Backing land reform as governor and as president shows just how loyal he remained to his principles throughout his life.

Nineteen sixty-eight would prove to be one of the most consequential years in American history. It began with the Tet Offensive, a surprise attack by the guerrilla Vietcong in major cities throughout the South. Although the American army and its Vietnamese allies ultimately decisively beat the Vietcong, the fact that the offensive happened at a time when the American public was being told the war was well in hand was shocking. The Johnson administration's resultant "credibility gap" fueled the presidential challenge of antiwar senator Eugene McCarthy. His shockingly close second-place finish in the New Hampshire Democratic primary convinced Johnson to abandon reelection. In April, the civil rights leader and icon Martin Luther King Jr. was assassinated in Memphis, Tennessee, and in June Robert F. Kennedy was also assassinated on the eve of what appeared to be a decisive victory over McCarthy in the California Democratic primary. King's murder triggered riots in over 120 cities (but not, Reagan proudly noted, in California). Antiwar protests grew in intensity, and when the Democrats met in

Chicago to nominate the incumbent vice president, Hubert Humphrey, tempers boiled over. Young protesters known as Yippies were teargassed and beaten on national television as Chicago police officers overreacted in the muggy summer weather. Similar student protests broke out in France, and the free world watched impotently as Russian tanks brutally suppressed young Czechs' effort to build "socialism with a human face" in their country. Rarely have Americans felt so pessimistic about the country's future.

Reagan's 1968 was less catastrophic, but in the long run was equally consequential. Despite his denials, he was engaged in a stealth run for the Republican nomination. He traveled the country giving speeches, wowing conservative and establishment audiences alike. Under the rules then in place, however, this enthusiasm could not translate into delegates. Most state delegations to the Republican National Convention would be selected by party bosses and leaders. Many of them, especially in the South, were conservatives, but more than anything else they wanted to win. They lined up behind former vice president Richard Nixon, who had risen from the political dead after his crushing 1962 gubernatorial defeat to become the prohibitive favorite.

Reagan studiously avoided announcing for president, but did run as a "favorite son" in California's winner-take-all primary. Such a run was a tradition at that time for many state leaders who wished to control their state's convention delegations; as many as sixteen favorite-son candidates had entered the 1968 race at one time. Reagan could then use his state's 86 delegates (667 were needed to win) as a base to springboard to the top.

In the end, Reagan's late entry into the race (indeed, he did not formally declare until August 7, the day the nominee was selected) and his recent entry into politics weighed against him. The conservative heavyweights Barry Goldwater, Texas senator John Tower, and South Carolina senator Strom Thurmond (the same man who had run for president in 1948 on an anti–civil rights platform; he had left the Democrats after the passage of the 1964 Civil Rights Act) lobbied conservatives for Nixon. In the end, they delivered for the former vice president: Reagan would garner fewer than 100 delegates from outside California, while southern states gave Nixon 298 votes.[48] Ever the astute showman, Reagan went to the podium and moved to make the nomination unanimous.

Two things stand out from Reagan's brief, unsuccessful foray into presidential politics. First, he had based his appeal on populist issues rather than the antigovernment themes that Goldwater had stressed. Reagan's name was placed into nomination by California State Treasurer Ivy Baker Priest, the first woman to nominate a presidential candidate, and she told cheering Reaganites that their man would "confront the radicals on campuses and the looters in our streets and say: The laws will be obeyed."[49] Reagan's million-vote 1966 victory proved he was "a winner," she said, and he would "fight to win" when freedom was threatened.[50] Almost no one wanted to make another political Pickett's Charge against the New Deal with Goldwater's electoral bloodbath still etched in Republicans' memories.

Second, Reagan's defeat also changed his approach to national politics. He had found that his rhetoric could move crowds but it could not move hardened pols. Future efforts, if any were to come, would require greater planning and organization than the slapdash, last-minute effort he had just employed. In his two subsequent contested races for the Republican nomination, Reagan would studiously reach out to local leaders to solicit their support well in advance of the actual vote. He would also work to unify the party's factions during the campaign rather than rely solely on the emotional support from one group.

The remainder of Reagan's first term offers little more than continued examples of his unique brand of conservatism. With revenue growth restored by his tax hike, Reagan's budgets dutifully increased spending in accord with state law for most programs while seeking to return some of the annual surpluses that had started to arise to the people in the form of tax rebates. He used his line-item veto to remove spending he thought wasteful, but this merely reduced the rate of government spending growth rather than make significant changes to sort of government that the state government provided. He vigorously (and successfully) opposed a tax-cutting initiative sponsored by Los Angeles County Assessor Phil Watson.[51] He continued to work for party unity, avoiding involvement in party primaries even when the contrast was clearly between a liberal and a conservative, as was the case in the 1968 primary for US Senate between the liberal incumbent, Tom Kuchel, and the conservative state superintendent of public instruction, Max Rafferty.[52] Hard-line conservatives may have been disappointed, but Reagan remained popular among most conservatives and among the working-class Democrats he assiduously courted.

Reagan's reaction to the rise of the environmental movement provides a fine example of his governing philosophy. In his first campaign he seemed to side with landowners and developers in their battles with the then-new environmental movement. His quip "If you've seen one tree, you've seen them all" haunted him throughout his career. But in office he surprised, and even shocked, many liberals with how often he used government to protect open space and clean up the air and water.

Some of his actions could be seen as refusing to use government to indirectly subsidize development. He stopped construction of two dams, for example, that would have provided water and electricity to surrounding regions.[53] But many others involved increasing the degree of regulation over landowners or businesses that many observers thought he would never sanction.

Perhaps the best examples of these efforts are his support for the creation of the Tahoe Regional Planning Agency (TRPA) and the California Air Resources Board (CARB). The TRPA regulates land development in the Lake Tahoe basin in an attempt to maintain the crystal clear blue water this alpine lake uniquely possesses. Reagan and a fellow conservative, Nevada governor Paul Laxalt, established the agency because the alternative was to spoil permanently this national treasure.[54] CARB, as the board became known, obtained the power to order pollution-control measures throughout California, including establishing regulations for automobile tailpipe emissions. In both cases, unelected men and women, people whom Reagan would otherwise likely have labeled as bureaucrats, told other people what they could or could not do with their property.

It's not hard to see why these environmental regulatory bodies have maintained their power decades after their creation. In each case, a large majority of people—Tahoe tourists in the first case, any resident of California's cities in the second—reaped significant benefits from the regulations these agencies promulgated. I vividly remember what life in Los Angeles's San Fernando Valley was like in the late 1960s. Brown smog would envelop the area, preventing people from seeing hills just a mile or two away, much less the majestic mountains to the east. My seven-year-old self would have to come inside on summer days, unable to breathe after riding my bike because of the toxins that invaded my lungs. Living in urban California may have been a good deal for most, but curbing air pollution would give those people a new—and better—deal.

Reagan's embrace of environmental measures has often been ascribed to his love of nature or to the strength of his adviser for environmental affairs, Ike Livermore. It's true that he demonstrated his love of the outdoors throughout his adult life, especially through his purchase of a series of ranches where he could stable and ride horses. It's also true that he followed the successful executive style he learned from Ralph Cordiner and delegated decision making to capable subordinates whenever possible. These explanations, however, presume that Reagan acted against his philosophy for purely emotional or personality-based reasons. Many on the left and right often have argued that Reagan's actions to expand or fail to dramatically shrink government resulted from these factors rather than his principles, hence the obsession among conservatives with White House personnel during his presidency. It's not that the people who make this argument are wrong; Reagan was an emotional man and he did trust his close advisers. But like "our liberal friends" whom Reagan chided in his "Time for Choosing" speech, there is just so much the people who make this argument know that isn't so.

Reagan's seemingly inconsistent decisions, as governor and as president, almost always can be explained by going back to his core beliefs. Throughout his life he believed in the dignity of the common individual and supported the exercise of governmental power to give that person the opportunity for a comfortable life of his or her own choice. With respect to environmental protection laws, those he favored were similar to the social welfare measures he supported: they gave a powerless many the voice to prevent harm from a powerful few. Where Reagan saw ordinary people on both sides of an environmental question, as he did with proposals to create a state redwoods park on the North Coast, he tried to find a balance so that workers whose jobs would be threatened and environmentalists could both benefit.[55] Neither Secretary Livermore nor any other aide ever took Ronald Reagan somewhere his principles did not already permit him to go.

Reagan entered the 1970 election in a very strong position for re-election. He ran unopposed for renomination, showing how popular he was among Republicans, and was opposed in the general election by his longtime nemesis, Assembly Speaker Jesse "Big Daddy" Unruh. Unruh tried to portray Reagan as a friend of the rich, someone who pushed through property tax cuts for his big business and wealthy backers' interests.[56] Reagan ignored these attacks, instead focusing on his opposition to drugs, his belief in welfare reform, and his environmental protection record.[57] The outcome was never really in doubt. While his margin was cut in half from 1966, Reagan won comfortably by a half-million votes.

Reagan again ran well ahead of Republican candidates. He won working-class cities like San Leandro and Lakewood that Republicans often struggled to carry.[58] He won most rural counties at a time when they still normally elected Democrats. In doing so, he ran well ahead of other Republicans. His old conservative friend George Murphy, for example, lost his reelection bid by over six hundred thousand votes, and the Republicans lost their tenuous control of the state legislature. Reagan's unique New Deal conservatism again attracted voters other Republicans could not.

Most conservatives are more familiar with Reagan's second term

as governor. He used his victory to focus on reducing California's exploding welfare rolls and campaign unsuccessfully for a constitutional
reduction of state taxes. Both efforts show Reagan's ongoing determination to ensure that government "helped the needy, not the greedy"
(a rhyme he would use often throughout the remainder of his career)
while protecting the taxpayer.[59] Both efforts were opposed by liberals
who believed sincerely in more redistribution and higher taxes, a shift
in thinking from FDR's days that Reagan's official biographer Edmund
Morris called a change from support for benefits to belief in entitlements.[60] In neither case, however, did Reagan's efforts involve an effort
to reduce the level of services available to most Californians.

California's welfare spending was increasing rapidly throughout the
late 1960s, but it accelerated dramatically in the final year of Reagan's
first term. The AFDC caseload, the number of people receiving checks
from the state's largest welfare program, went up from 769,000 individuals when Reagan took office to 1,150,687 in 1969 and a whopping
1,566,000 in 1970.[61] The caseload was going up by 40,000 people per
month. Spending on Medi-Cal was also going up rapidly, as anyone on
AFDC was also eligible for Medi-Cal. Unless spending on these and
other welfare programs was quickly curtailed, the state would need to
raise taxes again to meet its constitutional requirement of a balanced
budget.

Raising taxes without reducing welfare spending was not on Reagan's agenda. He had long thought that "the dole" could be a "narcotic"
that encouraged dependency, often quoting Franklin Roosevelt to that
effect.[62] "The dole," Reagan wrote privately, "except for the aged and
disabled, should be eliminated and a government work force be insti-
tuted for the able-bodied."[63] Failure to reform these programs would
force the state to cut back on "the types of things people should ask of
government—parks and everything else."[64]

Reagan convened a task force to study the state's many welfare programs and offer a comprehensive package of reforms. Under the direction of a trusted aide, Ed Meese, this effort produced a long report
offering hundreds of proposed administrative and legal changes to the

programs. These changes had four stated goals: increase assistance to the truly needy; require those able to work to do so or get job training; make Medi-Cal no more generous than private insurance; and strengthen a family's responsibility for its own welfare.[65] The Medi-Cal proposals were a reprise of the battle Reagan had fought and lost in 1967; the other goals were nothing more than a concrete expression of the principles he had articulated for years.

Reagan presented his ideas to the people in his second inaugural address. Recognizing the reality of Democratic legislative control, he said that bipartisanship was possible, citing environmental protection, infrastructure construction, and support for the mentally ill as examples.[66] He then turned to the need for welfare reform, telling the assembled legislators there would be no tax hike. His goal was to "eliminate waste and the impropriety of subsidizing those whose greed is greater than their need." The result, he said, would be programs that "maximize human dignity and salvage the destitute."[67]

The legislature sat on his proposals for months, coming around to negotiate only as time grew short for the passage of a timely budget. Reagan had made televised and personal appeals to Californians on this issue, saying he got the idea to bypass the legislature and go directly to the people from FDR's fireside chats. He would later ascribe the legislature's willingness to negotiate as a result of the calls and letters his efforts generated, saying that Democratic Assembly Speaker Bob Moretti told him on their first meeting to "stop those cards and letters from coming." Whatever the cause, the two men met frequently in mid-1971 to personally hammer out a compromise. The result included many of Reagan's proposals, including the reining in of Medi-Cal, stiffer eligibility requirements for AFDC, and a hike in benefits for those who remained on the rolls—the first since 1958.[68]

Reagan was proud of that latter achievement. He would refer to it frequently in the years ahead, writing one correspondent that

> our welfare reforms did not deny help to any deserving person. As much as anything, they were designed to enable us to do more

for those who truly needed help. There had been <u>no</u> increase in grants from 1958 to 1971. We increased the grants by 43 percent.[69]

This sentiment was not uniform on the right. In his autobiography, Reagan criticized unnamed conservatives who wanted him to end welfare instead of just cutting the abuses.[70] Doing so, however, would violate Reagan's long-held principle that government support of people who really needed help was entirely appropriate.

Welfare reform worked as advertised. The rolls started to drop almost immediately. By 1973 they had dropped from a high of 1,608,000 to 1,330,000.[71] Spending was curtailed enough that a second major tax hike was avoided. While a state Supreme Court decision on K–12 school spending[72] forced him to hike income and corporation taxes in 1972,[73] the rest of Reagan's final term was dedicated to reducing taxes and restraining the expansion of government power.

In 1972, environmentalists placed an initiative on the general election ballot to create a coastal commission to regulate the development of and public access to any privately owned piece of property on the California coastline. Governor Reagan opposed this initiative, arguing that existing state laws provided sufficient protection for the coast.[74] Despite his prestige and a large financial advantage for opponents of the measure, it passed by a 55–45 percent margin.

Reagan would meet another, more personal defeat at the ballot box in 1973. Still trying to reduce the cost of government and the tax burden of average Californians, he sponsored an initiative to limit state taxation and spending to a set amount of California personal income. The complex measure would have reduced over fifteen years the amount in personal income the state could take in taxes from about 8.75 percent to a flat 7 percent.[75] It would also have reduced state income taxes in 1974 by 7.5 percent and exempted from paying any state income tax all families earning less than $8,000 a year, which was then slightly less than the average family income.[76]

The campaign was hard fought. Groups benefitting from government spending like teachers' unions argued that the proposition would endanger spending on schools and other services people valued, while Governor Reagan said the government could keep spending rising and still cut taxes. The "Yes" campaign ran ads saying voters could "beat the politicians," get lower taxes, and still keep necessary state spending on things like "schools, the environment, and public safety."[77] Voters nevertheless opted to stick with their current system, rejecting Proposition 1 by a 54–46 percent margin.

Reagan afterward ascribed the loss to a misleading campaign by opponents that contended local taxes could go up, not down, in response to the limits.[78] But he may have been more accurate when he said, "It is an axiom of politics that when people are confused about an issue, many will vote No."[79] That's just another way of saying what he had told conservatives right after Barry Goldwater's defeat, that it is "human nature to avoid change and people will bend over backward to avoid radical change."[80] Reagan's proposal may have been reasonable, but it was radical. Enough Californians bent over backward that they continued to allow the legislature to tax and spend without limit whenever it wanted to.

Five years later, however, Californians had seen enough. The tax hikes Reagan had supported in 1967 combined with a hot economy to create a witches' brew of increasing taxes and rapidly rising property values. Reagan often fought to lower property taxes by using recurring state surpluses for property tax rebates, but he was never able to get the Democratic-controlled legislature to agree to a permanent tax cut. By 1978 the state was sitting on a record $5 billion surplus, equal to over a third of the state's annual budget.[81] Two antitax crusaders, Howard Jarvis and Paul Gann, placed a voter initiative on the ballot to cut property taxes nearly in half and limit their future increases dramatically. Reagan endorsed this measure.[82] Infuriated by years of inaction, California voters approved Proposition 13 with a nearly two-thirds majority. Californians took another step toward Reagan's vision in 1979 by passing Proposition 4 with 74 percent of the vote. The proposition limited state and local spending to the amount spent in 1979 plus increases for changes in the population and the cost of living. Since personal income normally increases at a faster rate than the sum of population increases plus inflation, Proposition 4 did through the back door what Proposition 1 tried to do up front: gently place the tax burden on Californians on a slow, downward glide. Once again, Reagan was ahead of the political curve, one that this time he had helped to shape.

The state's and the nation's turn to the right, however, was years in the future. Reagan's last year in office, 1974, would go down as one of the worst in modern history for the Republican Party. The Arab oil embargo, which lasted from October 1973 until March 1974, sent energy prices skyrocketing. Firms started laying people off, sending unemployment steadily up throughout the year. The economic downturn led to a stock market decline; stocks lost over 45 percent of their value between 1973 and 1974. To top it off, the Watergate scandal slowly strangled the Nixon presidency. Nixon's political viability was ended by the July 1974 release of some secretly taped Oval Office recordings that conclusively showed that the president had, despite years of denials, known of efforts to cover up a 1972 break-in by his campaign's operatives of the Democratic National Committee's Watergate hotel offices. On the evening of August 8, 1974, I, like millions of Americans, sat transfixed before my television as the only president I had ever known told us that he would "resign the Presidency effective at noon tomorrow."[83] Three months later, the GOP endured heavy losses in midterm elections, dropping forty-nine House seats and leaving it with less than a third of the total.

The Republican wipeout did not affect Reagan, however. He left office with his approval ratings on an upswing, with opinions about his performance in office higher than at any time since 1969.[84] His standing with conservatives was much higher both in and outside the state. Even though a Republican, Gerald Ford, had succeeded Nixon as president, many conservatives were encouraging Reagan to launch a primary challenge. Nothing he had done as governor had shaken their belief that he and his views deserved a promotion.

Reagan would soon heed their calls, and in doing so he would rely heavily on his record to prove he could put conservative ideas into action. In announcing his candidacy he said simply that

> for eight years in California, we labored to make government responsive. We worked against high odds—an opposition legislature for most of those years and an obstructive Washington bureaucracy for all of them. We did not always succeed. Nevertheless, we found that fiscal responsibility is possible, that the welfare rolls *can* come down, that social problems *can* be met below the Federal level.[85]

Each sentence is carefully worded; taken together, they are a succinct statement of Reagan's philosophy of government.

The object of government for Reagan was to ensure the popular will be heard and to take care of social problems with as little federal involvement as possible. Thus he sought to make government "responsive," not "smaller." He fought to reduce welfare rolls, but not to make welfare "a purely private concern" as Goldwater had argued in *Conscience*. Note also that he argues for fiscal responsibility, not tax cuts. It's not that he did not want taxes to be reduced: clearly his statement that "we did not always succeed" refers in part to Proposition 1's failure. But cutting government for its own sake irrespective of meeting social problems or providing citizens with the levels of education, environmental protection, and transportation they needed was not part of his agenda.

His more detailed defenses of his record in other speeches and private letters demonstrates this more fully. He often mentioned the $5.7 billion he had been able to return to taxpayers in refunds and temporary tax breaks.[86] But he also approvingly cited the dramatic increases in per student spending on K–12 education during his terms in office,[87] the increased spending on college scholarships and universities,[88] and California's "national model" of mental health treatment.[89] The rate of growth in both government spending and state government employment slowed under his leadership, but it neither stopped nor reversed.[90]

Welfare reform always figured prominently in Reagan's self-assessment, and his main point was always the balance he struck between the needy and the greedy. He had showed, he believed, that one could be generous to those who needed help while keeping those who didn't off the public's payroll.[91] Increasing welfare benefits might seem today like an odd thing for a conservative to tout, but neither Reagan nor his adoring audiences cared. Their conservative vision included caring for the poor at the same time as they wanted more of the able-bodied poor to enter the world of work. Self-government included responsibilities as well as rights.

Reagan's early movie career included a recurring role in a B-movie serial as Brass Bancroft of the US Secret Service. Charming and courageous, Brass always stood up for America, fought the bad guys, and brought them home to justice. As with any movie series of its day or the present, the audience didn't expect the character to change in each new installment. It came back precisely because it liked the star and wanted to see him meet new challenges and emerge on top.

Reagan left Sacramento to retire to his newly purchased "Rancho del Cielo," but no one thought he was riding off into the sunset. Reagan was not the retiring type. No one, least of all Reagan, knew what the next few years would bring, but everyone knew the last installment of his new serial had not yet been filmed. His conservative Republican and working-class Democrat fans wanted to see more of their hero, and he was never one to disappoint his fans. Only this time, Brass Bancroft wasn't going to be working for the higher-ups: he was going for the brass ring himself.

CHAPTER 6

REAGAN'S "DEATH VALLEY DAYS"

Many great statesmen have periods when they appear to be done for, has-beens whose careers ended before they had done anything notable. Lincoln despaired at the age of thirty-nine, a one-term congressman belonging to a failing party. Churchill looked washed up in the 1930s, an aging pol who appeared to increasingly embrace unusual or unpopular causes in a vain effort to reclimb the greasy pole of power. Even Franklin Roosevelt went through a time like this after losing his bid for vice president on the 1920 Democratic ticket, an eight-year period in which he contracted polio and wondered if he would ever walk again, much less satisfy his ambition to emulate his cousin, President Theodore Roosevelt.

The time between leaving the governor's office in January 1975 and winning the presidency in November 1980 was Reagan's lean period, his "Death Valley Days." He would run for president, openly this time, only to fall achingly short at the last actively contested convention of the twentieth century. He would nurse his wounds privately and slowly rebuild his public persona, not knowing if Republicans would accept him four years hence as a twice-defeated candidate. He would furthermore be sixty-nine years old when he ran again; if he won, he would be the oldest man so far ever to be elected president. Would Americans reject him because of his age, afraid he could not withstand the rigors of office?

One thing was certain as he entered this next-to-last phase of his political life: he would run as Ronald Reagan, on the ideas he had formed in days when atomic power and trips to the moon were mere fantasies presented in *Flash Gordon*, *Buck Rogers*, and other science fiction movie serials. Many who encountered Reagan for the first time in these years would hear the searing critiques of government, the calls for less bureaucracy and more freedom, and the firm, determined anti-communism and think there was little that government did that Reagan liked aside from fighting Russians. For the young antigovernment right, he was like Moses ready to lead them to the Promised Land. The progressive left, however, viewed him more as a false prophet.

It is easy to see why one could come to these conclusions. Many of Reagan's most memorable lines were uttered in these years: "The very heart and soul of conservatism is libertarianism";[1] "Raise a banner of no pale pastels, but bold colors."[2] Taken alone and out of context, these lines could create an impression that Ronald Reagan was an anti–New Deal conservative out to topple Roosevelt's legacy.

Context, however, matters, and in each case Reagan's most famous lines were part of an argument that was little different from the one he made in the 1950s and 1960s. If the heart of conservatism was libertarianism, reading the full interview in which he uttered that line made clear that his "libertarianism" was not what libertarians meant by that word. The "bold colors" Reagan offered were merely his innovative, New Deal–friendly conservatism.

The real Reagan was there for all who had eyes to see. In the 1975 interview he gave to the libertarian *Reason* magazine; in the speeches he gave during his 1976 run for the White House; in the speech he gave in February 1977 to the fourth annual Conservative Political Action Conference (CPAC), in which he gave his vision for the "New Republican Party"; and in speeches he gave in the 1980 campaign—in each case the man who had both attacked the growth of government and supported the goals and many of the programs of the New Deal was on full display.

Some on the right saw this. I recall one conversation I had as a freshman in college with an upperclassman who was supporting Illinois Congressman Phil Crane. Crane was running to Reagan's right, a much younger man who opposed government as much or more. As I waxed rhapsodic about Reagan, the upperclassman told me to look at Reagan's record as governor. If I did, he said, I would find that Reagan wasn't really in favor of cutting government. I laughed him off at the time, but I've come to see that from his ultraconservative perspective he was absolutely correct.[3]

Others took more concerted action. The then-new Libertarian Party nominated David Koch, one of the now-famous Koch brothers, as vice president on its ticket so that he could finance its presidential campaign. Running on a platform that was even more antigovernment than that of *The Conscience of a Conservative*, the party's presidential candidate, Ed Clark, made clear that if you wanted to really cut taxes and government, Ronald Reagan just wasn't good enough.[4]

Another Reagan quality was also on full display during this time: his rejection of ideology. Reagan's conservatism was founded on principles but rejected the type of litmus-test thinking that forced people into political boxes. Principles were not the enemy of compromise for him, but purity was the enemy of victory. This is especially clear in his 1977 speech to the CPAC convention. In 1960, Barry Goldwater had told conservatives to "grow up" and fight for their principles rather than simply complain. In 1977, Reagan essentially told conservatives to grow up and accept they had to work with people whom they disagreed with on many issues if they were going to save the country they loved.

You wouldn't be reading this book if the attacks on Reagan from the left and right had succeeded. The fact that they didn't, the fact that against all odds Ronald Wilson Reagan became the most important and consequential political leader of the last half of the twentieth century, was due entirely to what had started his political career to begin with: his ideas.

One would have received very low odds from a casino in early 1975 on the prospects of Ronald Reagan ever becoming president. The oil crisis, recession, and Watergate scandal had intensified the Democratic Party's dominance of American politics. Indeed, a GOP pollster, Robert Teeter, told the Republican National Committee that only 18 percent of Americans identified as Republicans.[5] Many of those considered themselves moderates or even liberals, and if Reagan did plan to run he would likely have to go through the sitting president, Republican Gerald Ford. The odds were indeed not in Reagan's favor.

Those poor odds did not deter Reagan, however. He immediately hit the mashed potato circuit, only this time he focused not on paying gigs before local groups but on talking to the conservative activists he would need if he were to run. His first major speech in this effort was made to a new gathering, the annual Conservative Political Action Conference. Addressing its second convention in March, Reagan laid out his agenda and his vision for a conservative future.

This speech is best known for his stirring phrase that a "revitalized" Republican Party should "rais[e] a banner of no pale pastels, but bold colors" that highlight the difference between the parties.[6] This is often considered to be a clarion call for hard-core conservatism. In fact, the principles Reagan discussed were quite mild in comparison with what Barry Goldwater had called for just a few years before.

Reagan listed nine principles that represented what a conservative Republican Party should stand for. They were

- ★ "fiscal integrity and sound money and above all an end to deficit spending";
- ★ "a permanent limit on the percentage of the people's earnings government can take without their consent";
- ★ "a genuine tax reform" that would allow people to figure out their tax payment "without having to employ legal help";
- ★ indexing of income tax brackets so people would not be penalized by inflation;

★ "our belief in a free market as the greatest provider for the people," a call that included "an end to the nit-picking, the harassment, and over-regulation of business and industry";

★ "ways to ward off socialism . . . by increasing participation by the people in the ownership of our industrial machine";

★ "holding those who commit misdeeds to personally accountable";

★ "mak[ing] it plain to international adventurers that our love of peace stops short of 'peace at any price'"; and

★ "maintain[ing] whatever level of strength is necessary to preserve our free way of life."

There's nothing here that any conservative today would find objectionable. There's also, however, nothing here that reiterates the attacks on the size and the scope of government that conservatives had made just a few years before—or that many make today. Reagan was softly presenting conservatives the same argument he had made ten years before in "A Time for Choosing": we could be for limiting the scope and growth of government without challenging the principles of the public New Deal.

Both Reagan's discussion of his record as governor and his critique of existing federal policy reinforce this conclusion. He presented his record as one of cutting welfare, implementing "a policy of 'cut, squeeze, and trim'" to reduce the cost of delivering government services, and returning over $5.7 billion in savings from both to the taxpayers in "rebates, tax reductions, and bridge toll reductions." While he did not tell his audience he had to raise taxes, he did mention that his welfare reform had increased welfare checks for the needy by an average of 43 percent while reducing the rolls by over 400,000. The clear implication was that conservatism in action was about getting more for less, precisely the attitude Goldwater had criticized as inadequate in *Conscience*.

His critique of federal policy was similarly limited. He argued for a free-market economy over socialism. He blamed then-rampant inflation on record-high deficit spending and argued for a balanced federal budget—without identifying any programs or spending that he wanted to cut. And he focused on foreign policy, contending that defense spending was being cut too much and that Congress's refusal to send sufficient arms to the South Vietnamese and Cambodians would embolden Communists and imperil US security. The direction he offered was clearly in opposition to the Great Society and its principle that only government planning, direction, and redistribution could solve America's problems. But that itself was merely proof that the descendants of Henry Wallace's Progressives were gaining more control over the Democratic Party itself. It was not proof that Reagan's conservatism represented a fundamental challenge to the New Deal doctrines underlying the shift away from pre-1932 Hoover Republicanism.

Reagan implied as much early on in his speech. He told conservatives that "our task is to make [the people of America] see that what we represent is identical to their own hopes and dreams of what America can and should be." Proof that this was possible was provided by a poll that showed a wide gulf between what delegates to the 1972 Democratic convention believed and what Democratic voters believed. Presumably these loyal Democrats had not suddenly been converted to Goldwaterism. Reagan is implying that conservatives believe the same things these Democrats do, which in turn implies that conservatism itself is consistent with the New Deal's social guarantees.

Conservatives received his message happily, but not all friends of liberty were so appreciative. Libertarians were wary of Reagan and wanted to find out just how far Reagan was willing to go in his attacks on government. They sent one of their leaders, Manny Klausner, the cofounder and then editor of *Reason* magazine, to interview the former governor to see just whose side he was on.[7]

The *Reason* magazine interview is today mainly remembered for a single Reagan line, "The very heart and soul of conservatism is libertarianism."[8] As one might expect, this quote is often used by libertarian organizations in their fund-raising to imply that Reagan supported their goals. But the truth is more elusive. To paraphrase Inigo Montoya from *The Princess Bride*: "Libertarian. I do not think Reagan thinks that word means what you think it means."

Reagan made clear throughout the interview that conservatism might share the libertarian love of individual freedom, but it differed sharply in its willingness to use government for positive ends. Whether the issues discussed concerned domestic and economic policy, social issues, or national defense, Reagan disagreed with his interlocutor on principle every time.

Their disagreements started at the outset over the very purposes of government. In response to a question to state what he believed the "proper functions of government" were, Reagan mentioned police and fire departments. Many libertarians believe that fire protection is simply a service that would be better provided on a private market, and it was no surprise to Reagan when Klausner jumped in to question his assertion that public fire departments were a "necessary and proper function of government." Reagan replied that he was aware of the libertarian argument that fire services had once been privately provided and funded, but that "because of the manner in which we live" public fire departments were justified "because there are very few ways in which you can handle fire in one particular structure today without it representing a threat to others."

This seemingly minor difference in fact exposed a major principled disagreement. For conservatives like Reagan, the social consequence of an individual's behavior was a legitimate justification for collective and government action. If an individual *could* harm you in the future, it was just and proper to restrain that person in some way so that the potential harm never came to fruition. Thus, because a person *could* choose not to insure himself against harm from fire, and hence could cause you harm if a fire erupted and inevitably spread to your insured dwelling, it was just to force that person to "purchase" fire insurance through taxation to establish a mandatory public fire department.

Libertarians like Klausner disagreed. Self-ownership, the inherent right of an individual to do whatever he or she wants with his or her own person or property, is a core principle for the libertarian. This right can be constrained only in the case of a direct violation of another person's right, such as physical violence. Prospective action to reduce the likelihood of harm coming to pass, or any effort to provide services that would empower one person at the financial expense of another, is to a libertarian inherently unjust.

Reagan and Klausner clashed again and again over these competing principles. A lengthy exchange occurred over the Food and Drug Administration. Reagan stated that he supported the existence of the FDA, a federal agency that is in charge of ensuring the safety of all food and drugs sold in America. The FDA, he argued, ensures "that some unscrupulous individual can't sell us canned meat that gives us botulism" and gives us "the protection of knowing that a drug on the shelf is not going to poison us or give us an adverse effect." In this and other fields, Reagan believed that "regulations that are for the protection of the people" were a legitimate function of government; only those that "tak[e] away the rights of management to make business decisions with regard to their competition" were improper.

Klausner disagreed. He pointedly asked Reagan if he thought "the Food and Drug Administration basically serves the Big Brother role, the protectionist role, and that the free market could adequately deal with it in the absence of regulations." Reagan replied that perhaps the free market would deal with it, but that government should remain a "Big Brother" to oversee private regulation to ensure that "industry did not, for profit, gradually erode the standards." Reagan again backed the principle that society acting through government could legitimately restrain others to prevent them from potentially committing harmful acts even when there was no evidence a particular individual was likely or even considering such action.

It is one thing to constrain people to prevent the commission of future direct harms. Some libertarians view these policies as extensions of the idea that government can protect people against the commission of directly harmful acts. It is quite another to argue that the government can legitimately tax one person to provide services to help advance another. Most libertarians deeply reject this principle and thus are opposed to government social insurance or welfare schemes, and in many cases are also opposed to government provision or financing of education and schools.

Not Reagan. As we have seen, Reagan always supported this principle even when supporting Barry Goldwater. He did not retreat from this principle when confronted in this interview.

Higher education was the arena in which this battle was waged. Klausner asked Reagan if he thought "there was a proper role for government in providing a university education" and if "it's proper to use tax revenue to finance higher education." While expressing sympathy for the idea of private education, the man who had long expressed approval of the "expansion of our public university system" and had told Eurkea College graduates that "no one would have it otherwise" politely said yes to both questions. He saw nothing wrong with government "'provid[ing] an education for the individual that can't provide for himself" and said "tuition should never be a block to anyone getting an education who could not otherwise afford to go to the university." While he wished that government had provided this education through "private sector universities," the fact they did not do so was not a violation of principle for Reagan. The major harm he saw that came from the expansion of the public sector was that higher education would be otherwise "far cheaper."

Here again we see the wide gap between the principles of Reagan and those of libertarians like Klausner and Goldwater. To the latter, using taxation to provide benefits that are intended to help a person advance in life was illegitimate and counterproductive (Klausner) or deeply suspect (Goldwater). For Reagan, it was a perfectly natural sentiment, one tied indelibly to the realization of the American dream of freedom and self-determination. On this, the core question that divided Hoover and Roosevelt forty-three years before, Reagan still stood with FDR.

Of course, FDR's vision is legitimate only if one considers indirect popular consent through elections to be a legitimate form of self-government. Libertarians even today are extremely suspicious of democratic government. They do not view democratic consent as legitimate in most cases, as it always leads to some people being coerced into a transaction through taxation that they did not personally agree to. Libertarians contend the only legitimate consent is, with the few exceptions granted for mutual self-protection, that which is granted individually and specifically to another individual for a specific purpose.

Reagan disagreed, and he and Klausner clashed over this principle as well. The clash started with a discussion about the income tax. Reagan said he was critical of progressive income taxation, but thought income taxation itself was "probably as fair a method of raising revenue for the government as any." He likened the income tax to an arrangement a hypothetical group of shipwrecked people might make on a desert island, assigning people certain tasks so that they spent a certain part of their time doing their share to keep everyone alive and safe. That led to the following exchange:

> **KLAUSNER:** Of course, if you're talking about starting from scratch—the shipwrecked people on the island—you're really talking about a voluntary approach, aren't you—as against taxation?
>
> **REAGAN:** Well, we're inclined to think our government here *is* a voluntary approach and that we've set up a government to perform certain things, such as the national protection, etc.
>
> **KLAUSNER:** Aren't we deluding ourselves in terms of consent, though? When we're talking about taxation, aren't we really dealing with force and coercion and nothing less than that?
>
> **REAGAN:** Well, government's only weapons *are* force and coercion and that's why we shouldn't let it get out of hand. And that's what the founding fathers had in mind with the Constitution, that you don't let it get out of hand.
>
> But you say voluntary on the island. . . . Now, what do you think would happen in that community if some individual said: "Not me; I won't stand guard." Well, I think the community

would expel him and say "Well, we're not going to guard *you*."
So voluntarism *does* get into a kind of force and coercion where
there is a legitimate need for it.

Klausner quickly moved on, but the fundamental disagreement had
been laid bare.[9] Reagan believed that indirect consent was true consent,
and that as such elected representatives had the legitimate right to enact
coercive laws for prospective protection and for individual advance-
ment regardless of the direct opposition some individuals might have
to those laws.

If libertarians exalt individual consent and denigrate democratic
consent, their opposition to social conservatism and hawkish national
defense becomes easier to understand. For the libertarian, the social
conservative seeks to deny individuals their right to self-government
by regulating abortion, drug usage, pornography, or any sort of sexual
expression. If democratic government itself is inherently suspect, the
fact that a majority or supermajority of people in a community think
such behavior is harmful to them has no weight. Those people are, in
a libertarian view, free not to engage in any of the behaviors they seek
to proscribe. In short, their only legitimate remedy is an individual one
rather than a collective one. Any attempt to impose a collective decision
in these matters is as illegitimate to a libertarian as attempts to restrain
a businessperson in the conduct of his business or to levy taxation on
someone to finance another person's service.

The same reasoning leads to a very restrictive view of international
engagement. For a libertarian, wars are just only in cases of direct self-
defense, and hence the sort of military engagement with the world that
America started to employ after World War II is both harmful and
unjust. Libertarians were vociferously opposed to communism: it was,
indeed, the very denial of every major premise of a libertarian society. Despite this, libertarians in the 1970s and 1980s tended to oppose
American military alliances and involvement overseas unless American
territory or lives were directly threatened.

It should come as no surprise that Reagan did not easily share the libertarian premises in either case. He had problems with what he called "sin laws" such as prohibitions on gambling or prostitution, but did not instinctively oppose them. For Reagan, a social prohibition was legitimate when it "protect[ed] us from each other," but not when it "protect[ed] us from ourselves." But while he would wrestle with whether a specific law was on one side or the other of that line, he was clear on his basic principle: "I cannot go along with the libertarian philosophy that says all of the sin laws can be ruled out as simply trying to protect us from ourselves."

Reagan clearly loved individual liberty, but some of the circumstances that he thought would place a "sin" in the realm of proper government regulation might be too broad for many libertarians. Gambling, for instance, involved the need for government to protect against "dishonest gambling" and the fear that a "father [could] gamble . . . his money away and thus leave his family dependent on the rest of us."[10] Prostitution involved the reality that prostitutes were not usually willing participants, that they were part of what Reagan said "in an earlier day was called white slave traffic" and which today we call human trafficking. It also involved public health concerns: Reagan cited the example of the military closing New Orleans's brothels during World War II because brothels reduced the cost of finding clients and thus increased the number of liaisons a prostitute could engage in, thereby increasing the risk a solider would contract venereal disease. Libertarians might argue that each of his examples either involve an unfortunate cost of liberty or self-protection measures better left to individuals. Reagan firmly disagreed.

Reagan was, as we might expect, less conflicted about America's foreign involvement. After saying that Republicans should say they would "do whatever is necessary to ensure that we can retain this free system of ours," Klausner asked if that meant "a Fortress America approach or a world policeman approach." Reagan firmly rejected the former, saying that "Fortress America is just what Lenin wanted us to have." He rejected the idea that "the war in Indochina" did not represent a threat to America, because the Russians were "sponsoring the aggression of the North Vietnamese." While Reagan said he would not have sent "American boys half-way around the world," once they had been sent there America had "a moral obligation as a nation to throw the full resources of the nation behind them and to win that war and get it over as quickly as possible." Reagan found reason to disagree with libertarians even on conscription (a.k.a. the military draft), which Reagan opposed during the time of the Vietnam War. He opposed it, however, because Lenin had said he wanted capitalist countries to maintain conscription "until the uniform became a symbol of servitude rather than patriotism." In short, Reagan opposed conscription because it was an unwise tactic in the fight against global communism rather than a violation of an individual's right to liberty.

Everything Reagan said in this interview was consistent with the views he had expressed so many times before.[11] He opposed government that tried to determine outcomes and plan society. He supported government when it genuinely sought to protect people against harm, no matter how hypothetical or indirect. He also supported government as a tool to help people advance in society (education) or to protect them against poverty that occurs "through no fault of their own" (the family "dependent on the rest of us" because of the gambling dad). Such a view of government may have been consistent with the ideals of most Americans at that time, but it was certainly more expansive than anything libertarians had in mind.

This did not mean that Reagan did not want to cut back government. As his thoughts on higher education—it would cost less if provided privately—show, he always believed that government spent too much in overhead for the services it provided or financed. This was especially true for the federal government and its many programs that it shared with states and cities. It was to this that he turned his attention as he prepared his nascent presidential campaign.

Reagan unveiled his thoughts in a speech he delivered to the Economic Club of Chicago on September 26, 1975. His speech included a specific, original proposal to end federal involvement in a host of policy areas broadly covering social service programs. Reagan contended this would reduce the federal budget by $90 billion a year—an enormous sum at a time when the entire annual budget was about $370 billion.[12] Cutting this would enable states and local governments to run programs in these areas by themselves, free from federal mandate or interference, while immediately balancing the federal budget and allowing for a cut to "the federal personal income tax burden of every American by an average of 23 percent."[13]

Reagan did not list specific programs to be eliminated in his speech, although he did name certain areas in which the federal government had "created more problems."[14] An addendum passed out by his campaign to reporters and attendees, however, gave indications of what might be on the chopping block. That document listed topics such as education, job training, community development, commerce, welfare, law enforcement grants, revenue sharing, Medicaid, and other unspecified health programs.[15] Specifically exempt were defense, NASA, Social Security, Medicare, energy, and transportation. Even some programs Reagan had long railed against, such as the Tennessee Valley Authority and farm subsidies, were on the exempt list.[16]

One may have thought that this would immediately have been severely criticized by the left, but that didn't happen. The speech was widely ignored even after Reagan formally entered the race in November. It garnered national attention only when President Ford's campaign drew attention to it, arguing that it would force voters in New Hampshire and Florida—two states without broad-based income taxes and two of the first states to hold presidential primaries—to create an income tax or raise other state and local taxes to take up the slack.[17] The political pressure forced Reagan to backtrack, first by proposing to transfer federal revenue sources to states to help finance the programs and then by dropping the specific $90 billion figure itself.[18]

Most of Reagan's biographers have focused on the speech's political effects, arguing that it cost him both early states and with them the 1976 nomination. Analyzing the speech's intellectual impact, however, is much more important. Some might contend that this address exemplified Reagan's libertarian or Goldwaterite philosophy, that it was an example of his supposed long-standing opposition to the New Deal and the principles of modern government it had initiated. A careful reading of the talk, however, shows nothing of the kind.

The New Deal's primary innovation was to enlarge the range of activities that government felt itself capable of addressing in order to give average Americans a hand up in life. Roosevelt and his followers sought to regulate and tax more in order to increase security and upward mobility for all. They differed among themselves as to how much to do and on the scope of private industry and charity within the new political order; the Truman and the Wallace wings of the post-FDR Democratic Party differed significantly on this point. But while much of their activity was directed to federal action, New Dealers struggled to win control of state and local governments too, precisely because it was less important where the action took place than that it did take place.

Thus, New Dealers fought to control the Democratic Party throughout the country and, once they were in control, to expand state and local governments' activities. G. Mennen Williams, David Lawrence, and Gaylord Nelson are obscure names now, but in the 1940s and 1950s they were the Democratic governors of Michigan, Pennsylvania, and Wisconsin, leaders in the effort to expand FDR's approach to governing to the states. California's Pat Brown was the Golden State's version of these men. Republican governors in large states, like Tom Dewey and Nelson Rockefeller of New York, George Romney of Michigan, and Earl Warren of California, also played their parts in hiking state aid to K–12 education, building new public universities and roads, and expanding social services and state parks.

We have seen that Reagan, in speech and in deed, as a private citizen in the late 1950s and early 1960s and as a public figure once elected governor, supported much of the expansion of government these men had wrought. He did not intend his Chicago proposal to result in dramatic cuts to these programs except insofar as cutting out the federal middleman would reduce bureaucracy. Rather, he believed that the care of the poor, education, policing, and local economic development were matters about which citizens of states and cities were in a better position to decide what should be done than representatives and bureaucrats.

These sentiments came through loud and clear when Reagan addressed the reaction to his proposal in subsequent speeches. The landmark collection of Reagan's handwritten, late-1970s radio addresses includes a "stump speech insert" dated January 22, 1976. That insert is a detailed refutation of the charges levied by critics against his Chicago speech and an explanation of what problems had arisen in these programs by lodging them at the federal level. Reagan's attack on the federal administration of these programs rested on two main critiques: waste and control.

Reagan's definition of waste was not limited to unnecessarily large levels of bureaucratic overhead or people who defrauded the programs. He mentioned both, the latter especially in the case of the infamous "Chicago welfare queen" who allegedly used multiple addresses, names, and phone numbers to collect over $150,000 a year from many different programs.[19] The major cause of waste, however, was people getting benefits who did not need them. Thus, he criticized the fact that existing programs allowed people "earning more than the median income" to collect food stamps, Medicaid, and welfare benefits.[20] With respect to food stamp eligibility, he criticized the fact that people could receive stamps even if they earned the median income, held substantial assets, or were children of wealthy parents.[21] He levied the same criticism of public housing programs, alleging that people with 80 percent of their area's median income were eligible for federal rent subsidies and that one-half of the units built by federal public housing programs "can only be afforded by upper-middle-class renters."[22] The problem for Reagan was not that government was taxing Peter to pay Paul, but rather than it was taxing Peter to pay Paul when Paul could provide quite well for himself.

His other primary criticism was that federal programs could force people to do what unelected bureaucrats wanted rather than what the people themselves desired. This was particularly true in federal education programs. Reagan's speech includes a variety of examples of "the lower level burocracy"[23] telling local schools what to do and higher-level officials telling colleges and universities they had to follow federal mandates to ensure the government would meet its social objectives.[24] In other cases, federal bureaucrats forced cities and states to spend money or hire staff they did not want in order to comply with federal mandates.[25] The problem was the same one he had identified since his early speeches in the 1950s: government was using the cloak of compassion to mask its true aims, social regimentation and the suppression of freedom.

Reagan's reaction to the criticism clearly shows that he saw nothing wrong with states or cities taxing their citizens to achieve social objectives that did help the needy. When asked about whether New Hampshire residents would have to adopt income or sales taxes for the first time to pay for any remanded programs they liked, Reagan did not respond with an attack on government or a pledge that taxes should never, ever be raised. Instead, he asked his interviewer, "But isn't this a proper decision for the people of the state to make?"[26] Indeed, as governor he had chosen to make that decision in 1967, choosing to substantially increase taxes rather than dramatically cut spending in the face of the record budget deficit. Eight years later, Reagan saw no reason why Granite State residents could not make the decisions he did regarding taxes if they wanted the same level of spending as Californians.

It is also worth noting that Reagan did not argue that the federal government had no legitimate role to play in these areas. His critique was not that the federal government *could* not do these things; it was that it *should* not do these things. And the reason it should not was because it was not in a position to know the problems and concerns of a state or city as well as its citizens. Thus, it was perfectly legitimate for the federal government to *fund* these programs or the general purposes that these programs were meant to address. Using the example of the Kerr-Mills Act, which gave the states money from the federal government to enact programs to assist the poor elderly with their medical bills, when pushed, Reagan quickly adopted the idea that a similar approach could be adopted for these programs as well. Libertarians who thought these programs were illegitimate, or old-guard conservatives who thought the federal government had no constitutional right to legislate in these areas, would find no comfort from Reagan's position.[27]

Reagan's own statements about why he ran in 1976 are consistent with this view. While he did not mention the Chicago speech in his autobiography, he did say he ran primarily because of a concern that Washington "was gradually but inexorably taking power from the states."[28] The federal government had done this by creating programs that tell "states, cities, counties, and schools how to spend this money." This in turn meant that "state and local governments [had] surrendered their destiny to a faceless bureaucracy in Washington that claimed to know better how to solve the problems of a city or town than the people who lived there." The Founders, he wrote, "never envisioned vast agencies in Washington telling our farmers what to plant, our teachers what to teach, our industrialists what to build."

These sentiments are entirely consistent with what Reagan had said in his private speeches in the late 1950s and early 1960s and in his Creative Society speech. The problem with big government was not that it was taxing or regulating one set of citizens to help others, as some conservatives and all libertarians argued. It was that under the guise of helping people and communities, power was flowing to an unelected group of people to guide and plan society according to this small group's wishes.

This was not an attack on the public New Deal, the sentiments that Harry Truman advanced in his 1948 campaign. Helping people in need and creating institutions and programs that gave average people a hand up in their quest to lead free and dignified lives was as perfectly acceptable to Ronald Reagan in 1975 as it had been in 1935 and 1955. It *was* an attack on the sentiments advanced by Henry Wallace and the Progressives in 1948, the view that private activity itself was inherently suspect and that a society had to be planned and regulated on a national basis from Washington, DC.

This crucial distinction between government activity and government planning allows us to understand why Reagan always made the bureaucracy the focal point of his attacks on government. Government activity could be, and often was, done by elected representatives. So long as their decisions arguably protected people from harm or gave them the ability to lead dignified lives of their own choosing, such activity was perfectly acceptable even if it led to higher taxes. Government planning, however, could not be done by elected representatives. The types of detailed decisions and interactions with individuals that carrying out plans required could only be done by professional bureaucrats.[29] Only unelected, professional bureaucrats could deal with the daily complexities that inevitably arose from conceiving and executing plans.

Since societal planning was the problem, bureaucrats had to become the enemy. Defeating them was Reagan's animating purpose; depriving them of power was his conservative goal. Reagan's interest in remanding programs to the state or local level derived from this impulse, not from any overriding belief that the activities themselves were inherently an improper exercise of governmental power.

Reagan's interest in reducing the amount of government spending was directly tied to these principles. As we shall see later in this chapter when we examine his radio broadcasts, the spending Reagan attacked always fit into one of two categories: it either enabled federal bureaucrats to advance their plans over those of ordinary citizens, or it gave money to people who did not deserve public assistance. Government then and now spends a lot of money that fits into one of these categories, and hence there was and remains great leeway to reduce the federal budget. But there was and is a lot of spending that does not fit into either category, spending that the early conservatives who rallied around Barry Goldwater and today's libertarians oppose as intolerable and unconstitutional impositions on liberty. On that ground, Reagan always stood with New Deal Democrats and against FDR's critics on the right.

Partly because of his Chicago speech, Reagan's campaign was on life support by late March. He had lost six straight primaries or caucuses, including the races in New Hampshire and Florida, where his federalism proposal had been a major issue. He headed into North Carolina as the underdog with little money but the support of the conservative Republican senator Jesse Helms. Helms's organization would help offset the lack of cash, but what the campaign really needed was a message that could rally support.

Reagan found that message by focusing on foreign policy. He started to emphasize his opposition to many aspects of the Ford administration's policy of détente—also known as "peaceful coexistence"—with the Communist Soviet Union. Most important, much as he had in 1966 when he found a populist issue to campaign on—opposition to radical student demonstrations at UC Berkeley—he picked up a populist issue that had not received much attention before: ownership of the Panama Canal. The canal, the only direct waterway connecting the Atlantic and Pacific Oceans, had been built by the United States, and the land surrounding it had been owned by the United States since 1903. The Ford administration was in negotiations with the Panamanian government, headed by the unelected strongman General Omar Torrijos, who was friendly with Cuba's Communist dictator, Fidel Castro, to return the canal and the surrounding Canal Zone to Panamanian ownership. Reagan would have none of it.

Waging the campaign on his familiar anti-Communist principles, Reagan pulled off a major upset and won the North Carolina primary. But his campaign was still starved of funds and he wouldn't have state organizations like Helms's to aid him elsewhere. Reagan needed money to wage battle in the states yet to come. So he took again to the airwaves on March 31, making a nationally televised address to appeal to the faithful for the money that would let him fight on.

Reagan's speech employed familiar themes, such as the threat from the Soviet Union and the problems with what he, quoting Cicero, called "the arrogance of officialdom."[30] It is notable, however, for three things: his direct attacks on President Ford, his invocation of Franklin Roosevelt, and his emphasis on protecting the security that some government-sponsored programs afforded millions of Americans.

In his autobiography, Reagan claimed that he entered the race against a sitting, albeit unelected,[31] Republican president only after he "pledged to follow the Eleventh Commandment."[32] While he claimed to have followed that pledge "not to speak ill of another Republican," in fact he attacked President Ford by name fifteen times in this crucial address. He blamed Ford for failing to stop inflation despite a pledge to "Whip Inflation Now," for signing an energy bill Ford had planned to veto that reduced American oil production at a time of energy shortages and rising gas prices, for preparing to give away the Panama Canal, and for failing to effectively fight Soviet communism.[33] Reagan had never before criticized a sitting Republican president in this manner, and the nature of his attacks were substantially identical to those he would levy against Democratic president Jimmy Carter four years later. The man who had a decade earlier called on all stripes of Republicans to make peace to fight the common foe was now directly responsible for dividing the party himself.

Of course, these attacks were coming from a man who himself had long been a Democrat. Reagan viewed the Republican Party not as an ancestral home as so many party faithful did, but as a vehicle in the current situation for maintaining American values. American values transcended party, and so when someone in Reagan's mind endangered American values, he saw no barrier to saying so. For Reagan, the Eleventh Commandment seems to have been a bar to the sort of personal attacks often levied against someone's character, not a barrier against talking about someone's record.

Ford's biggest sin in Reagan's eyes was that he was part of the "Washington Establishment." Reagan told the viewers of his March 31 speech that this establishment "is not the answer. It's the problem." And Ford had "for most of his adult life . . . been a part of the Washington Establishment." He was thus incapable of seeing how government and bureaucracy were harming America, and was unwilling to stand up when necessary to the establishment to fight for American values. Ford's Republicanism was thus more harmful than either Eisenhower's or Nixon's or even Rockefeller's, as Ford was simply the creature of the very enemy Reagan sought to defeat.

Looked at in this vein, Reagan's otherwise strange invocations of nonpartisanship make perfect sense. While he acknowledged he was seeking the Republican nomination, he started his speech by "hop[ing] that you who are Independents and Democrats will let me talk to you also tonight because the problems facing our country are problems that just don't bear any party label." The former New Dealer also invoked the Great Depression, saying that no one who had lived through that could "ever look upon an unemployed person with anything but compassion." When criticizing Ford for firing his more hawkish Defense Secretary, James Schelsinger, for suggesting America was weaker militarily than Ford wanted to let on, Reagan quoted FDR for the proposition that in dark times "it is time to speak the truth frankly and boldly." And he moved into the conclusion of his talk by again citing FDR's famous statement that Americans "have a rendezvous with destiny."

I doubt any other Republican would give a major speech while fighting for the Republican Party nomination that contained no positive references to any Republican president or figure, but did include direct and indirect references to FDR, the GOP's historic enemy, the man who had transformed America's majority party into a minority fighting for its life. No amount of political calculation or prudence can explain this. It is simply the case that even when he was launching a battle for the control of the Republican Party from that party's right, he was campaigning as the true inheritor of Franklin Roosevelt's mantle.

And so it was that FDR's heir went out of his way to reassure the Republicans, Democrats, and independents watching him that their hard-won social protections would be safe under him. He emphasized his commitment to "restore the integrity of Social Security," arguing that benefits were under attack from the inflation Ford wasn't stopping. He promised to appoint a presidential commission to "present a plan to strengthen and improve Social Security . . . so that no person who has contributed to Social Security will ever lose a dime." He noted how his welfare reforms had pruned rolls while increasing "grants to the truly deserving needy by an average of 43 percent." He even made a point of explaining how as governor he had taken a teacher's retirement fund with a massive unfunded liability and left office with it "fully funded on a sound actuarial basis." People who truly needed and relied on the social insurance and government programs enacted after 1932 had nothing to fear from Reagan.

Reagan's message started to resonate after North Carolina, and the rest of the year was a knock-down, drag-out battle between the two men. But in what was to become a pattern for the next forty years in intraparty battles, Reagan's victories in the South and Rocky Mountain West were offset by losses in the Northeast and most of the Midwest. When Reagan lost the Wisconsin and Ohio primaries by ten points each, the convention table was largely set in favor of Ford.

Reagan's gambit to overcome Ford's advantage was controversial at the time and remains so to this day. At that time, not all delegates were pledged to candidates coming into the convention. Hundreds of delegates in the bastions of liberal Republicanism, New York and Pennsylvania, were legally uncommitted and hence capable of changing their minds and backing Reagan. With that in mind, Reagan did something no candidate had done before and selected a vice presidential running mate before the convention: Pennsylvania senator Richard Schweiker.[34] Conservatives immediately erupted, as Schweiker had one of the most liberal voting records in the US Senate. Reagan, however, defended this pick as principled to the end of his life, arguing that he had once been a liberal and his discussions with Schweiker convinced him that his running mate was like he once was, someone on the verge of converting to conservatism.[35] Schweiker's voting record did in fact move noticeably to the right after his selection and remained so until he left the Senate in 1981 to become President Reagan's first secretary of Health and Human Services.[36]

Reagan's daring maneuver failed to dislodge liberal Republican delegates from their informal commitments to their state party leaders and President Ford. Despite thrilling millions, Reagan's second bid for the presidency fell short, garnering 1,070 delegate votes to President Ford's 1,187. Reagan gamely supported the Ford-Dole ticket, campaigning for it in many states. Ford roared back from a nearly thirty-point deficit after the close of the GOP convention in August, but fell just short, losing to the Democratic candidate, former Georgia governor Jimmy Carter, by about 2 percent in the popular vote and by a 297–240 margin in the Electoral College.[37]

Reagan was now in the political wilderness. He had lost two races for the presidency and no longer held elected office. He was already older than anyone who had been elected president since William Henry Harrison in 1840; if he were to run again in 1980, he would be the oldest man ever elected to his first term. Moreover, he would be running as the nominee of a party that was at its lowest ebb of fortune since the Great Depression. Republicans held only 143 of the 538 House seats, 38 of 100 Senate seats, and a paltry 12 of the 50 governorships. No one would have blamed Reagan if he and Nancy had retired to their beloved ranch and lived out the rest of their days riding horses and enjoying the California hills.

That was never in the cards. Reagan wrote that after he lost he told the California GOP delegation that "Nancy and I are not going back and sit on our rocking chair and say 'that's all for us.'"[38] He knew then and there he was running again. "I wasn't the reluctant candidate I'd been in 1968 and 1976," he wrote. "I wanted to be President."[39] It wasn't long before he presented himself once more to his loyalists.

The setting was the fourth annual Conservative Political Action Conference. His speech, delivered on his sixty-sixth birthday, is simply one of the most important, and perhaps the most underappreciated, of any talk he ever gave.

Reagan's speech was titled "The New Republican Party."[40] It sought to do four things at once. First, give conservatives hope that they could win despite years of defeat. Second, persuade them that their home was in the Republican Party, not in a new third party, as many prominent conservative intellectuals had argued. Third, show that this new party would be one firmly grounded in conservative principle. Fourth, and most important, show that devotion to ideology—even conservative ideology—was the enemy of everything they held dear.

He was able to accomplish the first two tasks easily. He started his speech by noting that many polls showed that either a large plurality or a majority of Americans described themselves as right of center or conservatives. He later briefly dismissed the calls for a "new political party" by noting that the Republican Party already included "the biggest single grouping of conservatives." "It makes more sense," he said, "to build on that grouping than to break it up and start all over."

The problem with that formula, however, was that not every self-described conservative wanted the same things. Reagan acknowledged this up front, saying, "Conservatism can and does mean different things to those who call themselves conservatives." If some conservatives viewed others as insufficiently conservative, and hence people with whom they could not work, then the whole project of "creat[ing] a political entity that will reflect the view of the great, hitherto [unacknowledged], conservative majority" would fail.

The enemy of that vitally important undertaking was ideology. Building this new party "will mean compromise," Reagan said, "but not a compromise of basic principle." Principle did not, however, mean "ideology." He said ideology "always conjures up in my mind a picture of a rigid, irrational clinging to abstract theory in the face of reality." Ideology in America was "a scare word." Marxist-Leninism, which "chopped off and discarded" facts if they "don't happen to fit the ideology," was a prime example of what was to be avoided. American conservatism was "free from slavish adherence to abstraction" and was "derived from willingness to learn" from present and prior experience.

The American conservatism Reagan believed in was not ideological. "The common sense and common decency of ordinary men and women, working out their own lives in their own way—this is the heart of American conservatism today." It supported ideas like a free market, balanced budgets, and moving government closer to the people because it was based on learned experience and example, not because some great theory told conservatives these ideas were right.

Reagan subtly told his audience of conservative activists that they must adopt these views if they were to win. "Our first job," he said, "is to get this message across to those who share most of our principles."

> Let us lay to rest, once and for all the myth of a small group of ideological purists trying to capture a majority. . . . If we allow ourselves to be portrayed as ideological shock troops without correcting this error we are doing ourselves and our cause a disservice. Wherever and whenever we can, we should gently but firmly correct our political and media friends who have been perpetuating the myth of conservatism as a narrow ideology. Whatever the word might have meant in the past, today conservatism means principles evolving from experience and a belief in change when necessary, but not just for the sake of change.

Lest anyone mistake his words, Reagan noted that "ideological fanaticism" could be found on the left or right. Ideological fanatics were "the enemies of freedom" and were people "who would sacrifice principle to theory, those who worship only the god of political, social and economic abstractions, ignoring the realities of everyday life. *They are not conservatives.*" (Emphasis added.)

Ever the politician, Reagan did not give his audience examples of who might qualify as "ideological fanatics" of the Right. But it should be clear from his words who he might have had in mind. The sort of libertarian for whom every political question was a matter of high principle, who would rest only when virtually every political program enacted in the past half century was repealed—that person would be a fanatic who sacrificed principle for abstraction. The sort of "ultra" whom Reagan had met in California, the type who would oppose a reasonable compromise given the circumstances to fight a hopeless battle—that person was a fanatic who sacrificed principle for abstraction. One might even say that the Goldwater of *Conscience* rather than the Goldwater Reagan knew personally was such a fanatic, as the entire book started from first principles and reasoned backward from them irrespective of "the realities of everyday life."

Recall that Reagan's arguments in his pre–"Time for Choosing" speeches were always based on facts, not theory. He was opposed to federal aid for education because no need had been shown, not because such aid was inherently opposed to liberty. He was for the Kerr-Mills Act because it met a legitimate need, helping poor senior citizens pay for needed medical care. He was against Medicare because in light of Kerr-Mills there was no need for it, unless the real purpose was to fit American life to preconceived ideological notions. Nothing Reagan said in his CPAC speech was any different from what he had been saying for years, before political office was even a glimmer in his inner eye.

We should therefore read his words here as ones of principle, not political pragmatism. Reagan was not advising conservatives to take this course solely because failure to do so would keep the divergent parts of American conservatism split from one another. He was subtly teaching his wards of the very roots of conservatism itself, roots found in the love of actual, ordinary people living actual, ordinary lives. "Most of us," he told his fellow conservatives, "like to think of ourselves as avoiding both extremes." It was these nonextreme conservatives who above all Reagan sought to bring into the New Republican Party.

These people were not businessmen, "makers," or strivers. These were ordinary people, "the man and the woman in the factories, the farmer, the cop on the beat." The current Republican Party was, "for reasons both fair and unfair" burdened with a "country club–big business image." These potential new Republicans were less interested in issues of big government and deficit spending; those concerned with that were already in the Republican Party. The new Republicans were called by some "social conservatives," people concerned with "law and order, abortion, busing, quota systems." The New Republican Party needed to address these people too if it wanted to unite the conservative majority into one political entity.

Reagan made clear that more than lip service was needed to address these people's concerns. "If we are to attract more working men and women of this country, we will do so not by simply 'making room' for them, but by making certain they have a say in what goes on in the party." Left unsaid was what that meant for the concerns of small-government conservatives for whom the New Deal and the "big government" it had created were at best problematic; their concerns would need to be soft-pedaled to make room for the new converts.

The true believers in small government for its own sake would always feel dismayed or betrayed when they came to realize that this was what was being asked of them. Those who were dismayed would grumble; those who felt betrayed would scream with outrage that their hero was not who they thought he was. The same cycle that arose in California with Schmitz and Steffgen would repeat itself throughout Reagan's 1980 run and his presidency.

But this sense of betrayal merely showed that such people had never listened carefully enough to Reagan's own words. This middle ground, this definition of American conservatism as an interpretation of the Roosevelt legacy rather than its repudiation, is where Reagan himself always stood. A limited but effective government that provided a robust defense of American freedom in the world and a hand up for American citizens as they confronted "the realities of everyday life" was what Reagan had offered America from the moment he launched his career as a political speaker. He had told the press in 1966 that if John Birchers voted for him, they were endorsing his views, not he theirs. In effect, he offered both discontented Democrats and conservative Republicans the same new deal: If you support me, you're backing my agenda; I am not necessarily backing yours.

Reagan gave listeners a sense of his agenda when he provided "my own version" of a "Declaration of Principles" for this New Republican Party. Largely quoting from the 1976 Republican Party platform, which many in the room had helped draft, it was exactly what he had proclaimed it should be, principled but not ideological and broad enough to include the concerns of all members of the conservative family. It stood for individual freedom, but not to the exclusion of government action that "assure[d] equal opportunity," and was "compassionate in caring for those citizens who are unable to care for themselves." It envisioned national governmental action to address environmental protection, a national transportation system, and for the safeguarding of civil liberties. It preferred "as a general rule . . . that government action should be taken first by the government" closest to the people, but did not establish federalism as a hard and inviolable barrier to action. The same balance was struck with regards to the actions of "voluntary organizations"; they "should have the opportunity to solve many of the social problems of their communities," but there would be no strict line between private and public action regarding social and economic issues.

A similar sense of balance pervaded his other principles. Family preservation was essential to America's future. Government must always ask "is it not better for the country to leave your dollars in your pocket," but no strict barrier would be imposed on how much or for what purposes it could take that money. "The American market system" was the most productive economic system imaginable, but the government still had the role to pursue "the elimination of unfair practices." In foreign policy, negotiation with adversaries was acceptable, but only within the framework of "maintaining a superior national defense, second to none."

Some conservatives might read this and conclude that Reagan offered conservatives "pale pastels" rather than "bold colors." But such conservatives, by defining conservatism too narrowly either in terms of principles or policies, were and are acting more as ideologues than as principled citizens. Purging conservatism of this tendency was the core of Reagan's message, and it was to this subject that he turned as he concluded his talk.

Reagan's New Republican Party, he said, would not be "based on a principle of exclusion." What followed should be read by today's conservative leaders and activists, for in so many ways they have failed to follow the guidance of the man whom they claim to revere:

> You do not get to be a majority party by searching for groups you won't associate or work with. If we truly believe in our principles, we should sit down and talk. Talk with anyone, anywhere, at any

time if it means talking about the principles of the Republican Party. *Conservatism is not a narrow ideology, nor is it the exclusive property of conservative activists.* [Emphasis added.]

That last sentence bears repeating and reexamination. Reagan told a roomful of conservative activists that they did not and could not define conservatism. If they wanted to act like they did, if they thought of themselves like some sort of supreme soviet that could define what was and was not conservative, then they would never be a majority party. Indeed, they would not even be conservative, for they would have abandoned principle for ideology, and in doing so would have ceased to be conservative at all.

For ultimately the enemy for Reagan was ideology, not big government. Big government could be the enemy, especially an ever-growing government that made itself the arbiter of all things great and small. That government exalted "centralized bureaucracy" and "government by a self-anointed elite." That government created "*extreme* taxation, *excessive* controls, *oppressive* government competition with business" (emphases added). That government, especially as found in the totalitarian and ideological Communist states, could threaten the most precious principle of all, "that each one of us maintain his dignity and his identity in an increasingly complex, centralized society."

Living through the Great Depression, however, Reagan had learned that an ideology insisting that government should do nothing could rob people of their dignity and identity as easily as one that said government should do everything. By ignoring the realities of everyday life in unregulated factories, by ignoring the realities of everyday life of people who despite their best efforts could not support themselves, the conservative and libertarian ideologies that hold liberty alone as a holy and inviolable principle also sacrifice the realities of everyday life on the altar of slavish devotion to abstraction. To that extent, the old Republican Party had fairly earned its image as the country club–big business party. Such a party and such an ideology no less than communism was abhorrent to Reagan.

Reagan spent the next three years applying his principles to the political problems of his time. His did so through a medium of his youth:
radio. He started broadcasting short, two-minute radio messages, a
modern version of FDR's fireside chats, to a nationwide audience. We
now know that he wrote many of these messages himself in longhand,
demonstrating again that he was literally the author of his own success.
These hundreds of messages together comprise the largest source of his
precise views on a variety of subjects. They are a treasure trove of conclusions that when sifted show exactly what his principles were.

It should not be surprising that even the most careful examination
of these short talks finds that Reagan's principles were the same as they
had been decades earlier. Recall what Nancy Reagan said: Reagan had
formed his principles years before he became governor.[41] What's noteworthy about his radio addresses is not his conservatism, it's how well
his clear but simple principles allowed him to formulate specific answers to questions that were entirely different from those facing America in the 1950s.

The realm of foreign policy was perhaps the least changed of any
policy realm over Reagan's active lifetime. He had started adult life an
ardent foe of one ideological, totalitarian state bent on world domination (Nazi Germany) and quickly moved on to become an even more
vociferous foe of the Soviet Union. By the 1970s, however, the Soviet
Union was on the march in ways not seen since the early days after
World War II, when it had gobbled up state after state in Eastern Europe. Marxist terrorist groups were active in Western Europe, even kid-
napping and murdering a former Italian premier.[42] Soviet-sponsored
"liberation movements" were actively destabilizing many countries
throughout the world, and Soviet client states like Cuba and Vietnam
had sent their militaries to support other new Soviet client states in
places like Angola, Mozambique, Ethiopia, and Cambodia. The USSR
meanwhile was building its nuclear and conventional armed forces to
numbers hitherto unknown, threatening America and its allies across
the globe.

Some quailed before this might, counseling negotiation and nonconfrontation. Not Reagan. He had opposed such temporizing since the early 1960s, and increased Russian might had merely confirmed him in his faith that communism was both inherently evil and inalterably expansionist. As adamantly opposed to war as he was, he was even more adamantly opposed to the idea that peace purchased at the price of freedom was worthwhile.

It is not surprising, therefore, that 30 percent of all his radio messages addressed foreign policy.[43] The vast majority was concerned with the threat from the Soviet Union, a nation Reagan called a "Godless tyranny" years before he famously labeled it an "evil empire."[44] In talk after talk he told listeners how America and its allies had fallen behind the Russians in conventional armaments.[45] Negotiations with the USSR over the limitation of nuclear weapons (SALT II) would result only in granting the Soviets the same sort of superiority in nuclear weapons.[46] He repeatedly quoted a speech given by Soviet leader Leonid Brezhnev in which he called the USSR's policy of détente a ruse and that by 1985 the Soviet Union would be able to work its will anywhere in the world.[47] "Only by mustering a superiority, beginning with a superiority of the spirit, can we stop the thunder of hobnailed boots on their march to world empire."[48]

This type of talk might seem unbelievable today, but it was not back then. We have now lived over a quarter of a century since the collapse of the Soviet Union. One needs to be nearly forty years old to have even the dimmest memories of a time when the Cold War was very real. President Jimmy Carter may have proclaimed an end to the "inordinate fear of Communism" in May 1977, but even he was proposing increased defense budgets after the Soviet Union's December 1979 invasion of its own client state, Afghanistan. Many intelligent and patriotic Americans thought Reagan was wrong and his rhetoric overheated, but few failed to see that the conflict with the Soviet Union was the most dangerous and important international issue of the age.

That was certainly my view when I met Ronald Reagan for the only time in my life. I had spent my high school years actively involved in my local Republican Party. When I went to Claremont McKenna

College in the fall of 1979, I immediately joined the school's College Republican chapter and joined them for the trek south to the state party's mid-September convention in San Diego.[49] The man then known as Governor Reagan gave a question-and-answer session for attendees and delegates prior to his speech to the entire convention. Since current and former students of my school were in charge of the Q&A, I was a shoo-in to get to talk with the man himself.

My moment came toward the end of the session. Standing in my blue polyester Sears suit to the candidate's right, I saw Jay Rosenlieb point at me to go ahead. My question was quick and to the point: "Governor Reagan, what do you think of the Non-Aligned Movement?" I was referring to a group of mainly Third World nations that purported to be unaligned between the two superpowers but whose criticisms were usually directed at America. As a staunch anti-Communist, I was hoping Reagan shared my views that this allegedly neutral group was in fact not our friend.

Reagan's reply was equally quick and to the point: "I don't believe there is such a thing as the Non-Aligned Movement. You're either for us or against us." Then and there I became a fan for life.

Reagan's clarity and courage attracted many more than died-in-the-wool conservative Republicans like me. Staunch anti-communism had also been a hallmark of the post-Roosevelt Democratic Party. Once Truman had defeated Wallace in the intramural fight over the immediate legacy of the New Deal, Democrats as well as Republicans lined up to mount a muscular defense against the Soviet Union. Truman himself organized the North Atlantic Treaty Organization (NATO) to combat Soviet expansion into Europe, and John F. Kennedy ran against Dwight Eisenhower's vice president, Richard Nixon, in 1960 in part by alleging that Ike's frugality had created a "missile gap" with the Soviet Union that imperiled American security.

Such views were increasingly unpopular within the Democratic Party, however. The 1972 Democratic nominee, George McGovern, had defeated the heir of the old Truman wing, former vice president Hubert Humphrey. Humphrey's backers lined up behind Washington senator Henry "Scoop" Jackson in 1976 only to see him trounced by former governor Jimmy Carter. As president, Carter quickly angered Jackson backers with a number of high-profile foreign policy moves and appointments that showed them the Democratic Party no longer shared their views. As the Carter presidency lurched from crisis to crisis, including the loss of an important ally when the Shiite cleric the Ayatollah Khomeini overthrew the shah of Iran, these "neoconservatives" increasingly turned a longing eye at the GOP to see if they could find a new home.

"Neoconservative" meant something much different in the 1970s. Today the term primarily refers to people who argued for and supported President George W. Bush's war in Iraq. Back then, it meant people who had been ardent New Dealers and had remained staunch anti-Communists while becoming less enamored of the continued expansion of government advocated by the increasingly dominant progressive Democrats. These men and women did not want to repeal most if any of the New Deal's substantive achievements, and hence looked askance on traditional Goldwaterite conservatives.

These intellectuals, activists, and academics were themselves important, but they acquired even more importance because their concerns mirrored those of an increasing number of working-class Democratic voters. These people had supported Nixon over the liberal McGovern in 1972, but remained leery of a conservatism they associated with anti-FDR sentiments and a corporate Republicanism they believed did not care about people like them. California's working-class Democrats had found a kindred soul in Reagan, however, and men and women like them in the rest of the country would get to examine him themselves over the next few years.

Reagan's radio messages broadcast the same, New Deal–friendly view of economic and domestic policy that he had been sharing for over twenty years. Not only were his principles indistinguishable from those he held in the 1950s, even some of the specific items he promoted came straight out of his old mashed-potato-circuit talks.

Fighting "bracket creep" is an excellent example of an idea Reagan had been promoting for decades. "Bracket creep" is an unintended by-product of a progressive income tax system that assesses higher income tax rates across ranges of incomes ("brackets") as income increases. If a worker gets a salary increase that covers only the cost of inflation, he might be worse off because his new income would be taxed at a higher rate if the increase forced him to move into a new tax bracket. So, for example, if incomes are taxed at 10 percent between $5,000 and $10,000 but at 20 percent between $10,000 and $15,000, a worker making $9,500 who gets a salary hike to $10,500 to offset high inflation would pay a much higher rate of tax on his income even though he is in fact no better off.

This was a big issue in the late 1970s, as America faced unusually high inflation. Workers would get 5 or 10 percent annual cost-of-living adjustments (COLAs) to offset inflation's effects, but end up worse off because they would be pushed into new tax brackets with higher income tax rates. Reagan proposed solving this by indexing the brackets for inflation, meaning that the ranges at which tax rates were imposed would rise with inflation.[50] This commonsense idea was quite popular and in fact was included in the tax cut legislation Reagan signed into law in 1981.

What few people realize is that Reagan had been proposing indexing for decades. He had argued against inflation as far back as his 1958 speech before the California Fertilizer Association[51] and specifically proposed indexation as a solution for bracket creep in his 1961 speech to the Phoenix Chamber of Commerce.[52] Few people cared back then, when inflation was only about 1 or 2 percent a year.[53] But when inflation rose to between 5 and 15 percent a year as it did in the mid- to late 1970s, suddenly Reagan's old idea seemed very relevant indeed.

Reagan's views on social insurance programs such as Social Security and Medicaid also had not changed. Back in the 1950s and 1960s, before there was a uniform federal health program for the poor (which is what Medicaid is), he had specifically said that any American without the money to pay for needed medical care should have it provided for him or her.[54] He espoused the same idea in his radio broadcasts, telling listeners that "we all want to insure [*sic*] that no one is denied needed medical care because of poverty."[55] Similarly, he had told Americans in his famous "Time for Choosing" speech that they could do better if they were allowed to invest their Social Security tax money themselves; he made the identical argument for his radio audience in the late 1970s.[56]

This is not to say that he never changed his mind on anything. By the late 1970s the union man who had long opposed right-to-work laws had changed his tune.[57] He said he "wholeheartedly" supported right to work, arguing that the "rank-and-file union member" felt that labor union leaders no longer represented his or her interests.[58] But this is the exception that proved the rule.

Reagan's core principles were no less changed than his specific ideas. We have already seen that he believed as passionately in a muscular defense of freedom abroad in the 1970s as he had in the 1940s or 1950s. With respect to his other core principles, he believed as much as he ever had in the goodness and the inherent dignity of the average American, the dangers of government planning, and the way in which legitimate need both required and limited government action.[59]

Government planning was always the ultimate foe, the manner by which America's unique fire of liberty could be stamped out and the rule of the many of themselves replaced by the rule of a self-appointed and unaccountable few. Those who encountered Reagan for the first time in these talks heard him say: "Our problem is a permanent structure of government insulated from the thinking and wishes of the people; a structure which for all practical purposes is more powerful than our elected representatives."[60]

Once that power is installed, people would be forced to conform to the dictates of others who were not accountable to anyone and accumulated power without regret.

Note that here, as throughout his career, the enemy is the unelected bureaucrat, not government itself. Reagan had been attacking this for decades because he believed free people could rule both themselves and their communities, choosing for themselves how best to live and what level of services to tax themselves to support. Individual freedom and collective, responsible government were not incompatible in Reagan's thought.

American government taxed too much, he thought, because it was aiding too many people who did not really need the aid, or encouraging otherwise decent people to avoid responsibility for their own fates. In his own retelling of the fable of the little red hen, Reagan describes a productive hen who is forced by government to share the proceeds of her baking with people who want the benefits of work without working themselves.[61] Reagan applied this insight to critique unemployment insurance, because lax standards[62] allowed people who didn't deserve it to get "generous tax free benefits."[63] Welfare taxed people to support "unconscionable administrative overhead"[64] while "injuring their diligence or providence."[65] Free food stamps were intended for the poor but instead were available to people in the lower middle class.[66] The result was a government that had gotten away from its legitimate function to support the "needy and disabled"[67] or "those who can't help themselves"[68] to one dedicated to "bigger government, less and less liberty, [and] redistribution of earnings through confiscatory taxation."[69]

No one familiar with Reagan's thought throughout the years can fail to see his remarkable continuity. He saw the same challenges and the same threats, and prescribed the same mode of addressing them in 1978 as he had in 1958. His values, moreover, were no different than they had been in 1938. He still believed in the possibility of a free America, of free Americans living lives of their own choosing, undergirded by a democratic and compassionate government unafraid to champion—and fight for—justice and peace at home and abroad.

His framework was flexible enough to permit him to incorporate new political issues into his worldview. American culture had changed a lot from that of his youth, and by the late 1970s the beginnings of what we now call the "culture wars" had arisen. Now-familiar debates over abortion, religious liberty, homosexuality, and the role of the sexes were then new. Reagan had largely not addressed those issues in the tamer, more cloistered days in which he formed his political opinions.[70] He was well aware, however, of the political possibilities these issues had, as his "New Republican Party" speech demonstrated. How to incorporate an appeal to voters concerned with these issues, however, may have perplexed a less thoughtful man. Not so Reagan.

Most social issues were, for Reagan, primarily another example of the self-appointed social planners ignoring the American people. Racial desegregation was fine, but forced busing of children to obtain a more even racial mix in public schools was not.[71] The Supreme Court ruling prohibiting prayer in schools was wrong,[72] as was federal involvement in K–12 education generally, because it removed power from local school boards and made public schools "society's agreed upon vehicle for social change."[73] Similarly, while laws barring discrimination "by virtue of sex or anything else for that matter" were acceptable, the Equal Rights Amendment was a bad idea.[74] "I'm for the E and the R but not the A" Reagan said in an October 1984 debate with the Democratic presidential nominee Walter Mondale.[75] In each case, he avoided making the issue about race or about Christian religion, rather viewing each action through the lens of an individual's or a family's right to live as they pleased.

Reagan's approach to homosexuality is an excellent example of his thinking on social issues. He did not support "the movement to abolish or lessen the present laws concerning sexual conduct," but he wrote an op-ed opposing an antigay ballot initiative in the 1978 California general election.[76] Proposition 6, known as the Briggs Initiative after its sponsor, State Senator John Briggs, would have permitted public schools to fire any teacher who "advocated" a homosexual lifestyle whether inside or outside the classroom. Reagan argued that this was "more government" and could lead to "over-enforcement."[77] He went on to disprove some of the assertions Briggs made about homosexuals, such as their alleged predisposition for child molestation, and contended that gay teachers could not model homosexuality for their students because "prevailing scientific opinion is that an individual's sexuality is determined at a very young age." Reagan took this position even though the initiative was part of a national antigay movement powered by the then-young Christian Right.

Reagan's stance toward the Briggs Initiative is indicative of how he approached social issues and the Christian Right more generally. His analysis of issues like abortion, prayer in schools, and the family always rested on his long-held principles rather than religion. He rarely if ever said America was a Christian nation or that Christian principles were essential to American identity or national well-being. He might speak about his own belief in God, but he almost never invoked Jesus. For Reagan, Christian conservatives were simply another group of citizens whose beliefs and values were being ignored or disparaged by the remote bureaucracy intent on imposing its views on America.

Reagan's voluminous private correspondence from this period shows he said the same things in private as he did in public. He would praise his ability as governor to increase "support for public schools eight times as much as the increase in enrollment" as much as his ability to "cut, squeeze, and trim" government spending.[78] He supported returning many programs to the states so that their citizens could decide whether to retain or eliminate them, not because he believed those programs were inherently not within the province of any government to address.[79] His discussion of issues of morality would mention God but not Christianity.[80]

There are a couple of letters that could be interpreted as showing a private Reagan who was more antigovernment than he let on. In a few notes, he said that the direction of America changed after FDR's election in 1932. He told "Philip," an otherwise unidentified young man, that "the Roosevelt era was characterized by a government takeover to an extent we've never known."[81] He also told his college girlfriend's father that he later realized "that we took a turning point back there in 1932 that has led to our present troubles."[82] Taken out of context, these lines could be said to indicate that Reagan now regretted his support for Roosevelt and had become an opponent of FDR's New Deal.

These views should be read in the broader context of Reagan's long public record. That record unequivocally stood behind the many public programs that legitimately helped people in need, provided for more opportunity, or prevented government from unfairly hindering a group of people from making their way in life. As we have seen, even Reagan's support of Goldwater was couched in the terms of a disappointed New Dealer looking to return to the true promise of that era rather than use the language of Roosevelt to implement the program of Lenin. The "government knows best" approach of the Henry Wallace Progressives was brought into being by that "turning point back there in 1932," but it was not the only interpretation one could give to that point.

Reagan's letters on health care coverage make that distinction crystal clear. Starting with a note to his longtime pen pal Lorraine Wagner in July 1961, Reagan specifically endorsed the idea that government—even the federal government—should pay for medical care for people who need help paying for it. His letter to Wagner was sent in response to hers asking about a record Reagan had made for the American Medical Association opposing proposals for Medicare. He told Wagner he was opposed to socialized medicine defined as "a compulsory medical-insurance program tied to Social Security for <u>all</u> senior citizens whether they need it or not." (Emphasis in original.)[83] Reagan went on to describe his full views in more detail:

> Very simply I'm in favor of helping those who need help. In the last session of Congress before this one we adopted a measure introduced by Senator Kerr (Democrat) and Congressman W. Mills (Democrat) known as the "Kerr-Mills" bill. This provides federal funds to the states to furnish medical care for the aged. The bill isn't actually working yet having only been passed eight months ago. Now I'm in favor of this bill—and *if the money isn't enough I think we should put up more.* . . . I am not opposed to providing medical care for those who really need it and can't pay for it but I do not believe in compulsory health insurance through a government bureau for people who don't need it or who have incomes or even a few million dollars tucked away. [Emphasis added.]

This was not an idea endorsed by all conservatives then, as we saw with Steffgen's opposition to Medicaid as itself "socialized medicine" in the last chapter. For Reagan, taxing Peter to pay for Paul's health care was all right so long as Paul really needed it.

This remained Reagan's view even as he was on the verge of announcing his 1980 presidential candidacy. Reagan wrote a letter in mid-1979 to Professor Vsevolod Nikolaev, a Russian American who had written him about his views on health insurance and Social Security. Reagan replied:

> While I am opposed to socialized medicine, I have always felt that medical care should be available for those who cannot otherwise afford it. I have been looking into a program whereby government might pay for the premiums for health insurance for those who cannot afford it and, at the same time, make such premiums for others a tax credit or deduction, preferably a credit to encourage more use of private health insurance. There is also the problem of insurance for those catastrophic cases where the medical care goes on for years at a tremendously high cost. I proposed a form of government insurance for that in California when I was governor, but we couldn't get any legislative support for it. I do believe this is a particular problem which must be faced and where government could have a hand.[84]

Pre-FDR conservatives and those who coalesced around Barry Goldwater in the early 1960s had always opposed federal funding for health care, except in the cases of veterans and federal employees. Taxing Peter to pay for Paul's doctor seemed both unconstitutional and unjust to them. Reagan had always quietly, but clearly, disagreed with them, and remained committed to his contrary conservatism throughout his political life.

That contrary conservatism had always formed the basis for his popular appeal, and it would be the basis on which his 1980 campaign would be founded. Reagan made this clear in his announcement speech, given on national television on November 13, 1979.[85] His first point was the poor economy of the period, which suffered from slow growth and high inflation now called "stagflation." While Reagan blamed the federal government's size and growth for this and said cutting taxes would restore economic health, he was careful to exempt a great deal of spending from his criticism. Getting "the waste out of federal spending," he said, "does not mean sacrificing essential services, nor do we need to destroy the system of benefits which flow to the poor, the elderly, the sick and the handicapped. *We have long since committed ourselves, as a people, to help those among us who cannot take care of themselves.*" (Emphasis added.)

That basic thrust, interpreting the New Deal's fundamental innovations to provide for less bureaucratic and government direction of American life, pervaded Reagan's other ideas. He proposed to solve the energy crisis not by adopting the bureaucracy's proposal that Americans make do with less but by getting government out of the way so individuals could produce more. Removing "government obstacles" to the increased "domestic production of oil and gas" would be accompanied, however, by continued efforts to create "more efficient automobiles." Reagan did not propose completely removing government from any role in addressing energy shortages; he merely proposed giving private companies and individuals the chance to solve those shortages through their own initiative in the marketplace.

Reagan's retrospective explanation for why he ran in 1980 provides further support for this view. The problem with the Democrats under Carter was that they wanted "national economic planning."[86]

> That meant one thing to me: The Democrats wanted to borrow some of the principles of the Soviets' failed five-year plans, with Washington setting national production goals, deciding where people worked, what they would do, where they would live, what they would produce.[87]

Whether Carter or the Democrats actually wanted to do that is beside the point. The point is that Reagan was taking aim at an excess of government control best described in the 1948 Progressive Party interpretation of the New Deal rather than the New Deal itself. Government help would be fine; government control and direction would not.

He also criticized the Democrats' commitment to a "'fairer distribution of wealth, income, and power."[88] Those were "code words that to me meant a confiscation of the earnings of people in our country who worked and produced, and their redistribution to those that didn't."[89] Again, whether Reagan's characterization is fair is not the issue. What is at issue is what Reagan saw as the problem with government. His answer, as it was decades before, was that government should not give money to people who did not contribute or deserve help. As his many other statements always showed, people who *could not* work or provide for themselves deserved government assistance. The problem came when government chose to use its power to create a society that was fairer primarily in the eyes of government planners and experts.

Reagan did not break any new intellectual ground in his race for the nomination, nor was his nomination ever really in doubt except for a very brief period in February 1980. That period indirectly shows why Reagan believed what he did, as the political experts were proved wrong twice and the power of individual initiative and character was shown to make all the difference.

Reagan's age and conservatism, not to mention his two previous defeats, meant that other ambitious Republicans were not hesitant to take him on. Some ran to his right, like Phil Crane, while the others ran to varying degrees to his left. Pundits, however, quickly settled on his two most important challengers.

The former Texas governor and treasury secretary John Connally was one. A Democrat turned Republican like Reagan, Connally was a favorite of the corporate set. He easily raised what was then a tremendous sum of money, $11 million, and as a southerner with extensive experience, he looked like the man who could steal the conservative South from Reagan.[90]

Senate Republican leader Howard Baker was the other. He had been an important figure in the Watergate hearings, regularly asking witnesses, "What did the President know and when did he know it?"[91] His Washington experience and leadership meant that many thought he could attract the type of moderate conservative who had backed Ford in 1976.

The experts were wrong about both men. Neither caught on with Republican voters, and both faded quickly from the scene. Instead, Reagan's primary competitors became two men who had registered as mere asterisks in the polls in the summer of 1979 but whose drive and ingenuity impressed voters.

George H. W. Bush caught fire first. The Yale-educated son of a Republican senator from Connecticut, he was a two-term congressman from his adopted Texas who had since held a series of political appointments, ranging from chairman of the Republican National Committee to ambassador to China to director of the CIA. Bush modeled his campaign on Jimmy Carter's successful challenge in 1976. He virtually camped out in Iowa, intending to use a victory there as a springboard to national attention just as Carter had.[92] He was moreover the sort of Republican moderate conservatives tended to like: experienced, non-ideological, socially moderate, and eternally geared toward balance. He was, for example, in favor of the ERA, was pro-choice on abortion, and criticized Reagan's plan for a major tax cut while increasing defense spending as "voodoo economics."[93] His campaign strategy initially worked, as he decisively defeated all other contenders and narrowly edged out Reagan to win the Iowa caucuses.

What happened next has gone down in political lore as one of the greatest political comebacks in history. Reagan abandoned the aloof strategy that his campaign manager, John Sears, had advised, and hit the campaign trail in New Hampshire with gusto. A few days before the primary, Reagan and Bush were scheduled to debate in Nashua at an event sponsored by a local newspaper. The newspaper was short of funds, however, and turned to the Reagan campaign to pay the bill. Effectively in charge, Reagan decided he wanted to invite all the contenders for a multicandidate debate rather than the one-on-one favored by Bush. At the debate, with most of the other contenders quietly lined up behind them, Reagan publicly fought with the moderator to have all the candidates included. Bush sat sheepishly by. When the moderator told the engineer to turn off Reagan's microphone, the candidate exploded with anger. "I'm paying for this microphone, Mr. Green [*sic*]," he shouted.[94] The contrast between Reagan and Bush—one man confidently in charge, the other standoffish and silent—told Republican voters all they needed to know. Three days later Reagan swamped Bush by 27 percent, 50–23.

Reagan's second surprise challenger then emerged, Illinois congressman John Anderson. While Anderson had started his career as a conventional small-town Republican, he had steadily moved to the political center over the 1970s. He was running as the most liberal of all the candidates, a man whose signature proposal was a fifty-cent-per-gallon tax hike on gasoline—at a time when gas had just hit a new high price of over a dollar a gallon. Anderson caught the eye of urban liberals unhappy with Carter and started to attract national attention, including a long-running feature in the comic strip *Doonesbury*. Moderates looking for an alternative to Reagan started to look at Anderson, and he proceeded to split the non-Reagan vote with Bush. This allowed Reagan to win decisive victories with pluralities in moderate states like Vermont, Illinois, and Wisconsin. By the time Anderson dropped out to pursue an independent campaign in the fall election, he had fatally wounded Bush's campaign. Bush would eke out a couple more narrow wins in moderate states like Pennsylvania and Michigan, but Reagan's delegate lead was too large to overcome. The race was over by the time we Californians voted on June 3.

"Third time pays for all," Bilbo Baggins told Thorin Oakenshield when contemplating facing the dragon Smaug at the end of their quest. So too now did Ronald Reagan, finally victorious in his third time seeking the Republican Party's presidential nomination, have to

confront the final foe in his decades-long quest: the Democratic incumbent, Jimmy Carter. General-election campaigns are never a good
time to begin something entirely new. So it was no surprise that Reagan largely rehashed his longtime themes in his acceptance speech to
the Republican convention. He had long told Americans that they
faced a time for choosing, that they had a rendezvous with destiny
that would forever determine whether freedom would endure. Only
now he had one thing he had never had before: he and his vision were
the choice he was asking Americans to make.

This version of "A Time for Choosing," like the version he delivered
sixteen years earlier on behalf of Barry Goldwater, would be focused on
the person whose votes he needed to become president: the disaffected
New Dealer. So it was perhaps not surprising that he started not just by
addressing the assembled delegates, but by also addressing "my fellow
citizens of this great nation."[95] He went on to say he would carry his
message "to every American, regardless of party affiliation," and that
his view of government placed trust "in those values that transcend
persons and parties."

This might sound like just good politics, but Reagan's opening few
minutes broke with most other recent nominees' traditions. Each of
the last three Republican nominees had either specifically mentioned
the word "Republican"; invoked past recent Republican heroes like
Nixon, Eisenhower, or Hoover; or done both within the first few paragraphs. In contrast, Reagan did not mention any other living Republican throughout his entire speech. He did not even mention the word
"Republican" until the fourteenth paragraph, and then mentioned it
briefly by calling Abraham Lincoln "the first Republican president."
He would not mention the word "Republican" again until his speech
was over a third complete—and then it was to tell his audience that
"we Republicans believe it is essential that we maintain *both* the forward momentum of economic growth and the strength of the safety
net beneath those in society who need help. We also believe it is essential that the integrity of *all aspects* of Social Security be preserved." In
short, he cloaked the GOP in the mantle of FDR, who had rested his

New Deal on the proposition that he could deliver both growth and security.

The next portion of his speech also stoked traditional Democratic themes rather than those Republicans were used to hearing. Instead of economic growth, he emphasized work, dignity, and jobs. Indeed, he did not use the phrase "economic growth" again, and he never mentioned entrepreneurs or called on job creators to make a better nation. Instead, he said it was "the American worker" who kept our economic system going. He pledged to cut taxes and reduce regulation, but not to create growth in the abstract: the result would be investment that would "put Americans back to work." He even pledged to "restore hope" and to "make America great again."

Reagan concluded his speech with a more direct appeal to the disaffected Democrat. He mentioned the word "Republican" only once more, when he said he had "thousands of Democrats, Independents, and Republicans from all economic conditions and walks of life bound together in that community of shared values of family, work, neighborhood, peace, and freedom." He said those people were the type of Americans Thomas Paine had in mind when he wrote, "during the darkest days of the American revolution—'We have it in our power to make the world over again.'" Reagan then turned his attention to another famous American who roused the nation from its slumber during dark times to reclaim its heritage: Franklin Delano Roosevelt.

He quoted FDR twice in the final part of his speech.[96] Immediately following his quotation of Paine, Reagan again told Americans that they had a "rendezvous with destiny." And to conclude he offered a long quotation from Roosevelt's own first acceptance speech, delivered in July 1932, in which he pledged to "abolish useless offices, eliminate unnecessary functions of government" and make government solvent again. He concluded his speech by telling Americans it was time "to recapture our destiny," to work together to carry out "these unkept promises," and to "pledge to each other and to all America on this July day 48 years later that we will do just that." Only those as old as Reagan or presidential historians would have realized that Reagan had just approvingly cited the speech in which FDR first used the phrase "New Deal." But the message was nevertheless clear: Today's Democratic Party has abandoned FDR's course; I mean to get us back on course.

I was listening to Reagan that night with many of my College Republican friends. While I was thrilled as ever to hear his words, what stuck in my mind for decades later came next. Reagan departed from his prepared remarks and talked about divine providence. He concluded with these words:

> I'll confess that I've been afraid to suggest what I'm going to suggest. But I'm more afraid not to. Can we begin our crusade joined together in a moment of silent prayer?

I was not then a particularly religious man, but the drama of the moment and the sense that we were all fighting together for a noble cause captured what I felt. It remained for many years my favorite passage from all of Reagan's speeches.

What I did not know then was that even here Reagan was interpreting Roosevelt. FDR had ended his speech on that July day forty-eight years earlier with an appeal for Americans to give him their help "to win in this crusade to return America to its own people."[97]

As Reagan left the podium to thunderous applause, the stage was set for his epic battle with modern progressive liberalism. But another force was mobilizing too. It would not be as powerful as Reagan, but it would attract the "conservative die hard" for whom nothing but a repeal of the New Deal would suffice. The Libertarian Party was moving, and it would offer a choice, not an echo.

The choice it would offer would have been considered extreme even by the most hard-line Goldwater supporters. Its platform pledged to repeal all entitlement programs such as Social Security, Medicare, and Medicaid, and to end all federal interference in the economy including the minimum wage and federal laws requiring employers to bargain with labor unions.[98] It also called for an immediate 50 percent cut in tax rates (Reagan was calling for only a 30 percent reduction) and pledged to work for the eventual elimination of all taxation and the repeal of the Sixteenth Amendment authorizing the federal income tax.[99] Add in the party's call for the repeal of all of what Reagan had termed "sin laws" and its opposition to American involvement in any military alliance, such as NATO, and you have a recipe that was beyond the pale for most voters.

The Libertarian Party nominated two lawyers for its ticket, Ed Clark for president and David Koch for vice president. It could not win, but it could deprive Reagan of enough votes in a close election to ensure President Carter's reelection.

This prospect did not trouble Clark, Koch, or other libertarians at all. They viewed Reagan the way Buckley used to view Dwight Eisenhower, as someone who offered the same old government solutions on the cheap. The party's national chairman, David Bergland, told the *Washington Post* that Reagan "talks about free enterprise and lowering taxes, but his record as governor of California is just the opposite."[100] Clark would later tell one audience that Reagan was the worst of the candidates running.[101] Much like Steffgen before him and many others during Reagan's presidency, Reagan's embrace of the New Deal's core principles made him unacceptable to self-described true friends of freedom.

The Clark-Koch ticket would end up garnering only a bit more than 1 percent of the national vote and did not cost Reagan a single state. While this was a higher level than any Libertarian candidate had received before or since until Gary Johnson's 3.3 percent in 2016, it conclusively showed what Reagan had known all along: Americans of all stripes were not willing to cast aside the core principles of the New Deal.

President Carter knew this too, and he spent the general election campaign trying to convince Americans that Reagan was in fact no different from Goldwater. He attacked Reagan's prior opposition to the Civil Rights Act of 1964 and Reagan's subsequent invocation of "state's rights" at a rally in Mississippi to revive Pat Brown's allegation of racism.[102] He argued that Reagan's staunch and vocal anti-communism could cause a war with the Soviet Union.[103] While Carter's attacks were so harsh that they were condemned, they succeeded in rallying Democrats to his banner after a bruising primary campaign against a liberal challenger, Senator Ted Kennedy.[104] The race was neck and neck as Carter and Reagan headed into their only debate, held one week before Election Day.

The key moment of the debate came toward the end, when Carter brought up Reagan's early opposition to Medicare. Carter had throughout the debate levied charge after charge against Reagan, trying to show that any Democrat who respected the accomplishments of FDR could not trust Reagan to keep them. But this final salvo pushed Reagan's buttons a bit too far. He started his response with the line that most conservatives today love to repeat: "There you go again."[105]

Conservatives rarely recall the next few lines, but they are crucial to understanding why this moment was decisive. After putting Carter in his place, Reagan went on:

> When I opposed Medicare, there was another piece of legislation meeting the same problem before the Congress. I happened to favor the other piece of legislation and thought that it would be better for the senior citizens and provide better care than the one that was finally passed. I was not opposing the principle of providing care for them.[106]

In the heat of the moment Reagan did not recall the name of the "other piece of legislation" he supported, but it was clearly the Kerr-Mills Act. Reagan had made clear all those years ago that he did believe that the federal government should pay for needed medical care for people who couldn't afford it themselves. He continued to make that clear in public and private for the entire time between those early days and the debate, as the 1979 letter to Professor Nikolaev clearly shows. When the chips were down, when the political battle was fiercest, Reagan won because he convinced the American people that he was what he said he was, the true heir to Franklin Roosevelt.

Reagan continued his invocation of FDR in his closing statement. He framed the choice voters would make simply:

Next Tuesday all of you will go to the polls, will stand there in the polling place and make a decision. I think when you make that decision, it might be well if you would ask yourself, *are you better off than you were four years ago?* Is it easier for you to go and buy things in the stores than it was four years ago? Is there more or less unemployment in the country than there was four years ago? Is America as respected throughout the world as it was? Do you feel that our security is as safe, that we're as strong as we were four years ago? [Emphasis added.][107]

Reagan's questions neatly set up the best case for him. A majority of Americans felt they were worse off, and that America was worse off, than when Carter had taken office. What only the oldest of them would have recalled, however, was that this was not the first time they had been asked to make such a choice.

Roosevelt had posed a nearly identical choice to Americans in his fifth fireside chat, given fifteen months after he took office. Compare Roosevelt's framing with Reagan's:

But the simplest way for each of you to judge recovery lies in the plain facts of your own individual situation. *Are you better off than you were last year?* Are your debts less burdensome? Is your bank account more secure? Are your working conditions better? Is your faith in your own individual future more firmly grounded?[108] [Emphasis added.]

Reagan didn't just borrow the famous question from FDR, he took the entire structure of the passage. First, both men pose the nature of the choice. Second, they pose the framing question: Are you better off than you were in the past? Third, they both pose exactly four follow-up questions that re-pose the initial question in terms of the specific items Americans were concerned about. This cannot have been coincidence. When Reagan was making his final appeal to the American people in the most important moment up to that time in his political life, he chose to cloak himself in Roosevelt's mantle.

The American people heard and understood. Private polls taken after the debate immediately showed Reagan rocketing ahead, although in that less technologically advanced time there were no public polls scheduled to show this. By the Monday before the election both candidates knew what was in store, but we who were following the race remained ignorant of what was to come.

I will never forget where I was and what I was doing a bit after 5:00 p.m. Pacific Time on Election Day. I was sitting in the student lounge running my College Republican club's get-out-the-vote operation, watching NBC news report the early returns while waiting for club members to come get their assignments. Suddenly the news anchor, John Chancellor, announced NBC was ready to make its projection. "Ronald Wilson Reagan—of California, a sports announcer, a film actor, the former governor of California—is our projected winner."[109] Like Chancellor and the young Tom Brokaw, I was stunned. Unlike them, I was ecstatic.

Reagan would go on to win a decisive Electoral College landslide, crushing Carter by 489 electoral votes to 49. Reagan's popular vote margin was also large, nearly 10 percent. Carter received only 41 percent of the popular vote, to this day the lowest level any incumbent Democratic president has ever received.[110]

The landslide was not just limited to Reagan, however. Republicans gained twelve Senate seats to take control of that chamber for the first time since 1954. They also gained 34 seats in the House to reach 192, the party's highest total since 1968. Many of those seats came from historically Democratic working-class districts such as Toledo's Ohio 9 and Providence's Rhode Island 2. By the millions, working-class Democrats who thought of themselves as conservatives but who still supported the New Deal voted for Reagan and Republicans up and down the ticket.

Working-class Democrats provided the votes for Reagan's margin just as they had done in his gubernatorial races in California. Their support was most evident in the South. The Democratic party had always had its electoral base in white, working-class southern regions from the days the party was founded in the 1830s. That support had eroded over time, but with a southerner at the top of the ticket the Democratic party was still very competitive in southern states. In fact, Carter had won in 1976 by sweeping all but one of the sixteen states in which slavery had been legal at the time of the Civil War.[111]

Reagan's backing from white southerners was so strong that he beat Carter in all but two of the fifteen states Carter had carried just four years before. His share of the vote was substantially higher than Ford's in every state, with increases ranging from 1.7 percent in the state with the highest percentage of blacks, Mississippi, to a high of 13.2 percent in Arkansas.[112] Reagan often ran even with or behind Ford in affluent cities or black communities, but ran even farther ahead of him in the smaller, white rural counties that then and now dominate the South. His brand of muscular, traditional, New Deal–friendly conservatism was exactly what these voters wanted.

White working-class northern Democrats also flocked to Reagan's banner. This is harder to discern in part because three states had a candidate on the ballot in either 1976 (Michigan—Ford) or 1980 (Illinois—Anderson; Wisconsin—former governor Patrick Lucey, Anderson's running mate). The results on these states were surely affected by the presence of these favorite sons, and Ford ran ahead of Reagan in each even though Reagan won all three. Despite this, Reagan outpolled Ford in many working-class congressional districts in each state in areas like northern Wisconsin, suburban Detroit, and rural Illinois beyond metropolitan Chicago.

Reagan's strength among working-class Democrats is best seen in other midwestern and northeastern states. He outpolled Ford in Pennsylvania, Ohio, and Iowa. He did particularly well in industrial counties like Luzerne (Wilkes-Barre), Lackawanna (Scranton), Lehigh (Bethlehem), Stark (Canton), and Summit (Akron). In these and other similar areas Reagan often ran 4 to 8 percent ahead of Ford. In more affluent counties, however, Reagan ran roughly even with or behind Ford.

The same patterns emerge from large northeastern states like New York and New Jersey. Reagan ran behind or roughly even with Ford in affluent or largely black communities, but ran well ahead of him in areas with large numbers of ethnic, working-class Democrats like Cumberland and Gloucester counties in New Jersey or the Catholic-dominated areas of Queens and Long Island. Reagan did especially well in Jewish neighborhoods in New York City, running as much as 20 percent ahead of Ford.[113] No matter where you looked, you found the same results: habitual working-class Democrats had crossed party lines to hand the White House to Ronald Wilson Reagan.

Reagan had emerged from his wilderness years triumphant. All the hard work, all the effort, all the long flights and the endless browbeating from the press: all of it had been worth it. We'll never know what he really thought at that moment when Nancy told Reagan while he was in the shower that President Carter wanted to speak with him.[114] But he must have felt vindicated.

Like Lincoln, Churchill, and Roosevelt, Reagan emerged from his time out of power because the nation was in crisis. Like those men, he also came to power only because he appealed to people who had long backed the other party. The four men all shared immense rhetorical gifts, but they also shared an ability to see big pictures when others saw only snapshots. Years before their competitors, they generated ideas that seemed out of place when they uttered them but which seemed completely natural when they had been proved right. And as with those men, the fight to get power was just the beginning.

Lincoln, Churchill, and Roosevelt had faced either an economic crisis or a military crisis. Reagan faced both. Moreover, unlike those men, his allies would not be in complete control of the legislature. Despite the Republican gains, Democrats still held the House by a commanding margin. Many Republicans also did not share his beliefs: only twenty-three of the forty-two incoming Republican senators who had previously served in Congress had received ratings above 80 from the American Conservative Union (ACU).[115] Seven had ACU ratings under 50, and six had ratings above 50 from the premier liberal ratings of the time, those of the Americans for Democratic Action.[116] Reagan had been given a mandate, but a still-wary populace had not given carte blanche to his party.

There were still more scripts to be written, more sequels to be shot. Reagan had been given the role he had long coveted, but it remained to be seen whether this leading man could carry the film. The challenges would be overwhelming, but one thing was certain: Reagan would approach them with the same ideas and the same confidence that had taken him from the mashed potato circuit to the Oval Office.

CHAPTER 7

PRESIDENT REAGAN

As if on cue, the sun burst through the morning clouds on January 20, 1981, just as Ronald Reagan stepped up to be sworn in as president of the United States. Reagan would go on to give a memorable speech, one that is still quoted decades later. But that morning all the world watched as the oldest man then ever to be elected president swore to uphold, protect, and defend the Constitution of the United States.

Perhaps more than any president in decades, Reagan had thought long and hard about what that oath meant. All of his intricately developed principles would be tested as he faced the challenges of the most powerful office in the free world. Moreover, he was taking office with the country faced by greater challenges, economic and military, than at any time since his boyhood hero, Franklin Roosevelt, had taken the same oath nearly forty-eight years before.

Reagan would meet those challenges and more. His then-radical economic ideas to cut income tax rates, reduce regulations, trim nonessential social spending, and control inflation helped spur the American economy to the greatest peacetime expansion in decades. Aside from a small recession caused by the first Gulf War in 1990–91, and aided by the cooperation between Democratic president Bill Clinton and a

Republican Congress in the mid-1990s, the economy grew rapidly for nearly twenty years. Tens of millions of jobs were created and incomes rose for people of all levels of education and income. But the economic miracle he unleashed was the least of his achievements.

Freedom and human dignity always mattered more to Reagan than wealth, and so the challenge of halting the Communist expansion was always foremost on his mind. When he took office, even his most rabid partisans were merely hoping that he could halt the decline in American might and prestige and restore hope that communism could be combated successfully. Instead, Reagan's foreign policy produced the most stunning reversal in fortune imaginable. Less than a year out of office, the Soviet Union had lost control of its satellites in Eastern Europe. By Christmas 1991, the Soviet Union itself had ceased to exist. The twin threats that had hung over the world for forty years, nuclear war between the world's two superpowers and Communist domination of the planet, were gone.

Millions of words have been written about how he was able to do this. This work will not try to recount all of the many decisions he made or trace who influenced what. There are many biographies that do that quite well. Instead, we will look at something else: the influence of Reagan's own ideas on the course of his administration.

Reagan displayed remarkable fidelity to these ideas even as he faced enormous pressure to cast them aside. His own staff would often pressure him to change course, but he would always refuse when doing so meant he would have to change his principles. This was as true of taxes as it was on fighting communism.

He would sometimes compromise or change course on specific actions. Thus he agreed to increase taxes as part of a deal to make Social Security solvent. More surprisingly, the old Cold Warrior would reach the most wide-ranging nuclear arms-control deal of any president when he signed the Intermediate-Range Nuclear Forces Treaty (INF) with Soviet leader Mikhail Gorbachev in 1988. These changes often perplexed his friends who equated a change in tactics with a change in principle.

Reagan therefore faced revolts from self-anointed conservative leaders. Frequently decrying the influence of supposed liberals within the administration, these leaders would protest that these staffers were diverting Reagan away from conservative principles. Toward the end of his second term, even some of Reagan's personal friends like Bill Buckley expressed misgivings over the INF treaty.

These leaders never understood the difference between principles and ideology. As Reagan had said in 1977, principles can adapt to new facts while ideologies cannot. For an ideologue every problem is a nail and every solution is a hammer. Reagan knew the hammer and the nail were merely means toward an end, putting two boards together. If he saw a different way to do that, he didn't hesitate to adopt a different course.

That course often flew in the face of ideological categories. He was an ardent free trader, but frequently imposed penalties on Japan and other nations he viewed as engaging in unfair trade. He loved immigrants, but signed a compromise immigration bill that he thought would reduce the flow of immigrants because controlling the border was more important.[1] He believed in lower taxes, but lower taxes for all, not just for the top 1 percent like the "supply-side" ideologues wanted. He could seek to cut unnecessary entitlement spending and also propose a government-financed catastrophic health insurance plan.

These supposed deviations often surprised people, no one more than the director of his Office for Management and Budget (OMB), David Stockman. Stockman's differences with his boss came out in two highly publicized episodes, one in 1981 and the other in 1986. In the first, Stockman's devotion to supply-side ideology led to public disagreement with Reagan. In the second, Stockman's tell-all book about his time in the Reagan White House depicted the president as too sentimental and swayable to lead the supply-side, libertarian revolution Stockman thought he had signed on for.

Stockman may have been shocked, shocked to learn there was politics going on in Washington, but his deeper failure was that he never understood what Reagan's principles were. Reagan had always said there is no such thing as left or right, there is only up or down. Armed with that belief, Reagan could and did act freely from ideological constraints in pursuit of his dream, the highest degree of liberty consistent with order and security. But to ideologues like Stockman, to whom only left or right mattered, Reagan was always a constant disappointment.

Reagan was never reliant on the people he had around him; he relied on his ideas. He had "come to Washington to put into practice ideas I'd believed in for decades," that unique mix of New Deal liberalism and freedom-loving conservatism combined with his principled, nonideological way of looking at the world.[2] With these principles, Reagan could retain popular favor when things looked darkest. He could navigate the rapids of politics, sometimes making mistakes but always keeping the ship of state on course. And with those ideas he could put together the political coalition of old-guard business Republicans, movement conservatives, and blue-collar Democrats and independents that he had first envisioned in the mid-1960s. The faith and love that Reagan had for America's people and ideals are what united this coalition; they are why you are reading this book today.

That faith and love were on full display that bright and chilly January afternoon when Reagan stood to give his first inaugural address. That speech is today best remembered by his line "government is not the solution to our problem; government is the problem."[3] That along with his condemnation of high taxes, overregulation, and deficit spending have led many ideological conservatives and libertarians to claim Reagan as their inspiration. They say that he, like they, intended to assault the very pillar of the New Deal, the guarantee that the government would step in to protect the material comfort and spiritual dignity of average Americans even in the face of the private sector.

It was apparent, however, that using the government to protect the comfort and dignity of ordinary people was Reagan's primary aim. He extolled America's farmers, policemen, miners, factory workers, teachers, homemakers, and doctors as "a special interest group that has been too long neglected . . . Americans." He said that "all must share" in

both the "productive work" and the "bounty of a revived economy."
His most moving praise of the average American came later when he
said:

> Those who say that we're in a time when there are not heroes,
> they just don't know where to look. You can see heroes every day
> going in and out of factory gates. Others, a handful in number,
> produce enough food to feed all of us and then the world be-
> yond. You meet heroes across a counter, and they're on both sides
> of that counter. There are entrepreneurs with faith in themselves
> and faith in an idea who create new jobs, new wealth and oppor-
> tunity. They're individuals and families whose taxes support the
> government and whose voluntary gifts support church, charity,
> culture, art, and education. Their patriotism is quiet, but deep.
> Their values sustain our national life.

Where too many conservatives, Republicans, or libertarians saw
losers or "takers," Reagan saw heroes.

These heroes came in all sizes and from all walks of life, and sometimes they needed government to help them out. Reagan told Americans that day that

> it's not my intention to do away with government. It is rather to
> make it work—work with us, not over us; to stand by our side,
> not ride on our back. Government can and must provide oppor-
> tunity, not smother it; foster productivity, not stifle it.

Later in his speech he elaborated on this.

> We shall reflect the compassion that is so much a part of your
> makeup. How can we love our country and not love our coun-
> trymen; and loving them, reach out a hand when they fall, heal
> them when they are sick, and provide opportunity to make them
> self-sufficient so they will be equal in fact and not just in theory?

Has any Republican since Reagan used the word "love" so freely and so unselfconsciously to describe his political philosophy? No one who could speak so movingly about the need to care for his fellow citizens could have intended to repeal or even significantly threaten the public New Deal they held so dear.

It was not fitting for an inaugural speech to place specific flesh on these bones of principle, but he would soon do that when he launched his economic recovery plan. He did just that in two speeches in early February.

Reagan laid the blame for unemployment, inflation, and high interest rates squarely on the government's doorstep. Decades of ever-increasing taxation, regulation, and deficit spending had created the economic witches' brew that was consuming America.[4] Drawing on themes he had first uttered decades earlier, he told Americans that bracket creep was decreasing the standard of living and that he meant to ignore those who said taxes shouldn't be cut until spending was reduced. He did mean to cut spending, but only for "those who are not really qualified by reason of need." He mainly meant to increase America's capacity to produce by cutting tax rates by 30 percent for everyone and by eliminating government wage or price controls and dramatically cutting regulations.

Reagan knew that most Americans valued social spending by government that gave the average person security in retirement and all Americans protection against undeserved poverty. Accordingly, he told Congress a few days later that

> we will continue to fulfill the obligations that spring from our national conscience. Those who, through no fault of their own, must depend on the rest of us—the poverty stricken, the disabled, the elderly, all those with true need—can rest assured that the social safety net of programs they depend on are exempt from any cuts.[5]

This broad principle placed a great deal of the federal budget beyond cutting. Social Security benefits and cost-of-living adjustments were protected from cuts, as were Medicare and the SSI program for the aged, blind, and disabled. Other social programs such as food stamps, disability insurance, and school breakfasts and lunches would only have their income levels for eligibility reduced so that "those without resources" could continue to receive benefits while those "who can afford to pay" did pay.

Reagan extended this principle of need to business too. Arguing that some subsidies were unnecessary because "the marketplace contains incentives enough to warrant continuing these activities without a government subsidy," he proposed eliminating the Department of Energy's synthetic fuels program and the Export-Import Bank.

The economic crisis did not force Reagan to go back on his lifetime commitment to the New Deal's social protections, and it also did not force him to go back on his commitment to fight communism. He told Congress that "my duty as president" impelled him to propose increased defense spending to combat the Soviet threat. He knew this might lead to more deficit spending, but he said if that were necessary he would choose that every time.[6]

The next few months were very difficult for Reagan. The political battle of his life would have been hard enough, but soon he was literally in the battle of his life. Shot by John Hinckley as he was leaving the Washington Hilton on the afternoon of March 30, Reagan was rushed to the hospital, where it was found a bullet had punctured a lung and was lodged inches away from his heart. Skilled surgeons pulled Reagan through, and the inevitable public sympathy increased when word of his calm wit in the operating room made its way to the American people.[7] By April he was back at work lobbying Congress for his economic program.

Reagan's lobbying, which included more televised speeches to push Congress into action, worked. By the end of July both his spending and his tax cuts had become law. The latter were even more generous than he had asked for, as congressmen had insisted he include indexation of the tax brackets to end bracket creep in the final proposal.[8] The so-called Reagan Revolution was on.

What that revolution entailed, however, differed depending on whom you asked. Liberals constantly argued that Reagan was tearing away the social protections initiated and inspired by the New Deal. This always infuriated Reagan. In his autobiography he complained that he "was never able to convince [House Speaker] Tip [O'Neill] that I didn't want to deprive the truly needy of the assistance the rest of us owed them; I just wanted to make government programs more efficient and eliminate waste, so that we no longer spent $2 for every $1 of aid we delivered to people."[9] When Democrats charged that one of his budget proposals struck at the heart of Social Security, Reagan called for a bipartisan commission to firm up Social Security's finances and ensure that recipients "continue to receive their full benefits."[10] "We can be compassionate about human needs," he told Americans, "without being complacent about budget extravagance."[11]

Disagreement over the scope of the revolution existed on the right too. This became painfully and publicly apparent in November when an article about OMB Director Stockman appeared in the magazine *The Atlantic*.

"The Education of David Stockman" rocked Washington.[12] The article's author, *Washington Post* editor William Greider, had held off-the-record discussions with Stockman for months with the understanding that nothing would be published until after the budget and tax bills were dealt with. Stockman had expressed his dismay to Greider over a host of issues in the White House, essentially airing some dirty laundry. He also admitted to fudging budget numbers and changing OMB computer models to hide how large the deficit would become if Reagan's proposals were approved. It appeared to many that the Reagan administration had engaged in a big con and the American people had been the mark.

Reagan's tax cuts had been the biggest con of all, if Stockman was to be believed. Stockman was an ardent believer in supply-side economics, a supposedly new theory about how markets worked and wealth was generated. Under supply-side theory, people responded heavily to marginal income tax rates. The higher they were, especially on the wealthiest people, the less they worked or the less inventive they were. The holy grail of supply-side theory, then, was to lower the top rate levied only on the richest taxpayers as much as possible.

Stockman cheerfully acknowledged this in his interviews, and went so far as to call Reagan's entire tax cut bill a "Trojan horse to bring down the top rate." This meant that "supply-side" wasn't meant to improve incentives or lighten the load for anyone except the richest Americans. Any tax cuts for anyone other than the wealthiest Americans was simply political sugar to make the supply-side medicine go down.

Greider noted that this meant the "new" supply-side doctrine was simply a new language to provide cover for the "hoary old" Republican doctrine that if one gave wealthy people and big businesses tax cuts, "the good effects 'trickle down' through the economy to reach everyone else." Stockman agreed that supply-side was "really new clothes" for old-style trickle-down economics. "'It's kind of hard to sell trickle-down,' he explained, 'so the supply-side formula was the only way to get a tax policy that was really 'trickle-down.' Supply-side is 'trickle down.'"

Stockman was only thirty-four at the time and had never been alive during FDR's presidency. So he likely did not know that the president's hero had directly attacked trickle-down economics in many speeches before and during his presidency.[13]

More important, Stockman was likely unaware that Reagan had been talking about tax reform for decades. Reagan was promoting the idea that all tax rates needed to come down for all people when Stockman was not even a teenager. Nor did Stockman seem to take note that Reagan as governor had increased the top rate for the wealthy and reduced taxes through rebates and property tax cuts for the working and middle classes. Stockman might have considered the president's tax cuts a "Trojan horse for trickle-down," but the president believed that everyone needed a lightened load and everyone's incentives needed to be improved.

This is probably why Reagan always resisted the "supply-side" label. He was proud that as governor he had increased the level of tax-free income for a family from $2,000 to $8,000 a year.[14] He thought that the best way to help the working poor was to reduce their taxes.[15] He told a then-prominent conservative publisher, R. Emmet Tyrell, "I'm not sure I really understood simon-pure 'supply-side' or that I agreed with every facet."[16] When asked directly by another letter writer about "supply-side economics," he said it was just common sense.[17]

The letter to Tyrell goes on to give Reagan's full thoughts on what he was trying to do:

> It's always seemed to me that when government goes beyond a certain percentage of what it takes as its share of the people's earning we have trouble. I guess a simple explanation of what I've been trying to do is peel government down to bare essentials—necessities, if you will, and then set tax revenues accordingly.
>
> If we then find that we overdid on the tax cuts [then] adjust—but it will take a lot more evidence than I've seen to convince me adjustment is needed.[18]

No real supply-sider could have written that passage. Supply-side was and is concerned with the incentives faced by the most economically productive citizens as expressed by marginal income tax rates. Instead, Reagan was simply reaffirming fidelity to the ideas he had first talked about in 1958.[19] Back then he said that economies that taxed more than a quarter of the national income faltered, that the people should set a rate of taxation they would accept and force government to spend no more than that, and that balanced budgets were essential to national health. Once again Reagan showed that when you supported him, as the supply-siders had done, he was not backing your agenda, you were backing his.

Reagan's final word on supply-side came in his autobiography. He said that he had not adopted supply-side theory "as the basis for my economic recovery program."[20] Instead, his experience with 94 percent marginal tax rates in Hollywood taught him that tax rates could suppress his desire to work. He went on:

The same principle that affected my thinking applied to people in all tax brackets. The more government takes in taxes, the less incentive people have to work. What coal-miner or assembly-line worker jumps at the offer of overtime when he knows Uncle Sam is going to take sixty percent or more of his extra pay?

And the principle applies as well to corporations and small businesses: When government confiscates half or more of their profits, the motivation to maximize profits goes down, and owners and managers make decisions disproportionately on a desire to avoid taxes.

Reagan was again showing he still believed what he had said decades earlier. He had indeed opposed high marginal tax rates even when he was a New Deal liberal, writing in 1951 in favor of a "human depreciation allowance" that would lower an individual's tax burden similar to the manner in which an oil company would use a depletion allowance to reduce its tax burden.[21] He had opposed tax rates above 50 percent as immoral in his mashed-potato-circuit speeches.[22] He had argued for years in favor of a tax reform that would lower the marginal tax rates for everyone, the Herlong-Baker tax bill.[23] So when supply-siders eagerly told each other in early 1980 that Reagan had "been successfully 'converted'" to supply-side, they were ignoring the evidence.[24] He was not coming over to them; they were coming over to him.

Supply-siders should have had another clue that Reagan did not share their ideology: his regular statements that the average person was the driver of the American economy. Supply-side theory holds that the entrepreneur is the person who drives the American economy. It is this person who builds new businesses, creates new modes of production, and invests capital most successfully who creates the wealth and jobs that then flow or trickle down to the rest of us. But Reagan always said the opposite. In his model, it was the average person whose savings provided the investment capital that allowed American business to invest. Put *them* to work, give *them* more money, and wealth would flow *up* to the businessman who would then cycle it back down. Presidential biographer Lou Cannon quotes Reagan as saying "America's natural economic strength" was its people: "My attitude had always been—let the people flourish."[25] Reagan held a conservative version of the theory FDR had announced in 1932, that "if we make the average of mankind comfortable and secure, their prosperity will rise upward, just as yeast rises up, through the ranks."[26]

Reagan mentioned the word "entrepreneur" only once in all of his major campaign and presidential speeches on the economy between November 1979 and the passage of the tax cut bill in July 1981. That was in his first inaugural, quoted at length above. The entrepreneur was simply one of many American heroes, listed after the shopkeeper, the housemaker, and the factory worker. The supply-siders were following Hoover and Goldwater in emphasizing the importance of the uncommon individual to American life. Reagan, as always, followed FDR and spoke lovingly of the common person.

This love for the real lives of everyday people also informed Reagan's trade policies. Reagan was an ardent free trader and believed people should be able to trade as freely between countries as they could within a country. He kicked off his 1980 campaign by proposing a free trade area encompassing Canada, Mexico, and the United States, an idea that Bill Clinton brought to fruition thirteen years later with the signing of the NAFTA accord. He also started talks for free trade with the Caribbean nations and with Central America, ideas that led to CAFTA and the Caribbean Basin Initiative. No one could accuse Reagan of being a protectionist devoted to a Fortress America view of the world.

His free-trade views did not, however, prevent him from taking firm action to protect American workers and companies from what he viewed as unfair trade practices. Nor did they prevent him from acknowledging political sentiment that was urging protection to help American workers. What Reagan did on trade is important proof that he always acted on principles, but was never an ideologue.

Japanese auto imports were the first trade issue Reagan had to deal with. American car manufacturers had held over 90 percent of the

US auto market in the early 1970s, but the massive increase in gasoline prices after the Arab oil embargoes of 1974 and 1979 had made fuel-efficient smaller Japanese cars attractive to American consumers. Chrysler, the smallest of Detroit's "Big Three" manufacturers, had been bailed out by the federal government in 1979, and auto companies and autoworker unions were pressing Congress to stop the flood of Japanese imports as Reagan took office.

An ideological free trader would have resisted these pressures to the last. Not Reagan. Reagan recognized that "the genuine suffering of American workers and their families made this issue intensely charged politically."[27] Reagan adopted an idea suggested by Vice President Bush, that he ask the Japanese to voluntarily restrict the number of vehicles they exported to the United States. He later did that in a meeting with the Japanese trade minister.[28] The Japanese adopted the suggestion later that year, reducing the pressure on American automakers.

Reduce, but not end. By 1982, Japanese auto companies had begun setting up "transplant" auto factories that assembled cars in the United States. This enabled them to get around the "voluntary" export limits, since the cars themselves were not exported. As more and more Japanese companies set up these plants, American auto manufacturers again came under pressure as consumers increasingly preferred cheaper, better cars designed in Japan but made in America. In effect, Reagan's move had created incentives for Japanese companies to share their wealth with American workers, defusing at least somewhat the pressures for protectionism. Reagan's nonideological engagement with the issue gave American consumers what they wanted while minimizing the downside to American autoworkers.

Reagan had focused on solving the nation's economic challenges throughout most of the year. But following the passage of the tax and spending bills, the country's military challenges took center stage. The Soviet Union had not been sitting idly by as Reagan had wrangled with Congress.

Communist forces were on the march everywhere. The USSR's Central American satellite, Nicaragua, was pumping arms into a Marxist

rebel group in El Salvador. Libya's dictator, Moammar Qadaffi, a mer-
curial figure who purchased weapons from the Soviets, tried to push the
United States out of the Central Mediterranean by claiming ownership
of the Gulf of Sidra, a body of water clearly in international jurisdiction.
Poland, the largest Communist country in Eastern Europe, had been in
turmoil since a visit by the first Polish pope, John Paul II, in 1979 had
unleashed anti-Communist sentiment. In May 1981, the Pope was shot
by a Turk who many believed acted in league with the Soviet KGB and
Bulgarian intelligence. Finally, in September, the Egyptian president,
Anwar Sadat, a man who had broken with the Soviets to move Egypt
into an alliance with the United States, was assassinated.

Reagan met these challenges with his characteristic resolve. When
the Libyan air force scrambled to intercept American naval planes
training in the Gulf of Sidra, Reagan ordered the US Navy to shoot
down any Libyan planes that tried to prevent the maneuvers. They did
and they were. Reagan marshaled quiet support for anti-Communist
Poles and kept America's European allies in line as they struggled to aid
their cause without provoking the Soviet Union. Reagan sent supplies
and training to El Salvadoran troops in their fight against the Marxist
rebels. And he began a wide-ranging global effort to combat Soviet influence wherever it existed, an effort that over his presidency would include support for anti-Communist guerrillas fighting in Afghanistan,
Angola, Mozambique, and Nicaragua.

By 1981 many Democrats viewed these acts as warlike and unusual,
but in fact Reagan was simply updating the same tactics that Democrat
Harry Truman had employed to fight communism in the late 1940s
and early 1950s. Truman had given aid to Greeks fighting Communist
guerrillas in that country's civil war and created the primary Western
military alliance of the Cold War era, NATO. When Soviet troops
blockaded West Berlin, a portion of the old German capital not under control of the Soviets, Truman ordered American planes to airlift
supplies over Communist-controlled airspace. And when Communist
North Korea invaded non-Communist South Korea in 1950, Truman
organized the United Nations to come to the defense of free Korea.

When Reagan was a New Dealer, Republican conservatives were isolationists and New Dealers were globally active. Reagan simply brought his old resolve into his new party and got to work.

Reagan had said for decades that Communists intended to conquer the world, and nothing he saw from the White House convinced him they had changed their stripes. Since the USSR's leader, Leonid Brezhnev, still claimed to desire a Communist world, Reagan felt obliged to fight back any way he knew how. Still, he sought to ease tensions without conceding American interests, and so he sent a handwritten letter to Brezhnev to see if there might be common ground in finding genuine peace.[29]

While Brezhnev brushed off Reagan's letter with a brusque reply, one paragraph Reagan wrote stands out as indicative of his deepest beliefs:

> The peoples of the world, despite differences in racial and ethnic origin, have very much in common. They want the dignity of having some control over their individual destiny. They want to work at the craft or trade of their own choosing and to be fairly rewarded. They want to raise their families in peace without harming anyone or suffering harm themselves. Government exists for their convenience, not the other way around. If they are incapable, as some would have us believe, of self-government, then where among them do we find people who are capable of governing others?[30]

What's striking here is the absence of a few words many might consider crucial to such a plea: liberty, freedom, free markets, and democracy. Instead, Reagan mentions dignity, choice, fair reward, and security. It's not that the first concepts are absent from his plea, but rather they are the means toward the more important ends. Freedom begets dignity; liberty begets choice, markets begets fair reward; and peace begets security. The ends, not the means, are what Reagan holds most dear.

Reagan's attitude toward El Salvador is a perfect example of his New Deal conservatism in action in the foreign sphere. In chapter 5 we discussed how the ultraconservative senator Jesse Helms opposed Reagan's support for the El Salvadoran president Jose Napoleon Duarte because Duarte had initiated land reform. Land reform is simply the curtailing of the freedom of some who are wealthy to provide enough land to the average person so they can have the "dignity of some control over their individual destiny" and be "fairly rewarded" for their work. Reagan went so far as to write that he would not have supported Duarte without his land reforms.[31] Reagan pushed El Salvador to adopt reforms such as this in order to give the average person a reason to support democratic regimes, exactly the argument he made in the 1940s to build public support against the resurgence of fascism.

The following year, 1982, was difficult for Reagan. The country lapsed into another recession as the tough monetary policy the Federal Reserve Bank had adopted, with Reagan's support, baked inflation out of the economy at the expense of jobs. Reagan had back-loaded his tax cut in order to gain congressional support, so the largest rate reductions had yet to occur. Unemployment rose, and with it Reagan's approval rating dropped.

For the most part Reagan toughed it out. He was under enormous pressure from his staff (especially Stockman, who kept his position after Reagan forgave him), the press, and congressional leaders from both parties to repeal much of his tax rate cuts.[32] But he had fought too long and too hard for his ideas to give up that easily. He resisted their efforts, but did agree to a compromise in which he agreed to increase tax revenues by closing some loopholes in exchange for promises to cut three times as much in domestic spending.[33] This, along with the continued economic doldrums, sparked the biggest revolt on the right Reagan would face until his 1987 arms-control treaty.

The conservative revolt was essentially one of ideology versus principle. Supply-siders like Congressman Jack Kemp were angry that Reagan would even consider raising taxes, much less push them through Congress. The fact that the deficit was exploding did not matter to them at all. Other conservatives such as the strategist Richard Viguerie were angry about a range of issues from the proposed tax hike to supposed failures to push the social conservative agenda.[34] Viguerie even devoted the entire July 1982 issue of his magazine, *Conservative Digest*, to attacking Reagan for his alleged leftward drift.[35] This in particular enraged Reagan, especially as Viguerie had first backed Phil Crane over him and then supported John Connally,[36] and had even tried to persuade General Alexander Haig to run against Reagan.[37]

This dispute was yet another example of what Reagan called "ultra-pure conservatives" coming to the belated realization that Reagan was not one of them. Reagan had always said it was better to get some of what you want and then come back for more, but that sort of reasoning never worked with these ideologues. Reagan could not convince Kemp to back his tax hike even though he told Kemp "the tax increase is the price we have to pay to get the budget cuts."[38] In fact, Kemp at this time believed wholeheartedly in the supply-side idea that tax cuts alone would generate so much revenue the budget could be balanced without any spending cuts. Reagan had never agreed with Kemp on this, and the fact of ballooning deficits had convinced Reagan that he needed to slightly change course.[39] But new facts never influence an ideologue, as Reagan had noted to CPAC in 1977, and Kemp was nothing if not ideological when it came to taxes.

It was also true, however, that Reagan's principles were always different from those of these people. Viguerie, for example, attacked Reagan for signing an extension of the Voting Rights Act that guaranteed blacks the right to vote in the South. As we have seen, Reagan himself was always unprejudiced and came to understand that government action was needed to ensure that African Americans had the same opportunities to live dignified lives of their own choosing as other Americans. He was proud of his role as governor in changing civil service rules to help blacks rise in state employ and in increasing the share of blacks employed by state government.[40] Reagan had changed his mind about government's role in the fight to eradicate race and sex discrimination decades earlier when he decided not to back full repeal of the Rumford

Act, even though such repeal enjoyed overwhelming popular support from whites. He was not going to change his mind back now.

These ideologues blamed Reagan's staff for leading him astray, but in fact they failed to see that Reagan himself was the "problem." Many of the participants in the revolt were former Reagan White House staffers, but note that these people were all former Reagan Administration staffers who had left only a bit more than a year after he had taken office.[41] Former assistant treasury secretary Paul Craig Roberts claimed "there were more Reaganites in that room [a meeting of the revolting conservatives] than there are in the Administration, and ten times as many as there are in the White House."[42] They believed the president had not assembled a winning team. But perhaps, to paraphrase what Reagan had said so many years before, it's not that his conservative friends were wrong, it's that so much they knew just wasn't so.

Reagan had always been a man who interpreted rather than opposed Franklin Roosevelt. He had always been a man who conciliated different factions rather than drove people apart. He had always been a man who changed course when it seemed to be appropriate, a man who was more wedded to his goal than his method. The fact that these people were on the outside while others, purportedly more "liberal" were on the inside, may have been a clue that Ronald Reagan just wasn't that into them or their ideologies. The California conservative who saw this first, Kent Steffgen, would not have been surprised.

Reagan's lobbying won the day and his tax bill passed narrowly. He noted drily in his diary that "again some of our ultra-pure conservatives deserted."[43] He won another tax hike battle later in the year, a five-cent-per-gallon gasoline tax increase, again over a Senate filibuster waged by hard-core conservatives such as Jesse Helms.[44] The failure of Democrats to keep their commitment to him to reduce spending, however, meant that he would never again back a tax hike without his priorities written into the same bill.

Reagan's beliefs about communism were much less nuanced and thus much less susceptible of misunderstanding. Conservatives were always thrilled to hear him denounce the "evil empire," and so it is that even today conservatives love to quote the speech he gave before the British Parliament in June 1982 at the Palace of Westminster.

That speech is best remembered for his belief that "the march of freedom and democracy" would leave "Marxism-Leninism on the ash-heap of history."[45] That, however, is merely his conclusion, reached after he provided an acute and prescient analysis of human nature and politics. It is to that which we now turn.

Reagan made clear that he both believed that human nature desired freedom and that there could be many interpretations of how that freedom could be exercised. He noted that none of the Soviet-supported client states in Central and Eastern Europe were immune from unrest, as the brutal suppression in December 1981 of Poland's drive for some freedom had shown. "Regimes planted by bayonets do not take root."

They could not take root because of the natural human desires he had told Brezhnev about in his private letter just months before. People want to be free to choose their own way of life, and those who are denied this do not produce for those who make the choices for them. Thus, the Soviet Union was faced with its own inevitable conflict between a political order and an economic one, only this time it was the reverse of what Karl Marx had predicted. It would not be the democratic nations that would succumb because of the internal contradictions of capitalism; those nations had shown themselves able to adapt through free elections such that even the least skilled person had hope and dignity. It was the Soviet Union itself that faced the internal contradiction of its order, one caused by the inability of an unfree people to produce enough to compete militarily with the free nations of the West.

Thus Reagan told Britain to remain strong and courageous. If the West maintained its resolve, its faith in the inviolate nature of human rights, and kept the military strength to resist Soviet threats, then victory was inevitable. "The Soviet Union is not immune from the reality of what is going on in the world. It has happened in the past—a small ruling elite either mistakenly attempts to ease domestic unrest through greater repression and foreign adventure, or it chooses a wiser course. It begins to allow its people a voice in their own destiny."

It is easy today to see the wisdom in his words. Less than a decade later the Soviet Union had collapsed under the weight of its contradictions, just as Reagan had foretold. But at the time it seemed to many to be hopelessly naive. Reagan's call for international efforts to plant democracy was scoffed at; his honest assessment of Soviet intentions called a throwback to the 1950s.[46] But Reagan was never one to shrink from conflict when his core beliefs were challenged.

The freedom that Reagan spoke of, however, was not the sort that libertarians champion. Reagan knew that even the American government that he thought was too big was small in comparison to that of Britain and the other European allies. And so he was careful to note that his criticisms of government and collectivism did not include them:

> Now, I'm aware that among us here and throughout Europe there is legitimate disagreement over the extent to which the public sector should play a role in a nation's economy and life. But on one point all of us are united—our abhorrence of dictatorship in all its forms, but most particularly totalitarianism and the terrible inhumanities it has caused in our time—the great purge, Auschwitz and Dachau, the Gulag, and Cambodia.

This was surely a politic thing to do, but it was also a principled one. By noting that disagreement over the exact role of the state in public life was legitimate, Reagan demonstrated that he did not share the libertarian allergy to government. And by noting that all democracies shared an opposition to ideological dictatorship, he established once again that this, not the specific tax level or whether any particular government program existed, was the primary target in his decades-long warnings about government power.

The next two years contained many political challenges for Reagan, but none that really tested or illuminated his core beliefs. Each year he would propose more spending cuts than Congress would pass. Each year he would resist urging from Congress and his staff to cut military spending or increase tax rates.[47] Each year he would be told that he was provoking the threat of nuclear war with the Soviet Union by forcefully resisting its expansion. Each year he would go on carefully and skillfully to do the best he could under the circumstances to see his vision through.

It's not that he wasn't making important decisions. He rejected intense public pressure for a freeze on nuclear weapons development (the so-called nuclear freeze), an idea he said would lock in a Soviet advantage. He and the NATO allies followed through on their scheduled deployment of Pershing II intermediate-range nuclear missiles to combat Soviet SS-20 intermediate missiles even as the Soviets stormed out of arms-control talks in protest. Reagan announced a research effort to build a defense against nuclear missile attack, an idea the press labeled "Star Wars." He even ordered an invasion of the tiny Caribbean island nation of Grenada in October 1983 when a bloody Marxist coup threatened to install another Communist regime in America's backyard. It's just that each of these decisions, as important as they were, simply demonstrated to the nation and the world that Reagan had meant what he had said for the past three decades about fighting communism.

Reagan's major domestic achievement during this period also showed fidelity to principle. Reagan's original budget had included a plan to reduce Social Security benefits for people who retired before age sixty-five, but Congress rejected that idea overwhelmingly. Since Social Security was on the verge of bankruptcy, Reagan proposed creating a bipartisan commission to create a comprehensive plan to save the popular program. The commission's plan was a classic compromise, including increases in tax rates for workers, eventual benefit cuts for retirees by raising the retirement age in small stages to reach age 67 in 2027, and taxing some Social Security benefits for the first time for retirees with above-average incomes from sources other than Social Security.[48] With Reagan's support, the bill quickly sailed through both houses of Congress in less than two months.[49]

Reagan had promised Americans he would not jeopardize core New Deal programs like Social Security. The compromise showed that he was true to his word even if it meant increasing taxes. Indeed, he

believed one part of the tax hike, the taxation of Social Security benefits for wealthier adults, was a welcome change. This tax, he wrote
Mr. Phillip Robertson, was "a step toward correcting a mistake in the
program—there should have been a means test from the beginning."[50]
Reagan again showed that his opposition to government was not an
absolute, and that his belief in tax cuts was not a barrier to financing the
social safety net Americans had come to depend on.

The economy was already improving by the time this compromise
passed. Unemployment peaked in early 1983 and plummeted throughout the year. When the final installment of Reagan's three-year tax
cut took effect midyear, the economy was turbocharged. Real GDP
growth was over 7 percent in 1983. Unemployment had dropped from
10.4 percent to 8 percent, and the inflation that had peaked at nearly
15 percent in the winter of 1980 had dropped to a mere 3 percent by
year's end. Reaganomics had worked so well that Reagan noted "they
don't call it Reaganomics anymore."[51]

The roaring economy helped Reagan's reelection campaign im-
mensely. Reagan's approval rating rose from a low of 35 percent in
January 1983 to break the 50 percent barrier by November.[52] This dramatic turnaround put him in the driver's seat for the 1984 campaign.
By January 1984 he led the likely Democratic nominee, former vice
president Walter Mondale, by 10 percent.[53] The man once regarded as
an extremist washed-up actor was on the cusp of a historic reelection.

It's easy to credit material factors for his political success. People
do vote their pocketbooks, and presidents rarely if ever lose when the
economy is growing quickly. But Reagan had always said that what
troubled him most about America in the late 1970s was its spiritual, not
its material, malaise. He was proud, therefore, when he saw America's
confidence springing back. "The spiritual rebirth I had hoped for was
under way, as vigorous and as robust as the nation's economic turnaround. America was coming back, becoming proud of itself again,
becoming confident about the future," Reagan wrote in his autobiography.[54] He noted this was happening, but rarely claimed direct credit for
helping nurture this spiritual renewal. He was too modest.

Throughout his life Reagan's guiding light was a genuine love for the American people. In private he could be remote and difficult to know, but that masked a deep love for individuals, which came through in the politics he professed. Reagan had always opposed the rule of a self-proclaimed elite few whether those people were tyrants, bureaucrats, or tyrannical bosses. Unlike ideologues of the Left, who placed their hopes in government planning, or ideologues of the Right, who placed their hopes in the entrepreneur or the successful businessperson, Reagan always viewed America's people as the source of its greatness and its potential.

We have seen this throughout his career already, how he extolled average people as "heroes" in his first inaugural address and said conservatives represented "the forgotten American" after Goldwater's 1964 defeat. Reagan displayed this love of the common person again and again in the run-up to the 1984 election. It was the crucial element that let people know he was on their side even when things were looking bad, the element that allowed his popularity to rebound so quickly when things started to turn up even a little.

Reagan's faith in and love for the average American is on full display in his best-known speech from this era, the speech given on the shores of Normandy to commemorate the fortieth anniversary of the successful D-day invasion.[55] He could have focused on the great issues at stake in that war and spoken of abstract principles of freedom, slavery, and tyranny. Instead, he started by recounting the individual feats of bravery that Americans and soldiers of other countries had performed in storming the cliffs under withering enemy fire. "These are the boys of Pointe du Hoc," he said. "These are the men who took the cliffs. These are the champions who helped free a continent. These are the heroes who helped end a war."

One could say that this was an obvious political move that any president would have made. But that's just not so. Compare Reagan's focus on individual courage with the words President George W. Bush made when he thought the war in Iraq was "mission accomplished."[56] Bush focused on the objectives of the war, the love of liberty that animates

Americans and people everywhere, and the continuing resolve of America to fight al Qaida. He does mention the soldiers' "courage" and their "willingness to face danger for your country," but there is no mention of individual courage. The soldiers are important because they are part of a "we," part of a plan they did not create. For Reagan, it was only the uncommon acts of individual bravery accomplished by common people that made the "we" possible.

Reagan's deep belief in the uncommon heights that common men and women could surmount was a recurring theme of his. In his 1982 State of the Union speech, he praised the heroism of a government employee, Lenny Skutnik, who had jumped into the icy waters of the Potomac to save someone trying to survive an airline crash.[57] He spoke of the "countless, quiet, everyday heroes of American life," the parents who sacrifice for their children, the volunteers who "feed, clothe, nurse, and teach the needy," and the "millions who have made our nation and our nation's destiny so very special." He would tell attendees at the ninth annual CPAC convention that "'Main Street' Americans . . . blue-collar workers, blacks, Hispanic, shopkeepers, scholars, service people, housewives, and professional men and women" were "the backbone of America."[58] He would conclude his 1983 State of the Union address by telling Congress that it was the ordinary American who was "laying the foundation" for recovery and "a better tomorrow."[59]

> From coast to coast, on the job and in the classrooms and laboratories, at new construction sites and in churches and community groups, neighbors are helping neighbors. And they've already begun the building, the research, the work, and the giving that will make our country great again.
>
> I believe this, because I believe in them.

In the final analysis, Reagan's political success came down to this. Americans loved him because they knew he loved them.

Reagan's reelection was nearly assured by the time of the Republican Convention in August. Mondale had been seriously challenged by an outsider, Colorado senator Gary Hart, and this battle hurt him deeply. Mondale trailed Reagan by 17 percent in the Gallup poll taken before the Democratic Convention, and even with the customary post-convention bounce was able to cut his deficit only to 12 percent.[60] The Summer Olympics then took place in Los Angeles, and for two weeks the nation went through a display of patriotic pride I hadn't seen in my lifetime. Night after night Americans won gold, and the chant "USA, USA" spontaneously roared through stadiums and homes alike. Reagan had been America's cheerleader for years, so it was no surprise when this era of national good feeling worked to his benefit. He was ahead by 19 percent as the Olympics closed and the Republican Convention started.[61] He wasn't looking at just a reelection; he was looking at a historic landslide.

Reagan's acceptance speech did not need to break new ground, and it didn't.[62] His speech recited his long-standing theme of a virtuous people fighting against a party that wanted to control their lives through overregulation and overtaxation, and he drew on the renewed pride in America to whip the crowd into a patriotic frenzy. The crowd spontaneously burst into the "USA, USA" chant that was sweeping the nation; Reagan clearly enjoyed every minute of this lovefest.

Reagan had always focused his attention on the forgotten American, that New Deal supporter who had grown disenchanted as the Democratic Party seemed to become more like Henry Wallace's party and less like Harry Truman's. His acceptance speech was again devoted to wooing that person, with a clear depiction of the current Democratic leadership as out of step with traditional Democratic values. He noted that some Democrats had likened the Grenada invasion to the Soviet invasion of Afghanistan or "the crushing of human rights in Poland." "Could you imagine Harry Truman, John Kennedy, Hubert Humphrey, or Scoop Jackson making such a shocking comparison?" He went on to close his speech by again noting he had cast his first ballot for FDR, asking the crowd, "Did I leave the Democratic Party, or did the leadership of that party leave not just me but millions of patriotic Democrats who believed in the principles and philosophy of that platform?" Since the Democratic Party leadership had left behind their voters, Reagan said, "it's no surprise that so many responsible Democrats feel our platform is closer to their views, and we welcome them to our side."

There was a glaring omission in Reagan's argument: the word "Republican." He mentioned that word only once, when he referred to an anticrime bill that had "passed the Republican Senate" but was being held up by the Democratic House. As in his first acceptance speech, Reagan mentioned only one former Republican president by name, Abraham Lincoln. Reagan was clearly a partisan Republican by this point in his political career, but he would take no chances as he tried to woo the voter for whom "Republican" still meant "Hoover" or "uncaring boss."

Reagan also returned to the theme he had mentioned so long ago in his TV speech for Goldwater, the argument that there is no such thing as left or right but only up or down. He elaborated on this theme, explaining what he meant by "down" and "up":

> Isn't our choice really not one of left or right, but of up or down? Down through the welfare state to statism, to more and more government largesse accompanied by more government authority, less individual liberty, and, ultimately, totalitarianism, always advanced as for our own good. The alternative is the dream conceived by our Founding Fathers, up to the ultimate in individual freedom consistent with an orderly society.

Libertarians and Goldwaterites could jump on his inclusion of "the welfare state" in the category of "down" to argue that in his heart Reagan was as far right as they. But that just doesn't hold water.

Reagan's "down" category has three stages; "welfare state," "statism," and "totalitarianism." One of his early speeches that attacked collectivism also broke down the enemy into three stages; "liberalism," "socialism," and "communism." Just as in 1984 Reagan said the "welfare state" can lead to "statism" and "totalitarianism," in 1962 Reagan said "liberalism" could lead to "socialism" and then "communism."[63] The pure symmetry between the two arguments strongly suggests that Reagan's 1984 statement was simply a truncated version of the argument he made so many years ago, so it is to that speech we turn to help us understand what Reagan meant.

That speech to the Conservative League of Minneapolis, "Losing Freedom by Installments," made a simple argument. Liberalism was a cousin to socialism and communism because each ideology saw solutions to society's problems through government. But this did not mean that Reagan thought government should do little or nothing. In the same speech he endorsed the idea of public housing. He also specifically endorsed federal government aid for medical insurance for needy seniors, saying, "As one conservative, let me say any person in the United States who requires medical attention and cannot provide it for himself should have it provided for him." He made clear he opposed only a "compulsory government insurance program regardless of need."

This distinction between government help for the needy, which was good, and government direction of society, which was bad, is crucial to understanding Reagan's thought. This is why he could support the basic innovation FDR introduced, the legitimization of direct government assistance to help the truly needy advance in American life, while opposing the interpretation of that innovation that placed government at the center of everything and gave aid to people who neither needed it nor deserved it. Thus he would famously write in his diary that

the press is dying to paint me as now trying to undo the New Deal. I remind them I voted for F.D.R. 4 times. I'm trying to undo the "Great Society." It was L.B.J.'s war on poverty that led to our present mess.[64]

The "welfare state" for Reagan was always the Great Society and its attempt to transform American society in accordance with the ideas of

Henry Wallace. It never included legitimate help for deserving people, the principle that underlay many of the major programs the federal and state governments funded.

The rest of the campaign was a cakewalk. Reagan's overpreparation for the first debate caused him to stumble, raising fears he was showing signs of age, but he bounced right back in the next debate with his characteristic poise and humor.[65] I watched eagerly with millions of other worried Reaganites as the moderator asked Reagan if he thought he could bear up under the strain of office at his age. After saying he could, Reagan quipped, "I am not going to exploit for political purposes my opponent's youth and inexperience."[66] Millions of us, including Mondale, laughed out loud. We all knew that the campaign had just ended.[67]

Reagan won his reelection in a massive landslide. Reagan beat Mondale by over 18 percent, and Mondale received a lower share of the popular vote than Carter had four years before. The Electoral College margin was even greater, 525–13. Mondale had carried only the heavily Democratic Washington, DC, and his home state of Minnesota, the latter by less than four thousand votes out of 2.1 million cast. To this day only one person has bested Reagan's Electoral College vote margin: Franklin Roosevelt in his first reelection in 1936.

Reagan again won large shares of the working-class Democratic vote he had long courted. His share of the vote skyrocketed throughout the South, increasing over his 1980 showing by a high of 19.2 percent in Carter's home state of Georgia to a low of 8.3 percent in more metropolitan Texas. Throughout the rural South, Reagan's vote leaped up by 10 to 20 percent. Reagan's blend of a muscular foreign policy and a compassionate yet restrained government was just what these voters wanted.

He also bested his total among working-class whites in the Midwest, although by smaller margins. Auto-dependent Michigan, probably benefiting from the respite the industry received from Japan's export restraints, was Reagan's best state in the region. He received 59.2 percent of the vote there, 10.2 percent higher than in 1980 and a larger share than in traditionally more Republican Ohio. Reagan also did over 7 percent better in Ohio than in 1980, and between 2 and 6 percent better in the other states in the region.

Reagan's vote share increased almost everywhere, but it jumped the most in suburban areas where families had benefited a lot from the dramatic decline in inflation. His vote share jumped by nine and thirteen points in predominantly suburban counties in Ohio and by six to nine points in Pennsylvania's suburbs. It rose by a more modest three to four points in working-class northeastern Pennsylvania and by one to eight points in most working-class Ohio counties. In both states, the heavily unionized steel regions barely budged—their industry remained in decline. More prosperous Michigan saw the greatest increases, with increases between 7 and 15 percent in the Detroit region and 7 to 9 percent in more working-class counties.

Democratic partisans saw what Reagan had done and despaired. The core of the New Deal coalition had been shattered, drawn over to a man most of them still considered coldhearted and bellicose. But their voters had disagreed: Reagan's view of FDR's legacy was just fine by them.

Had the seventy-three-year-old Reagan died suddenly right then, his presidency would have been considered a success. Instead, he went on to conquer new heights in his second term. He ushered in a comprehensive tax reform that eliminated many tax shelters, gave families tax relief, and lowered the top income tax rate to a mere 28 percent, the lowest it had been since before the Great Depression. He continued to spar with Japan over trade, slapping penalties and quotas on Japanese imports as he strove to make free trade fair trade. He even went on to survive the Iran-Contra scandal to forge an unprecedented and wholly unexpected partnership with a new Soviet leader, the young Mikhail Gorbachev.

That effort scared many of his strongest supporters and made many wonder if the Gipper truly had moved left in his dotage. But the old man won again, as the trust he had forged with Gorbachev gave the Communist the political room to begin his programs of glasnost and perestroika. Just as Reagan had predicted in the Westminster speech, once the bayonet was removed, the subject peoples of the Soviet empire wanted nothing to do with communism.

Reagan's push for tax reform started with his second inaugural address. Saying that "freedom and incentives unleash the drive and entrepreneurial genius that are the core of human progress,"[68] he called for tax simplification to make the tax code "more fair and bring the rates down for all who work and earn." He followed up that brief call with a more detailed call in his State of the Union address.[69] Speaking for "the American farmer, the entrepreneur, and every worker in industries fighting to modernize and compete," he asked Congress to reduce tax rates by removing tax preferences. He proposed reducing the top marginal tax rate, which had been 70 percent when he took office, to "no more than 35 percent, and possibly lower." He also urged that "individuals living at or near the poverty line be totally exempt from Federal income tax." "To restore fairness to families, we will also propose increasing significantly the personal exemption."

These simple principles might seem to be supply-side inspired, with their discussion of the top rate and the mention of entrepreneurs. But they are in fact simply the same ideas Reagan promoted in the 1950s and 1960s, when the supply-side godfather Arthur Laffer had been a college undergraduate. Reagan had attacked any progressive taxation as immoral, arguing instead for what he called proportionate taxation and what we today call a flat tax.[70] He had long believed the best way to fight poverty was to stop taxing the poor and the working poor who needed that money to raise their families.[71] He had always said that the floor Americans were building to ensure all people could live with comfort and dignity should also not create a ceiling above which people with energy and inspiration could not rise.[72] The words and details may have been new, but the ideas themselves, like their author, were quite old indeed.

It took nearly two years for Congress to hash out a bipartisan tax reform bill, but when it did the results looked very similar to Reagan's principles. The number of tax brackets was reduced from fifteen to effectively two, lowering the top rate from 50 percent to 28 percent.[73] The standard deduction and personal exemption amounts were raised, removing over six million poor families from the income tax rolls and giving substantial tax relief to most middle-class households. Many tax shelters, especially with regard to real estate ownership and speculation, were eliminated, as were deductions for state and local sales taxes and consumer interest payments on credit cards and nonmortgage loans.

Interestingly, the capital gains tax was *raised* from 20 to 28 percent. The predominantly wealthy people who earn a large share of their income from selling stocks and collecting dividends saw a very significant tax hike thanks to Reagan's bill.

Reagan's remarks on signing his landmark achievement reflect the different goals he had. He praised the reform for encouraging "risk-taking, innovation, and that old American spirit of enterprise" and removing the "steeply progressive nature" of the old code, which punished "that special effort and extra hard work that has always been the driving force of our economy."[74] He gave equal weight to the bill's increasing the "freedom of expression of the entrepreneur" as to "fairness for families" and to the restoration of "America's promise of hope and opportunity, that with hard work even the poorest among us can gain the security and happiness that is the due of all Americans." He praised the facts that "millions of working poor will be dropped from the tax rolls altogether, and families will get a long-overdue break with lower rates and an almost doubled personal exemption" as well as the fact that "flatter rates will mean more reward for that extra effort."

For Reagan, tax reform was not primarily or even significantly an exercise in lowering the top rate to empower entrepreneurs and job creators. Instead, it was the culmination of a long dream to help people of all backgrounds and from all walks of life be economically free to live dignified and secure lives of their own choosing.

Other second-term initiatives were less successful, but were no less equally intended to prune government so that it helped the people who needed it but *only* the people who needed it. Reagan laid out those plans in a televised address to the nation in early 1985. Arguing that "Government began to take over America . . . in the name of the Great Society," he urged Congress to adopt a series of spending cuts that would "bring spending down into line with tax revenues."[75] These cuts would not touch "the safety net for needy Americans." Instead, they would target the programs that went "not to individuals needing help, but to thousands and thousands of bureaucrats, researchers, planners, managers, and professional advocates who earn their living from the great growth industry of government." He advocated eliminating Amtrak passenger railroad subsidies, loans to business through the Export-Import Bank and the Small Business Administration, and farm subsidies.[76]

He expanded on this in his 1986 State of the Union speech.[77] Budget balancing, he said, should not be accomplished "by taking from those in need. As families take care of their own, government should provide shelter and nourishment for those who cannot provide for themselves." But that did not mean that welfare should not be reformed to help people to "escape the spider's web of dependency." Quoting Franklin Roosevelt that "welfare is a narcotic, a subtle destroyer of the human spirit," Reagan proposed reforming welfare to increase the number of people who became independent of it. But he also went further than that.

Reagan had long believed that people should not be denied needed medical care because of a lack of funds, and that government had a role to play to help ensure people got the care they needed. Even with the massive budget deficits facing the country, he believed it was time to start to fulfill this dream. He announced that he was directing his secretary of Health and Human Services to work to see "how the private sector and government can work together to address the problems of affordable insurance for those whose life savings would otherwise be threatened when catastrophic illness strikes."

Most conservatives supported or at least tolerated these initiatives. But one man could hold his tongue no longer. David Stockman finally left the Reagan administration in August 1985 and started work on a book that would prove to be his parting shot against the president he had served.

The Triumph of Politics, published in the summer of 1986, was Stockman's effort at biting the hand that fed him. It followed the path of the time-honored Washington tell-all insider book explaining why all the people you served with in government were fools and incompetents. But it offered two things that were different that make it essential reading even today for any libertarian or libertarian-conservative. First, Stockman proclaimed that he was the biggest fool and incompetent of them all. Second, he was foolish precisely because he tried to push an ideological anti–New Deal revolution that nobody else really wanted.

Stockman proclaimed loudly that he "joined the Reagan Revolution as a radical ideologue."[78] He had searched his whole life for an all-encompassing worldview that made sense of all things, passing through a Marxist phase in college before settling on supply-side libertarianism.[79] His new ideology preached the virtues of a dynamic capitalism and minimalist government, "a spare and stingy creature which offered even-handed public justice but no more."[80] He came at his beliefs from a different source, but Stockman's ideology preached the same thing as Goldwater's *Conscience of a Conservative* and the early anti-Eisenhower conservative movement.

Like Goldwater, Stockman believed that he—with the exception of pro-entrepreneurial measures like supply-side tax cuts—had come to Washington to cut government, not improve it. The Reagan Revolution he sought to lead required a "frontal assault on the American welfare state."[81] That meant such things as an end to subsidies to farmers and businesses, an end to welfare for the able-bodied, and an end to permitting people to collect more in Social Security benefits than they had contributed in taxes.[82] Americans as a whole were "getting more than they deserved, needed, or owed."[83] He meant to cut them off from the government that had helped them since the New Deal.

Stockman believed Reagan should have led the fight for this revolution from the start. But what's telling is not that Reagan didn't support this, it's Stockman's rationale for why he did not. Reagan, he wrote, was "too kind, gentle, and sentimental. Despite his right-wing image, *his ideology and philosophy always took a back seat* when he [learned] some individual human being might be hurt."(Emphasis added.)[84] Stockman, like other disappointed conservatives, and most liberals, assumed that Reagan in his heart was as antigovernment as he and Barry Goldwater were.

We have seen that Reagan never endorsed the view of minimalist government that Stockman, Goldwater, and today's libertarians and libertarian-conservatives advocate. From the moment he stepped onto the stage as a conservative speaker, Reagan made clear that he supported government measures that offer genuine help to people with legitimate need. He did not abandon his ideology when he saw that people would be hurt; his entire philosophy was informed by that fact from the outset.

Stockman's views on Social Security benefits demonstrate this in spades. His principle of "no more benefits than you put in" would mean Social Security was little more than a forced savings program. If you were poor or part of the working poor, you would get very little in terms of benefits. You would remain poor, perhaps even poorer, in "retirement" in Stockman's world even with these "benefits." But preventing "poverty by reason of old age because of unemployment," as he put it in the "Time for Choosing" speech, was exactly what Reagan believed Social Security was supposed to do. Reagan *wanted* those better off to provide those worse off "through no fault of their own" with "comfort, and even a few luxuries" in their old age—and he wanted to tax the rich to make sure the deserving poor got their benefits.

Reagan and Stockman ultimately disagreed on principle. Reagan believed that you deserved a certain minimal standard of living so long as you contributed according to your ability. You *deserved* that "help" because you were a human being living in America. Stockman believed you deserved only what you could compel others to give you in a free-market exchange. If you were neither talented nor fortunate enough to be able to afford a comfortable retirement, you did not *deserve* it—and thus should not get it.

It's no surprise that Stockman so fundamentally misunderstood Reagan. He had held him in contempt at the outset of the 1980 campaign, saying he believed Reagan to be a "cranky obscurantist" and an "antediluvian."[85] He identified Reagan's "political base" with "every kook and fringe group that inhabited the vasty deep of American politics."[86] That included the social-issues conservatives of the New Right, "the Bible-thumping creationists, the anti-Communist witch-hunters, and the small-minded Hollywood millionaires to whom 'supply side' meant one more Mercedes."[87] Stockman was, if it were possible, even more unfamiliar than the liberal was with Ronald Reagan, his views, and the people who loved him.

But even those familiar with Reagan's views could be surprised at what he did. Reagan's dealings with Gorbachev are the primary example of this, as even personal friends who had known him for decades were shocked when the virulent anti-Communist shook hands with a Communist leader to eliminate American weapons that had helped hold Soviet expansion in check.

Reagan always noted that every Soviet leader had reiterated the goal of worldwide Communist domination, and that their actions in fomenting revolution and spreading their ideology showed they were serious. Thus he called the Soviet Union an "evil empire,"[88] and even joked before a nationwide radio address that "I've signed legislation that will outlaw Russia forever. We begin bombing in five minutes."[89] While he sought to engage the Soviets in arms-control talks to discuss significant reductions in nuclear weapons, none of these leaders seriously engaged his proposals. The world thus continued to watch what it had watched for seventy years, a Soviet Communist leadership that steadily and aggressively marched toward what it said history itself dictated, the installment of worldwide Communist rule.

Mikhail Gorbachev assumed power in early 1985. Gorbachev was different from prior Soviet rulers: young (fifty-four years old when he took power), sunny in temperament, and well dressed and familiar with Western ideas. He was the first Soviet leader to have been born after the Communist Revolution, and from the outset he preached change rather than continuity. British prime minister Margaret Thatcher, Reagan's philosophical soul mate, had met him in 1984 and famously declared "we can do business with him." Reagan was eager to find out if he could too.

Reagan started by sending Vice President Bush to Gorbachev's predecessor's funeral with a letter inviting the new leader to a summit meeting in Washington. Gorbachev turned him down, as expected, but "expressed less hostility than I had come to expect from Soviet leaders."[90] Despite that, Reagan was not yet sold that Gorbachev was truly "a *different* sort of Soviet leader."[91] He didn't begin to come to that conclusion until he met him face to face in Geneva, Switzerland, that November. After spending some time alone with him by a roaring fire (Reagan, ever the FDR devotee, called this a "fireside chat"[92]), he decided that Thatcher had been right and he could talk with Gorbachev. Most important, he later noted,

> not once during our private sessions or at the plenary meetings did he express support for the old Marxist-Leninist goal of a one-world Communist state or the Brezhnev Doctrine of Soviet expansionism. He was the first Soviet leader I knew of who hadn't done that.[93]

This was the first set of new facts that the principled Reagan would note to chart a new path to his old course, replacing the Soviet Union with a regime that respected human dignity and freedom.

Reagan continued to get new facts in early 1986 that gave him further hope that the decades-old conflict could be turned around. The Soviet economy had started to sputter, perhaps shocked by the massive collapse in world oil prices that occurred between November 1985 and February 1986.[94] The Soviet Union was heavily dependent on revenue it gained from selling surplus oil abroad to pay for the grain and other imports it used to offset its nonmarket economy's inefficiencies.[95] These economic problems were quickly followed by the unexpected nuclear disaster at a nuclear power plant in the Soviet city of Chernobyl.[96] Poor design and an incompetently administered stress test sent radioactive material into the ground and the air, the latter spreading contamination throughout Western Europe. Reagan continued to press Gorbachev to meet and pushed nuclear negotiators to find common ground on a verifiable treaty reducing nuclear-armed missiles. A proposal by Gorbachev led Reagan to agree to meet him in Reykjavik, Iceland, to see if a deal might be concluded.

Reykjavik proved to be an unsuccessful, yet important, summit. Gorbachev and Reagan nearly agreed to a landmark treaty to dramatically reduce strategic and intermediate-level nuclear missiles, and Gorbachev volunteered to reduce the Soviets' conventional military to offset desired reductions in tactical nuclear weapons.[97] But he insisted that Reagan agree to stop American research into a defense against ballistic missiles. Reagan was not willing to do that, arguing that this "was an insurance policy to guarantee the Soviets kept the agreements."[98] Reagan offered to share the fruits of the research to the Soviets to prove the United States had no intention of using this defense in an offensive manner, building an impregnable shield behind which it could launch a devastating first strike on Russia.[99] When Gorbachev refused to budge, Reagan angrily stormed out of the meeting.

Many conservatives distrusted Reagan's outreach, but he saw things differently. He noted that Gorbachev was trying to change the Soviet system. Gorbachev had started to encourage private ownership of businesses (perestroika) and to reduce internal repression and interference in the affairs of other countries (glasnost). Reagan had always believed, as the Westminster speech showed, that the Soviet Union would have to do this or fall because of internal dissent. As he noted these developments he moved forward with private diplomacy to reengage with Gorbachev.[100] He maintained public condemnation of the Soviet system, telling Gorbachev in an address before the Berlin Wall to "tear down this wall!"[101] The Wall stayed up, but behind the scene the walls were starting to crack. Reagan received word while he was accompanying his wife at his mother-in-law's funeral that the Soviets were willing to discuss the Reykjavik measures without insisting on the Americans' elimination of missile defense research.[102] By December, the old Cold Warrior sat in the White House to sign the Intermediate-Range Nuclear

Forces (INF) Treaty, pledging both sides to eliminating an entire type of nuclear weapon from the globe.

Conservatives had been suspicious of this development for months. In May, Reagan's close personal friend William F. Buckley Jr. published an issue of his influential magazine, *National Review*, condemning what the cover called "Reagan's Suicide Pact."[103] Buckley's disapproval did not go away despite many private discussions with Reagan.[104] Reagan moved to reassure other conservatives, telling the New Hampshire newspaper publisher "Nackey" Loeb that "the evil empire is still just that."[105] He said that Gorbachev was sincere about glasnost and perestroika and that he truly was different although still a solid Communist.[106] Reagan was impressed that the head of an officially atheist state had twice referred to God in their private meetings[107] and by Gorbachev's failure to reaffirm "the Marxian concept of a one-world Communist state."[108]

Whatever their private misgivings, conservative senators quickly fell in line. The treaty was ratified in May, opposed only by a few ultra-conservatives, including North Carolina senator Jesse Helms.[109] Thus, the man whose support in the 1976 North Carolina primary did more than any other person's outside the Reagan campaign itself to save the Californian's flagging hopes became in the end yet another ultra who found Reagan wasn't the man he had thought he was.

We will never know if conservative fears about Gorbachev, that he or a successor might renege on the treaty or invade Western Europe once American missiles were destroyed, would have come to fruition. Gorbachev was prepared to use the domestic power the treaty gave him to test Reagan's premise that a free people would never choose communism. Within two years, he would find to his dismay that Reagan had been stunningly right.

Gorbachev first removed Soviet troops from Afghanistan in 1988 and 1989, the first time Soviet troops had retreated since World War II. He then announced that the Soviet Union would not use its military to prop up satellite regimes in Eastern Europe, and he allowed mass protests within the Soviet Union to occur without repression. Reagan thought the latter development confirmed he had been right about Gorbachev, telling his old friend and colleague the former California senator George Murphy as much in a letter in July 1988.[110] But 1988 was only the spark that lit the Soviet empire ablaze.

Poland was the first to go. By April 1989 the Polish Communists had agreed to partially free elections with the anti-Communist trade union Solidarity. Solidarity won every seat it was eligible to compete for in the June election, and by fall a non-Communist was prime minister. By September the Hungarian Communist party had agreed to free, multiparty elections to take place in 1990.

The most important and symbolic revolt occurred in the Soviet-occupied portions of Germany, known as the German Democratic Republic, or East Germany. Tens of thousands fled the country by the fall of 1989, and thousands more took to the streets to demand change. By November 9, 1989, the East German regime had seen enough. It opened the border with West Germany directly, and East German citizens started to tear down the wall that Reagan had asked Gorbachev to dismantle just two years earlier.

The final nail in the Soviet coffin was hammered into place in Czechoslovakia. Inspired by their neighbors, hundreds of thousands of Czechs surged to Wenceslaus Square in the center of the capital of Prague. Czech Communists caved in quickly, forming a coalition government with non-Communists in late December.

I will never forget where I was on December 30, 1989. I was in Munich, Germany, that morning on my first trip to Europe. I can read German, and so as I was in the main train station headed to Regensburg I looked up at the electronic bulletin board that flashed news headlines. There I saw it: the Czechoslovaks had appointed non-Communists to lead the interior (police) and defense (army) ministries. For the first time since Vladimir I. Lenin had seized power in 1917, a Communist government had given up control of the guns. Reagan had been proved right. The Cold War was over.

I often think about that day as I have furthered my understanding of Reagan. I have come to learn that the deepest political belief he had was a love of individual human beings and a belief that each person is capable of living a life of dignity and worth. Many of us mouthed those words, but we remained caught in ideological webs of our own spinning, seeing only left or right. He, however, saw neither left nor right, but only up or down. He saw that human beings may differ on much, but the love of self and the love for others are parts of the human soul that cannot be removed no matter how powerful a government becomes.

I was surprised decades later when I saw the epitaph he had chosen for his gravestone proclaiming his belief in the "purpose and worth in each and every human life." But I should not have been. That was what he had been telling us all along, from his early days as a New Dealer to his mashed-potato-circuit days refining his views to his life as governor and then as president. We *are* capable of self-government, he told us. We *can* choose to restrain our greed while we feed every person's need. We *can* choose, as British prime minister Theresa May recently said, to "reject the ideological templates provided by the socialist left and the libertarian right."[111] We can choose to do this, because we are human beings and because we are Americans.

Reagan often told his audiences that they faced a "time for choosing" and a "rendezvous with destiny." The truth is that every generation of Americans, every generation of conservatives, faces times for choosing and rendezvouses with destiny. That is because self-government is a constant choice: we must always choose to feed the better angels of our nature and restrain the demons of greed and faction. We Americans, we conservatives, we Republicans: we all face this time for choosing today. Our national politics is riven by deep disagreement and partisanship, but all that sound and fury is not about nothing. It is simply we, the people, trying to decide how best to interpret our national principles in light of the challenges we face today as individuals and as a nation.

We conservatives and Republicans have a particular choice ahead of us because too often we have chosen to often ignore Ronald Reagan's real political and intellectual legacy. We have too often implemented his specific words while ignoring or forgetting the spirit behind those words. Too often we have behaved as political Pharisees, following the letter of the law while losing sight of its spirit.

We have reached the end of our examination of the real Ronald Reagan. The next, final chapter will look at how we conservatives and Republicans lost our way by forgetting him and how we can find it and him again. The election of Donald Trump has led many to conclude we are witnessing the de-Reaganization of the Republican Party. In fact, it is just the opposite. The spirit that Trump awakened and the constituency that spirit attracted is essentially the same in each case as that Reagan communicated and attracted. Trump's election gives the conservative movement and the Republican Party its last, best hope to finally build Reagan's New Republican Party and once again make America a shining city on the hill.

THE TIME IS NOW: REAGAN

Ronald Reagan left us in 2004 when his soul "slipped the surly bonds of earth to touch the face of God."[1] His spirit, however, remains with us today. Just as Democrats wrapped themselves in the mantles of FDR and JFK for decades after their untimely deaths, so too do Republicans today all seek to run as Reagan's true heir. Even President Obama understood that we live in Reagan's shadow, telling his fellow Democrats that "Ronald Reagan changed the trajectory of America."[2]

Unfortunately, for most of the time since Reagan's departure conservatives and Republicans have been wearing the wrong mantle. Conservatives and Republicans thought Reagan had given them a cookie-cutter formula—cut taxes, promote traditional morality, maintain a strong defense—rather than a deep conservative philosophy. They left the most crucial element of his appeal behind: the love of average Americans and the willingness to always use government to express their values. Republicans and conservatives spoke his words, but they did not carry his tune.

The result was that the Republican presidential nominee has failed to win a majority of the popular vote in six of the last seven elections. That is the GOP's worst showing since the party was created in 1854.

It has won unprecedented strength in Congress and the states, but that has largely been a result of the progressive wing of the Democratic Party consistently pushing an updated version of the Henry Wallace, government-centric, 1948 Progressive Party agenda. Big Republican wins have always come when a Democratic president or nominee expresses those unpopular values. When Democrats try to challenge for FDR's mantle by running even slightly toward the center, they have continued to win in the post-Reagan era.

The Republican and conservative failure is painfully evident in partisan self-identification polls. Republicans are not often aware of how badly and for how long they have trailed Democrats. Since the New Deal, more people have said they were Democrats than said they were Republicans in every single year except one.[3] That margin has declined since Reagan's day: Democrats outnumbered Republicans by a 45 to 23 percent margin in 1980, compared with a 36 to 33 percent margin in 2016.[4] But despite Reagan's best efforts, the Republican Party still suffers from its eighty-four-year-old brand problem.

The 2016 Republican deficit is not simply a case of California and New York drowning out "the real America." Democrats outnumbered Republicans in each of the three key midwestern states—Michigan, Pennsylvania, and Wisconsin—that gave Donald Trump the presidency.[5] Ronald Reagan sought to create a "New Republican Party," but it is evident that his successors have failed to finish the job.

It's not too hard to figure out why, either. As we saw in chapter 1, working-class voters did support Republicans in the pre–New Deal era when the GOP was the party that spoke for their values. But the Great Depression broke that bond. The party's refusal to do everything in its power to mitigate the massive poverty that followed by reason of unemployment in the wake of the crash convinced the average American that the GOP cared more about the wealthy than it did about them. Republicans still fight against that image to this day.

The party's problems are nicely summed up in a skit from the most popular comic in Reagan's youth, Jack Benny. Benny's shtick was that he played a miser who was always pinching pennies. In the skit, Benny is held up by a mugger who says, "Your money or your life!" Benny doesn't answer at first, but growls when the mugger repeats the demand: "I'm thinking it over!"[6]

Benny's answer is hilarious because it is absurd. No rational person would prefer her money to her life. But too many Americans think that when the chips are down, Republicans and conservatives are like Benny: they care more about money than about life.

That perception becomes even worse when applied to government policy. Since government programs are paid for by taxes on wealthier people, many Americans think the GOP cares about rich people's money than they do about their lives. No wonder they're not Republicans!

Party strategists often talk about how to surmount the various "gaps" the GOP faces. Republicans do much better among men than women—the "gender gap." They do much better among whites than nonwhites—the "racial gap." They do much better among married than among nonmarried voters—the "marriage gap." But each of these gaps exists because of the elephant in the room that flows from the perception mentioned above. Each of the groups that Republicans do worse with wants something from government that it believes will help give it a hand up in life, something Republicans usually oppose.

The Republican Party does not suffer from a gender gap, a racial gap, or a marriage gap. It suffers from an empathy gap.

Ronald Reagan always worked to show what he felt, genuine empathy for the problems of everyday life that people faced. He always empathized with "the forgotten American," and when he learned that some groups of people needed a little extra help to achieve the American promise, he changed his mind and gave it to them. Not all Americans were convinced he loved them, but enough were that he won their trust to change America.

This chapter is the story of how the conservative movement and the Republican Party lost its way after Reagan left office and how it can find its way back. It's the story of a movement that thought Reagan was just a more attractive version of Goldwater and thought it could get on with the job of cutting down the New Deal. It's the story of an establishment party that never thought it needed to make room at the table for the working person, a party that thought those voters could simply be bought off with God and guns. It's the story of a party that owes its post-2008 resurgence to the political obtuseness of President Obama, who thought his and his party's return to power was a mandate to push through a modern version of the Henry Wallace agenda. And it's the story of a party that owes the presidency to the most unlikely of men, Donald Trump, who has no deep philosophy but whose vision of an energetic government dedicated to the values of the working person brought the Reagan Democrat temporarily back into the fold.

This chapter is ultimately about something much more. It's about how we can finally realize our vision of making American conservatism the governing heart and soul of our land. No one can know for sure how Ronald Reagan would have addressed today's problems: his willingness to change tactical course in the face of new facts makes it impossible to know for sure what he would do today about taxes or trade. But he left a clear enough legacy behind that we can know the spirit with which he would approach those problems.

It would be a spirit that looked beyond left or right and toward up or down. It would be a spirit that took the average American's real life as its touchstone, and it would be one that made his or her well-being, not the devotion to abstract ideals, the final measure of success. It would be a spirit, I believe, that would finally convince a large plurality of Americans that conservative Republicanism cares more about life than money. It would be a spirit that would end the party's eighty-four-year status as the second party in American life and give us the political power to begin the world anew.

Ronald Reagan's campaign slogan in 1980 was simple yet profound: "The Time Is Now: Reagan." That is as true today as it was back then.

The drift away from Reagan started with his successor, George H. W. Bush. Reagan's loyal vice president campaigned as a populist in the Reaganite tradition. Although he started well behind the Democratic candidate, Michael Dukakis, by Election Day Bush was easily the victor. He received over 53 percent of the popular vote and won the Electoral College by a thundering 426–111 margin. He carried Michigan, Ohio, and Pennsylvania as well as the entire South except heavily unionized West Virginia. Bush largely reconstructed the Reagan coalition of traditional business Republicans, southern whites, and blue-collar ethnic midwestern and northeastern Democrats.

What no one knew then was that Bush would be the last Republican to carry Michigan, Pennsylvania, and Ohio in one election, and the last Republican to win over 300 Electoral College votes, until Donald Trump twenty-eight years later.

Pundits were so impressed with Bush's win that they started to speak of a "Republican lock" on the Electoral College.[7] But that lock existed only as long as the Republicans held the key. By 1992 Democrat Bill Clinton had picked the lock because he, not Bush, understood that the American voter wanted a president to continue to interpret FDR's legacy.

Clinton became the most vocal champion of the "New Democrats." They often were people who had supported Humphrey or Scoop Jackson in fights with Democratic progressives, and they meant to offer a modern version of Harry Truman's interpretation of FDR's legacy. Decried by many progressives as conservatives in Democratic clothing, New Democrats nonetheless attracted working-class Democrats back to the party and elected Clinton in 1992. Bush lost six states in the South and every state in the Midwest except rock-ribbed-Republican Indiana to the young, centrist Democrat. The Reagan Democrats had gone home to their party.

Clinton nearly gave back his advantage by governing more from the left than he had campaigned. He tried to push a comprehensive national health care bill through Congress, got the Democratic-controlled Congress to raise taxes, and let welfare reform proposals languish. Many blue-collar Democrats felt they had been abandoned, and Republicans rode anger over Clinton's move to the left to gain fifty-four seats in the House, giving them control for the first time in forty years and making the firebrand Newt Gingrich Speaker of the

House. The GOP also gained control of the Senate for the first time since 1986 and won a net ten new governorships. Many of the seats lost were in blue-collar and rural territory, the sort of places that had been Democratic congressional mainstays since the New Deal. Republicans looked like they were back.

Just as Clinton had misread his victory as an endorsement of the Left, however, the congressional Republicans misread their victory as an endorsement of the Right. They came out of the box clamoring for big budget cuts in entitlements and the elimination of a number of cabinet departments. Clinton shrewdly cast aside the progressive agenda, and wrapped himself in FDR's mantle in his 1995 State of the Union address.[8] He portrayed himself as the protector of cherished programs—Medicare, Medicaid, education, and the environment—while working to cut fat in government through his Reinventing Government initiative. When Republicans shut the government down in the winter of 1995 rather than agree to reduce their proposals, Clinton waged a public relations campaign to recast himself.[9] He soon forced them to back down, and Democrats regained their traditional advantage in partisan identification polls.

Republicans proclaimed they were following Reagan, when they were actually ignoring key elements of his thought. "Human nature resists change," Reagan had told conservatives in 1964, "and it bends over backward to resist radical change." But these conservatives wanted nothing but radical change. Republican revolutionaries had vastly overestimated the public's desire to cut valuable programs in the name of saving money. While many polls showed that majorities of Americans disliked the budget deficit, wanted to cut spending rather than hike taxes, and wanted smaller government over large government, when the chips were down they would not support saving money over saving lives.

The failed Republican assault on the federal budget reinforced the long-held view that Republicans—and now conservatives—cared more about their money than your life. Faced with a choice between a Congress they didn't trust and a president they didn't trust, voters in

1996 made the sensible choice and split the difference. They reelected the Republican Congress while also reelecting Bill Clinton by a comfortable margin over Senate Republican leader Bob Dole. Clinton won by 49–41 percent in the popular vote and with a 379–159 margin in the Electoral College. Clinton had again carried six southern states and every state in the Midwest except Indiana. He had also carried previously GOP-leaning California, New Jersey, and Connecticut twice. The Republican lock had not only been picked, it had been completely shattered.

The two-term Texas governor George W. Bush, the son of George Herbert Walker Bush, stepped up in 2000 to try to recapture the center for the GOP. "W," as he became known, tried to run as, one adviser once told me, "not Clinton and not Gingrich." Running as a "uniter, not a divider"[10] and a "reformer with results,"[11] Bush tried to address the Republican Party's long-standing empathy gap with his faith-influenced "compassionate conservatism."

Bush won, but only because of a left split between the Democratic nominee, Vice President Al Gore, and the Green Party's nominee Ralph Nader. Bush's southern background and unabashed invocation of his evangelical Christian faith (he said in one debate that Jesus was his favorite political philosopher[12]) was music to these voters' ears. Bush won all seven southern or border states that Clinton had carried in 1996, and in each the left-wing (Democratic + Green) share of the vote was down.

The Midwest, however, did not cotton to Bush. These states have fewer evangelical Christians than the Southern and border states, and even those that are evangelical tend to have larger shares of German, Scandinavian, or Dutch rather than British heritage. Bush lost almost all the midwestern states Clinton had carried in 1996, and the share of the vote for the Left (Gore and Nader) went *up* in each state. Bush carried Ohio, the least Democratic and most evangelical of these states, but even there the share of the combined vote for the Left or the center Left went up, not down.

Bush lost the nationwide popular vote, receiving only 47.9 percent.

He won a narrow Electoral College victory, 271–267, only because enough progressives backed Nader to throw New Hampshire and Florida to Bush. The combined Gore-plus-Nader vote was over 50.5 percent in each state. Even then Bush required a miracle, as he won Florida's 25 electoral votes by only 537 votes out of nearly six million cast. But for the infamous "butterfly ballot," a poorly designed ballot in an elderly and heavily Democratic area that caused thousands of Democrats to inadvertently spoil their ballot or vote for the Reform Party candidate, Pat Buchanan, Gore would have won Florida and with it the presidency.[13]

Republicans did even more poorly down ballot. The GOP lost another two seats in the House, giving it a razor thin 222–213 advantage. It lost four seats in the Senate, making the chamber a 50–50 tie where control was decided only by the tie-breaking vote of Vice President Dick Cheney. Twelve years after Reagan left the White House, his New Republican Party was still struggling to unite all the various strands of conservative and nonprogressives under one big tent.

Bush's compassionate conservatism was supposed to solve that problem. Bush's embrace of his evangelical identity along with his muscular foreign policy, especially his immediate and militant reaction to 9/11, did attract many southern and southern-descended voters. Those former Reagan Democrats were happy in this party, and the GOP's domination of the South really starts from this time period.

But compassionate conservatism ultimately failed as a political strategy because it broke faith with antigovernment conservatives and offered nothing to the working-class whites whose votes determined the outcome in midwestern states. Its embrace of some expansion of government and lack of interest in budget cutting made many libertarian-conservatives and old-line Goldwaterites angry. Midwestern working-class whites, on the other hand, still wanted a government that was limited in its aspirations but aggressive in putting itself on the side of the average working person. They weren't members of Baptist, Methodist, or nondenominational Christian churches. They weren't poor, so the Bush administration's focus on helping the poor didn't affect their daily lives.

The ultimate question every voter asks is "Do you care about people like me?" Compassionate conservatism failed because it did not, and could not, answer that question positively for enough people. For working-class midwesterners, it failed what I call the "truckers and cashiers test." Driving a truck is the job that employs the largest number of white working-class men. Being a cashier or a waitress is the job that employs the largest number of white working-class women. Suppose you were a nonevangelical trucker or a cashier listening to the radio while "W" spoke about compassionate conservatism. Did you hear anything during the talk that made you think he cared about people like you?

Reagan never failed this test. Virtually every speech had this person in mind, and virtually every speech had something that person could uniquely relate to. The frequent invocations, acknowledged or hidden, to Roosevelt were one example of how he did this. The regular praise of the average worker rather than that person's educated boss was another. Reagan could attract both kinds of disaffected New Dealer, southern and northern, because he always made his love for them the staple of his thought.

Bush won reelection, riding a recovering economy and his victory in the Iraq War (the guerrilla war that ultimately fought the United States to a draw was just getting under way) to a narrow victory. He barely topped a majority of the vote, receiving 50.7 percent, and won by 286–252 in the Electoral College. He lost only one state he had carried in 2000, New Hampshire, as the progressives who had backed Nader largely voted for the Democratic nominee, Massachusetts senator John Kerry. He picked up two, winning Iowa and New Mexico by less than a percentage point in each state.

Bush's popular-vote margin was heavily dependent on southern votes. The combined share of the vote for the Democrats and the Greens dropped by between 2 and 5 percent in each of the seven southern and border states that Bush had gained from Clinton. But that share dropped very little in the midwestern and northern battleground states, with Iowa's 2.2 percent drop leading the way. Despite compassionate conservatism, economic recovery, and perceived victory in war, Bush's Republicanism remained unpopular among the midwestern Reagan working-class Democrats needed to entrench a GOP majority.

One would have thought that a narrow win would have given rise to a cautious agenda. But Bush was riding high and thought he could do more. The compromise Reagan had signed saving Social Security was nearing the end of its intended life span. All projections showed that the program would begin to run out of money in the decade or two ahead without another plan to save it. Bush decided he was just the guy to tackle this challenge. But how he did it spoke volumes about how his vision differed from Reagan's.

Social Security is perhaps the enduring legacy of the New Deal for most voters. It offers them comfort, dignity, and peace of mind for their retirement years. No longer would they have to depend on charity, their children (if they had any), or the kindness of their neighbors when they grew too old to work. Thanks to that basic monthly check, they would not, to borrow Reagan's words, have to worry about poverty following unemployment as a result of old age.

Bush's 2005 plan to reform Social Security called those values into question. Instead of security, Bush offered risk by proposing to allow people under the age of fifty-five to use some of their Social Security tax money to fund personal retirement accounts. Since current taxes pay for current retirees' benefits, this idea would have reduced the tax revenue needed to pay for older people's checks. Bush's plan failed to provide details on how that gap would be eliminated, meaning that people began to wonder whether the benefits they relied on would be secure. Bush also ruled out raising any new tax revenue to pay for this gap, instead suggesting that benefits could be cut for wealthier retirees or annual benefit increases could be reduced.[14] Where Reagan had always stressed that current retirees would get what they earned, Bush's plan called that guarantee into question.

Democrats were meanwhile tacking back to the center. The House and Senate campaign chairs strategically recruited more moderate candidates to run in the states and House districts they needed to retake control. They would thus look more like Clinton at a time when Bush was looking more like Gingrich on domestic issues, and would furthermore be aided by the increasing quagmire in Iraq.

The election of 2006 was a Democratic landslide. They gained thirty House seats to retake the majority and won nearly every contested Senate seat up for grabs, picking up a net six seats to return Senate control to them. Republicans also lost six governors' chairs. The New Republican party looked very much like the old, pre-Reagan Republican Party: tired, out of ideas, and out of power.

The man the Republicans nominated in 2008 to succeed Bush, Arizona senator John McCain, also showed he misunderstood Reagan's ideas. He proposed eliminating the exemption from income taxation of health insurance premiums paid by employers, effectively raising the cost of health care for every American who got health insurance through his or her job. Employer-provided health insurance had been free from income tax since World War II; it continued to work for most people even though many economists argued it encouraged unnecessary medical spending.

Reagan had warned against the "slavish devotion to abstraction" and knew that "human nature bends over backward to avoid radical change." McCain's radical change to a system that provided secure access to the basic necessity of health care was the polar opposite of the change people wanted. It seemed to be exactly the type of thing a Republican would propose who cared more about abstractions than the "realities of everyday life," more about their money than your life.

The Democratic nominee, Illinois senator Barack Obama, did not ignore this opportunity. Despite an extremely liberal voting record as a state senator, he campaigned as someone who could unite rather than divide. So he leaped at the opportunity to attack McCain's proposal. One of the ads he aired attacking McCain's health care plan was even determined to be the most aired ad of the prior decade.[15]

Obama had come to national attention when he gave a well-received keynote address at the 2004 Democratic National Convention.[16] The best-remembered lines of that talk are those in which he argued that the political differences among Americans did not detract from their fundamental unity of American purpose:

> There is not a liberal America and a conservative America—there is the United States of America. There is not a black America and white America and Latino America and Asian America; there is the United States of America. The pundits like to slice-and-dice our country into Red States and Blue States; Red States for Republicans, Blue States for Democrats. But I've got news for them, too. We worship an awesome God in the Blue States, and we don't like federal agents poking around our libraries in the Red States. We coach Little League in the Blue States, and yes we've got some gay friends in the Red States. There are patriots who opposed the war in Iraq and there are patriots who supported the war in Iraq. We are one people, all of us pledging allegiance to the stars and stripes, all of us defending the United States of America.

Progressives saw someone who could communicate their values in a language average Americans might respond to. The seeds of his presidential campaign were born that night with those words, and he was careful during the campaign to avoid giving people a different impression. On election night, 50 percent of Americans told exit pollsters that Obama's views were "just right"; only 42 percent, almost all of them partisan Republicans, said they were "too liberal."[17]

The 2008 election was the worst defeat for the Republican Party since 1974. Obama beat McCain by a 53–46 percent margin in the popular vote and a 365–173 vote margin in the Electoral College. He carried the swing state of New Hampshire and every midwestern state, including Indiana, which went Democratic for the first time since LBJ's 1964 landslide over Barry Goldwater. Obama also won the former Republican western strongholds of Nevada and Colorado and took three coastal southern states; Virginia, North Carolina, and Florida. Virginia also had not voted for a Democrat since 1964, and North Carolina had voted Republican every four years since 1976.

Obama's midwestern strength was due in part to his ability to keep whites without a college degree. Exit polls show he carried working-class whites in Iowa, Michigan, and New Hampshire and performed better among them than among college-educated whites in Indiana.[18] He lost them in Ohio by only 10 percent, a development that allowed him to ride massive margins among the sizable African American population there to victory.[19] Evangelical voters were still largely Republican, but other whites of all educational backgrounds were very open to the apparently centrist Democrat.

The carnage was even worse in other races. Republicans lost another 21 House seats to drop to a mere 178, their lowest total since before the 1994 victory. The party lost an astounding eight Senate seats, reducing them to 41, the smallest number since 1978. When a liberal Pennsylvania Republican switched to the Democrats in April, the party held a filibuster-proof 60 Senate seats. Democrats looked like they were back.

We all know what happened after that.[20] Obama had campaigned as a healer, a person who could mix red and blue in pursuit of a common American vision. When he instead governed as a progressive (albeit as one never pure enough for the faithful), pushing a trillion-dollar government spending program sold as an "economic stimulus," climate change, and Obamacare as his major priorities, he broke faith with the independents and moderate blue-collar Democrats who had elected him and given Democrats the largest House and Senate majorities they had possessed since before Ronald Reagan.

These were simply unwise priorities to push when the nation was wracked with a massive, worsening recession. But that did not matter to the forty-seven-year-old who had already authored two autobiographies. According to the *New York Times*, Obama's first treasury secretary, Timothy Geithner, told him early on that his legacy would be preventing a second great depression. Obama replied, "That's not enough for me."[21] That, plus encouraging a fast recovery, would have been enough for most Americans.

Obama's progressive advisers, ignoring the counsel of his first chief of staff, Rahm Emanuel, believed the reason Bill Clinton's Democrats had been wiped out in 1994—after they had sought to pass a progressive wish list—was that they had flinched and not rammed their priorities through Congress. Do that, they told Obama, and Americans will reward the bold. Instead, Democrats lost even more seats in the House in 2010 than they had in 1994, dropping to their lowest level since 1946.

Devastation dogged down-ballot Democrats too. Democrats lost six Senate seats, and probably would have lost three more had not poorly qualified, Tea Party–backed candidates defeated more capable, and more moderate, opponents in the Republican primaries.[22] Republicans picked up five governorships, winning in the large states of Wisconsin, Michigan, Ohio, Pennsylvania, and Florida. They gained an incredible 720 state legislative seats, picking up majority control in twenty-one legislative chambers. In two years, Democrats had gone from their strongest position in forty years to their weakest in over eighty.

The reason for this reversal of fortune was not hard to see: the white working class, especially those from nonevangelical backgrounds, had voted Republican en masse. By Election Day, President Obama's approval rating among whites without a college degree was only 30 percent, or only a few points higher than when Richard Nixon resigned in disgrace.[23] These voters had been making it clear in election after election since 1966 that they did not want the rapid expansion of government programs and did not trust the government's management of the economy. Their revolts had fueled Nixon's 1972 landslide, Reagan's epic 1980 victory, and the 1994 Republican tsunami. They had come back into the Democratic fold when they had been promised the progressives wouldn't be running the show. To find that the opposite was true, at a time when their jobs were drying up and their paychecks had been declining or flat for years, was just too much.

Fully forty-four of the sixty-three seats Republicans gained in the House were from the South or the Midwest. Some were from Republican-leaning seats that had fallen in the last two Democratic landslides, but many were long-held Democratic seats from white working-class areas. These were places like Duluth's Minnesota 8, western Wisconsin's

7th District, Illinois's 17th on the Mississippi River, the Appalachian coal country of Ohio 6, and northeastern Pennsylvania's 10th and 11th Districts. If one lays a map of those seats and others like them over the map of 2016 presidential county-level election returns, one would find an eerie overlap between Democratic seats like these and places where Donald Trump gained the most compared with Mitt Romney. Trump's victory was presaged by the 2010 working-class revolt against Obama and his progressive politics.

These voters were saying no to Obama, but the Tea Party, anti-government Right thought they were saying yes to it. Inspired by House Budget Committee Chairman Paul Ryan's 2008 "Roadmap for America's Future," House Republicans adopted a revised version of that plan—the "Path to Prosperity"—as their answer to Obama's progressive expansion. But this seemed to miss the popular mood. Voters had just bent over backward to avoid the radical change Obama wanted. The Roadmap and, to a lesser degree, the Path, promised radical change in the precisely opposite direction.

The original Roadmap could have been cooked up in David Stockman's laboratory.[24] It promised a tax plan that focused on cutting the top income tax rate to 25 percent and eliminated any income taxes on "unearned income": capital gains, interest, and dividends. It adopted a version of the Bush Social Security plan, permitting people under fifty-five to divert up to a third of their payroll taxes into a private account without specifying where the revenue to pay current benefits would come from. It also endorsed lowering current benefits by adjusting the way the annual increase was calculated as well as cuts to future benefits by raising the retirement age. It promised to replace Medicare for those under fifty-five with a set payment with which they would be expected to purchase their own coverage. It would end Medicaid, the federal-state shared program that provides health care coverage for the poor, disabled, and elderly people who need to live in nursing homes, replacing it with a set payment those people could use to buy their own care. And it reproposed the McCain health insurance plan, replacing the exclusion of health insurance premiums from income and payroll taxes and replacing it with a set credit amount that was meant to help people buy their own, individual health insurance plans.[25]

In one fell swoop, every major social insurance program would be revamped to decrease an individual's security and increase his or her risk and choice. At the same time, billionaires who get much of their income from unearned income would pay virtually no federal income taxes. Mitt Romney, the man who selected Ryan to be his 2012 presidential running mate, would have benefited enormously from this latter provision. His 2011 tax return shows that nearly all of his income, over $13 million, came from unearned income.[26] Instead of paying nearly $2 million in income tax, Romney would have paid nearly nothing under the Roadmap.

These sweeping changes were proposed to avoid any tax increases, reduce federal spending to 18.5 percent of GDP (the post–World War II historical average) and keep taxes level at 19 percent of GDP forever. The Roadmap promised to "ensure a safety net, maintained by government if necessary," but its heart was clearly on the side of a small, limited government of the sort not seen since before the New Deal.[27]

The Path to Prosperity scaled back the Roadmap's ambition but retained its basic structure, priorities, and approach. It dropped specific endorsements of the Bush Social Security and McCain health insurance plans.[28] Elimination of income taxes on unearned income was removed.[29] It also replaced the fixed contribution for low-income Medicaid recipients with a block grant of the entire program to the states.[30] It retained, however, both the emphasis on reducing the top personal income tax rate to 25 percent,[31] and the conversion of Medicare into a fixed-payment system as opposed to the fee-for-service it has always been.[32]

Whatever the merits of these plans, polls made it clear this was not the change the working-class white Democrats and independents whose votes fueled the 2010 election wanted. At the same time as Ryan was unveiling the Path, the Pew Research Center released its triennial analysis of the American electorate, "Beyond Red vs. Blue."[33] That analysis breaks voters into different groups of shared views and demographic characteristics. One group was primarily made up of whites without college degrees making the median income or below. Pew called these voters "Disaffecteds." What they wanted was not what the Roadmap or the Path promised.

The Ryan agenda was premised on the idea that the rising federal budget deficit was the most important issue facing America: get that under control now, and in the future America would prosper. On this Ryan was in accord with the Republican base: 50 percent of the group Pew labeled "Staunch Conservatives" thought the federal budget deficit was the biggest economic worry.[34] Disaffecteds disagreed: only 9 percent thought the deficit was the biggest worry.[35] They were worried about jobs: 43 percent said "the job situation" was the biggest worry.[36]

That priority made sense in light of their experiences in the Great Recession. Seventy-one percent of Disaffecteds had experienced unemployment in their household during the prior year, the largest total for any of Pew's groups.[37] Sixty-three percent said the recession had had a major impact on their household from which they had not yet recovered.[38] This was also the largest total for any group. Eighty-three percent said they often didn't have enough money to make ends meet.[39] This experience had made them pessimistic: almost half said hard work was no guarantee of success, again the largest total for any group.[40]

As one might expect, these voters did not want cuts to programs they relied on. Eighty-two percent opposed changing Social Security and Medicare, the heart of Ryan's Roadmap.[41] Only 17 percent thought the best way to tackle the deficit was to cut major programs, compared with 59 percent of Ryan's Staunch Conservatives.[42]

Disaffecteds also wanted more government help than Staunch Conservatives were willing to provide. Sixty-one percent of Disaffecteds said the government should do more to help the needy even if it meant going more into debt; only 9 percent of Staunch Conservatives agreed.[43] Members of the former group believed that poor people had hard lives because government benefits didn't go far enough to help them live decently.[44]

Despite these differences, Disaffecteds leaned Republican in their voting preferences. They agreed with other Republican-leaning groups on questions of government efficiency, and stood between the most conservative and liberal groups on a host of foreign policy and social issues. But they thought of themselves as independents: 63 percent chose to call themselves that while only 25 percent said they were Republicans. This is the classic definition of a swing voter, someone who sees himself between the two coalitions and can be swayed either way.

Accordingly, one should not be surprised that 60 percent had a favorable view of Bill Clinton while only 28 percent approved of Obama.[45] They were open to New Deal Democrats like Clinton or Republicans who approved of the core elements of the New Deal like Reagan. They opposed both progressives and Goldwater-style conservatives.

The Pew data made clear what savvy politicians like Reagan and Clinton had realized for decades: the Disaffecteds were the key to either party forming a durable majority. They were the only group that could be swayed to join a party's base without irrevocably fracturing the new coalition. Despite this, they had either been betrayed or ignored by both parties' ideological leaderships for decades. Their frustration was building up and they were losing hope. Eighty-two percent told Pew that elected officials didn't care what people like them thought, again the highest total for any group.[46] The seeds for Trump were being sown.

There were other hints in these data that a Trump-like candidacy could excite these voters. Disaffecteds were suspicious of immigrants, thinking by large margins that immigrants took American jobs and threatened American customs and values.[47] They were the most anti–free trade group, with 59 percent saying free trade agreements were bad for the United States.[48] They were anti–Wall Street, with 59 percent saying Wall Street hurt the economy more than it helped.[49] They were the most isolationist group, saying the United States should focus more on domestic problems, and believing Obama wasn't pulling out of Afghanistan fast enough.[50] All of the themes Trump used to excite these voters and distinguish himself from the GOP field in 2016 could be found in the 2011 Pew survey.

The path to rebuilding the Reagan coalition was wide open, but once again the Republican Party refused to walk down it. The key group it needed to win was economically and educationally downscale, disliked Wall Street, was concerned about jobs rather than growth, felt elites didn't care about them, didn't want big cuts to entitlements, and were opposed to free trade. So the GOP nominated a rich, MBA-educated financier who was the son of a former auto company CEO and governor. That man liked Wall Street and free trade, was concerned about growth over jobs, and picked the author of the GOP's entitlement cuts, Paul Ryan, as his running mate. Republicans were not offering working-class whites a choice, they were presenting an echo of the persona and policies the Dissaffecteds had rejected for a very long time.

Romney and Republicans were oblivious to this. The Republican Convention was an orgy of enthusiasm for businessmen and bosses. "We built this" became a convention theme, praising the entrepreneur and businessman for his daring and risk taking.[51] Romney's remark that the 47 percent of Americans who paid no federal income tax were therefore dependent on the federal government for benefits deepened this negative image.[52] Ryan compounded this when it was discovered that he had previously said that the battle in America was between "makers" and "takers," people who work hard and pay income taxes versus those who don't and get benefits. Millions of working Americans like the Disaffecteds, however, work very hard for very little money. They pay payroll, sales, and gas taxes even if they don't pay income taxes. They may get by with some help from government programs, but they don't view themselves as "takers." Romney and Ryan had not only failed the "truckers and cashiers test"; they had told those voters they really didn't care much about people like them.

Obama surprised the entire Republican establishment by winning comfortably. He won 51 percent of the popular vote, the first time since FDR that a Democratic presidential candidate had won two popular-vote majorities in a row. He won the Electoral College 332–206 by again winning most midwestern states and New Hampshire, along

with Nevada, Virginia, Florida, and Colorado. Democrats also dashed
the Republicans' Senate hopes by gaining two seats when earlier many
observers thought they would lose control. Once again, the failure to
come to grips with what working-class, nonevangelical whites wanted
from government cost the GOP dearly.

One answer to the exit poll tells you everything you need to know
about why Romney lost. Voters were asked which of four personal characteristics they thought was most important in a president.[53] Seventy-
four percent of voters selected either "shares my values," "strong leader,"
or "vision for future." Romney won each of these categories by between
9 and 23 percent. He lost the presidency because 21 percent selected
the fourth category, and he lost among those voters by 63 percent, 81–
18. That category: "cares about people like me."

Eighty years after the New Deal, Republican leaders finally woke
up and saw they had an empathy gap. Or so they tried to tell you.
Establishment and conservatives alike tripped over each other to show
how much they cared about people. There was just one problem with
their approach: they forgot the words "like me."

The establishment, business wing of the party expressed its views
in a comprehensive analysis of what went wrong in 2012. Known officially as "Growth and Opportunity Project" and colloquially as "the
autopsy," the report spent most of its space analyzing the party's campaign tactics and infrastructure and offered sound ideas for reform.[54]
But tools are only useful if you have a good idea how to use them. In
politics, that means knowing who might vote for you and what you
need to promise to get them to do so. On this question, the report was
fatally flawed.

The party establishment uncritically accepted the Democrats' and
the media's explanation for the Obama victory: what the Democrats
called "the Rising American Electorate."[55] This theory, first propounded
by the progressive thinkers Ruy Teixeira and John Judis in their 2002
book *The Emerging Democratic Majority*, noted that people of color
(black, Hispanic, Asian, and multiracial individuals), college-educated
whites working in information industries, and unmarried women were

all growing in voting strength.[56] Every four years these voters grew in number, and the groups that supported Republicans, especially older whites without college degrees, shrank. While Judis and Teixeira argued that Democrats still had to do well enough with working-class whites to get their majority, most Democrats did not note this. Instead, they argued that by the 2008 election the Rising American Electorate would be large enough in size that they could win a majority without moving away from progressive policies because the conservative Republican coalition—focused on smaller government, lower taxes and traditional religion—could not compete for these voters.

The authors of the autopsy saw this future and decided the GOP had to compete with Democrats among these groups. But they did not understand that the reason these voters didn't like Republicans was because they disagreed with the party's underlying philosophy of caring more about what they viewed as abstractions (small government) or money (taxes) than life. The autopsy's authors presented what I call the "barrier" explanation of why these voters did not like the GOP. According to the autopsy, Republicans held certain views on a couple of issues that these voters held to be unacceptable. The report noted two: opposition to immigration and same-sex marriage.[57] Remove these "barriers," the report argued, and these voters would be open to the underlying philosophy.

This short, superficial analysis ignored two important points. First, a very large share of the Republican voter base cared intensely about immigration and same-sex marriage. Casting aside these issues meant dividing the party in the hope that Republicans could then reunite it and gain new voters. The other point is even more important: the groups the barrier explanation were meant to attract wouldn't want what the authors desired to sell them even if the barriers were removed.

Take Hispanic voters. Polls show that immigration actually ranks low on the voting priorities of Hispanic voters. They care much more about education and health care than they do about immigration. Their views tended to side more with Democrats than Republicans on these issues.

Many Hispanics also disagree with the fundamental, core tenant of the Republican Party establishment, that helping business and the wealthy with lower taxes helps everyone. The Public Religion Research Institute's 2013 Hispanic Values Survey showed this clearly. It asked Hispanics which of two sets of policies would help grow the economy more: higher taxes and more government spending on education and infrastructure, or lower taxes on individuals and business and reduced government spending. By a nearly two to one margin, 58–33 percent, Hispanics agreed with the higher taxes, more spending approach.[58]

The electoral crisis the autopsy was meant to solve was the fact that Mitt Romney received only 27 percent of the Hispanic vote. But the evidence shows that even if the "barrier" of immigration were removed, an "autopsy-friendly" Republican candidate would add only 6 percent to Romney's measly total. A move that tiny would only have helped pick up Florida, leaving the GOP nominee well short of the 270 Electoral College votes he or she would need to win.

Paul Ryan's move to embrace caring was better thought out and more comprehensive. He spent over a year traveling the country, visiting poor neighborhoods and meeting with experts on poverty. The result was what I call "Ryan 2.0," a comprehensive vision to reform the safety net and help move people out of poverty.[59] He also gave a speech to accompany that vision in which he explicitly endorsed the concept of the modern safety net in which he said that "earned success and earned *security* go hand in hand."[60] (Emphasis in original.) Finally, he retracted his "makers versus takers" formulation.[61] Ryan had heard the message of 2012; he cared about people.

I know Ryan and I also know that he has always cared about people. But his post-2012 statements and policies did not address the GOP's political problem well enough. Like the authors of the autopsy, he showed that he "cared about people" and forgot the last two words: "like me."

The working-class, nonevangelical white voters who had elected Reagan and had largely left the GOP since heard nothing in Ryan's words to reassure them. They wanted someone who would share their values, and those values included more than caring about the poor. These voters were not poor. They might have been afraid of becoming poor, but they were more afraid about the changes that were buffeting their lives that no politician seemed to see or care about. They wanted someone who would see the world as they saw it, tell them they were right, and promise them he had their backs. Ryan has a noble vision. But it fails the "truckers and cashiers test," big league.

In effect, Ryan had a different barrier theory, only his idea was that the barrier that kept people from voting Republican was a perception that Republicans did not care about people at all and that working-class voters had been offended by his clever rhyme. But that was not, and has never been, the case. These voters do not, and have not since 1932, liked to vote for a Republican whose underlying philosophy is explicitly or implicitly in conflict with the New Deal's core promises.

Ryan's and the autopsy's approaches to addressing the 2012 election are what I call "clothes and cosmetics conservatism." The theory in each case was different, but the result was the same. Republicans hoped that by changing the packaging a bit, putting on nicer clothes and some good makeup, people would change their minds about who they were. Clothes and cosmetics conservatism fails because underneath the fancy packaging is the same old stuff these voters have not been buying for decades.

Not all Republicans thought that they needed to show they cared, however. Some conservatives didn't think the voters rejected them because they were too antigovernment; they thought the voters rejected them because they hadn't been clear enough about the fact they *were* antigovernment. This view, centered in the Republican's Tea Party wing, argued that only people who were militantly unrepentant about their opposition to the status quo could mobilize voters who had chosen Obama over Romney or who had sat out the election entirely. These people advocated what I call "louder and clearer conservatism," and their leader was Texas senator Ted Cruz.

Cruz was elected in 2012, and he wasted no time in making a national name for himself. By the summer of 2013 he was leading a crusade to shut down the government rather than fund Obamacare's Medicaid expansion and subsidies for people to purchase health insurance. He told Republican senators that if they opposed him they were supporters of Obamacare.[62] After this quixotic effort predictably failed, he turned his attention to the debt ceiling. In 2015, he urged another government shutdown—and an American default on its bond obligations—if the legislative authority to borrow money to fund the government did not include cuts in future spending.[63] In the course of these fights he worked with like-minded congressmen to undermine House Speaker John Boehner and called Senate Republican leader Mitch McConnell a liar on the Senate floor.[64]

Cruz's theory was that Romney had lost because millions of conservative Americans had not voted in 2012 because of Romney's moderation. He told conservative audiences that they were a majority if only they would rally the troops with "bold colors, no pale pastels."[65] Compromise was the enemy of victory, he argued; only consistent, unwavering, hard-line conservatism would defeat liberal Democrats.

It's not just that Cruz was wrong; it's that so much he knew just wasn't so. Take his claim that over two million conservatives stayed home in 2012, and that an increase of "less than a million votes would have produced 84 electoral votes, more than enough to win."[66] This was, at best, a distortion of the facts. Turnout was down in 2012, but not in six of the seven swing states Cruz cited. Of those seven, only Ohio cast fewer votes in 2012, and the difference (128,000) was smaller than Obama's margin in the state. Moreover, in three of the swing states Cruz cited, voters actually cast *more* ballots in 2012 than in 2008.

Nor did the conservatives and Republicans who did vote abandon Romney. Romney carried 93 percent of Republicans, which tied for the all-time high since exit polling began in 1972. His 82 percent among conservatives sounds low until you compare it with the percentages other GOP nominees won. Only George W. Bush in 2004 bested that share, with 84 percent, and the only other candidate who even equaled it was Ronald Reagan in his 1984 landslide.

Republicans of all stripes were clearly missing the point about the 2012 election, but so too were the Democrats. Their faith in the Rising American Electorate theory meant they thought moving further to the left was the best way to win. President Obama therefore pushed on climate change, signing the Paris Accords. He made a deal with Iran and made light of the new terrorist group ISIS, calling it "the JV." He bypassed a Congress unwilling to approve comprehensive immigration reform and issued an executive order that effectively legalized the status of millions of undocumented immigrants. And he pushed forward on negotiating free-trade agreements like the Trans-Pacific Partnership (TPP). The result: Republicans took control of the Senate in the 2014 midterms, picking up nine Senate seats. ·

The House election results were less dramatic but more ominous for both parties. Republicans gained thirteen seats, pushing their total to 247 and besting their previous post–New Deal high set in 2010. Six of those seats were in working-class white Democratic territory in the Midwest and Northeast, including seats in Iowa, Maine, and New York that president Obama had won with large majorities. As with 2010, laying the map of these seats over the 2016 county election returns map shows another eerie similarity: these seats also contained the areas where Trump would gain the most over Romney. The Trump train was getting ready to leave the station, and none of the major strategists in either party had any idea it was on the tracks.

Everything Trump did and said from the minute he entered the race in summer 2015 was, by luck or by design, music to the working-class whites' ears. He blasted immigration's economic and cultural impacts. He attacked free trade agreements, saying that China and Mexico were eating our lunch and stealing our jobs. He reminded these voters how these problems had been developing for years (i.e., both parties were to blame) and that the elites who ran the country hadn't been listening to them. Only strong, active leadership would make America great again, and he was just the man to provide it.

Even the things he supposedly did wrong worked with these voters. His lack of enthusiasm about traditional religion and his flip-flops on abortion might have hurt him with the party's evangelical, social-conservative wing, but nonevangelical working-class voters (and, we discovered, many evangelicals who did not attend church often) didn't care. They were what the Canadian conservative political strategist Patrick Muttart called "morally moderate": they may have held traditional views on social issues, but those views did not motivate their votes.[67] Trump's running feud with Jeb Bush reminded these voters of the defeat and depression his brother had brought them. His lack of coherent tax cut or spending cut plan didn't bother these voters; they didn't care about the size of government. His statement that he did not want to cut Social Security or Medicare earned the scorn of the GOP's antigovernment warriors and budget hawks, but as the Pew survey showed, these voters loved Trump's position.

Trump would add one element to his appeal that proved decisive: his proposed ban on Muslim immigration. Trump's national poll numbers were stuck in a narrow band between 25 and 30 percent prior to the Paris and San Bernardino terrorist attacks in late 2015.[68] His appeal skyrocketed after he proposed the ban on December 7. Polls taken after that date showed him in the mid to high 30s, a position of dominance he never gave up.

The exit polls confirm this interpretation. The ban was highly popular among Republican primary voters, with between 63 and 78 percent approving it in every state where the question was asked. Trump normally won between 45 and 50 percent of these voters. But this actually understates the import of the issue to his candidacy. Between 80 and 90 percent of his voters backed the ban, meaning that it united his backers more than any other concern.

The Republican race started with seventeen candidates including Trump, but it effectively boiled down to a race between four men. Cruz ran as Cruz, the "louder and clearer" conservative. Bush was the autopsy candidate, stressing his tax cuts and his openness to Hispanic immigration even though many conservatives disagreed with him.[69] Marco Rubio was effectively the Paul Ryan "clothes and cosmetics" conservative, displaying a strong interest in poverty while endorsing a Ryanesque tax cut and economic growth plan. Each ran in his own way as Reagan's true heir. But the man who beat them had a bead on an element of Reagan's appeal that every one of his competitors missed: citizenship.

Citizenship is another way of expressing what Reagan called self-government. At its most basic level, self-government meant governing yourself, or personal responsibility. But it always meant more than that for Reagan. As we saw in chapter 4, self-government for Reagan included a sense of obligation to and for one's fellow Americans. You were not their master or their keeper, but you did have an obligation to be their helper. For this reason, self-government for Reagan always required some sense of obligation to help citizens who "through no fault of their own" were in genuine need, whether that help involved getting out of their way, providing monetary assistance, or levying trade sanctions on the Japanese to punish unfair practices.

Trump's appeal to the working-class, nonevangelical white electorate was rooted in this idea. Trump voters believed they had played by the rules and had been unfairly punished because political elites simply didn't care about people like them. It's against the rules to manipulate a national currency to gain a trade advantage or steal intellectual property, but nothing happens to the Chinese when they do that even when it costs Americans their jobs. It's against the rules to come to and work in this country without permission, but nothing seems to happen to the millions of people who do that or the businesses that hire them. It's against the rules to open fire on your neighbors, but some Muslims, whether immigrants or natives, do just that repeatedly on American soil, and it keeps on happening. In the eyes of these voters, the elites of both parties had broken the bonds of trust and obligation that bind Americans to each other. Once Trump said he understood their pain and had their backs, they tuned out anything those elites said to try to change their minds.

Trump had electrified one of the elements of the Reagan coalition, but the other elements—antigovernment conservatives, social conservatives, and business conservatives—were wary. Once he clinched the nomination, however, he pledged to support something they each cared deeply about, such as a conservative Supreme Court nominee for social conservatives, deregulation for business conservatives, and a big tax cut for antigovernment conservatives. He also argued that they had nowhere else to go: if they did not back him, they implicitly backed Hillary Clinton. In effect, he was banking that "Never Hillary" would be a stronger pull for most Republicans than "Never Trump."

Hillary Clinton could have done something about this, but it would have required her to imitate her husband and tack to the center to compete for working-class Democrats or the moderately conservative business voters who disliked Trump. She did neither. She was always wary of the progressive wing of her party, which had backed Bernie Sanders in the primaries against her and some of whom were backing the Green Party's Jill Stein. Hillary Clinton also had the Rising American Electorate theory in her camp. All she had to do was encourage turnout among these groups, she was told, and they would deliver her a victory. No one seemed to notice that many of those voters lived in states she was already going to carry, like California and New York. Running up the score in these states left open the thin possibility that Trump's strategy of reuniting the Reagan coalition with positive appeals to the former Reagan Democrats and negative, "I'm better than Hillary" appeals to the others would let him win where it counted, in the Electoral College.

We all know what happened next. Trump lost the popular vote by nearly three million votes, but that was due to Clinton winning large margins in states with large numbers of members of the Rising American Electorate. Trump won narrow victories in places where voter demographics were not changing as quickly and where Trump and Clinton had focused their efforts. He won the Electoral College by 306–232 because he won Florida, North Carolina, and the five midwestern states that Obama had carried twice. The Reagan Democrats were back.

Trump won whites without a college degree by 37 percent, 66–29. Moreover, unlike Bush, McCain, and Romney, he did nearly as well among midwestern working-class whites as among southern ones. Trump carried working-class whites in the five midwestern states he took from the Democrats' column by over 30 percent in each.[70] Recall that Obama in 2008 had *won* working-class whites in three of these states and lost them in the two others by only ten and fifteen points. Even in 2012 he had won these voters in Iowa and lost them by no more than ten points in most of the others.[71]

Trump's laser-like focus on the concerns of the white working class had another side-effect that remains unnoticed by most partisans: he handily beat Romney among "cares about people like me" voters. Romney had lost by 81–18 among this group; Trump lost by only 57–35.[72] Trump did as well or better on this question in each of the five midwestern states he gained; Romney, if one can believe it, lost "cares about people like me" voters by even more than 63 points in each of those five states. The media said Trump was nasty, bigoted, misogynistic, rude, and a fascist. For his core voters, though, he was the only one who really cared.

Progressive analysts have argued that these voters empathized with Trump because he expressed their own closeted racist or sexist thoughts. This is hard to swallow in light of these voters' proved willingness to vote for blacks (Obama), or women.[73] One can see this best when one looks at Wisconsin. Trump carried the Badger State by only 22,758 votes. He carried twenty-one working-class counties by a total of 34,300 that just four years had given comfortable majorities to both President Obama and the only openly lesbian US senator, Tammy Baldwin.[74] Had Clinton simply run even with Trump in these counties, still doing worse than Obama and Baldwin, she would easily have won.

Even Trump's record appeal with white working-class voters is not enough on its own to fulfill Reagan's dream of a majority New Republican Party. That's because Trump, unlike Reagan, did not try to build a positive coalition including all the New Party's elements. As mentioned, he primarily relied on the party faithful's hatred of Hillary Clinton to build his coalition. Even then he fell short, winning only 46 percent of the popular vote. While he was gaining millions of working-class two-time Obama voters, he was losing millions of upper-class McCain-Romney supporters.

Trump fell well short of Romney in votes and in percentage of votes cast almost anywhere there were highly-educated, prosperous people. He lost California's Orange County, the first time a Republican had lost that conservative bastion since 1936. He lost congressional districts with high levels of education and incomes in Virginia, Texas, Illinois, and California that Romney had carried.[75] He nearly lost a similar district represented by his nominee to become the Health and Human Services secretary, Tom Price, in Georgia. He saw his winning margins drop in a host of high-education, high-income areas even in places like Oklahoma, Indiana, and South Carolina.

This was true even in swing states that Trump actively contested. Trump carried the Milwaukee suburbs by 28,000 fewer votes than Romney did. He lost the Philadelphia suburbs by nearly 65,000 votes more than Romney did, and he lost the educated and affluent areas of Colorado by 54,000 votes more than Romney did. The Trump victory may point the way to a national Republican majority, but it does not deliver it automatically.

Nor should conservatives and Republicans expect to rely on Trump himself to deliver it. He has shown no inclination to develop the type of comprehensive philosophy that drove Reagan's political ambitions. He also seems to think of the party and its members as pieces on a chessboard, of value only so long as they are of use. But it would be unwise for conservative Republicans to rely on Trump to deliver that majority even if he wanted to or could.

Imagine if Trump were to leave office, for whatever reason, tomorrow. Where would conservatism and the Republican Party be? Would voters across the broad potential Republican coalition have started to think of themselves as Republicans? Or would they view a Trump-less party as just what it was before, something that excited hard-core conservatives and business types but seemed cold and uncaring to others who would prefer not to vote for progressive Democrats?

Republicans and conservatives need to face some facts. We have been a minority party and movement in America for eighty-four years. We have won elections in that time, but never have we really taken hold of government and changed the debate in our direction for more than a couple of years at a time. In the end, it always seems that government remains big, it remains run by progressives or those espousing progressive values, and the only debates we influence are on the margin or about cost. Unless we change this, unless we change the very nature of the political debate, we will forever be little more than tax collectors for the liberal welfare state.

Ronald Reagan had a grander vision. He envisioned a new majority party, one that embraced every broad strain of conservative thought. It was a party that expressed and acted on the majority sentiments in the country, a majority that did not fall neatly on the left or the right. It was a party that embraced freedom without forgetting human dignity. It was a party that praised initiative without denigrating the average. It was a party called all to its banner regardless of creed, gender, or race, but did not treat everyone as merely an individual without a family, a community, or a nation to call home. It was a party that had a robust view of what American self-government entailed without placing government at the center of American life.

It was a party that interpreted rather than opposed the New Deal.

Some of you will surely wonder why I return to this theme. Doesn't everyone today pay homage to the New Deal, pledging to retain its core elements like Social Security? At a surface level that is true: all but the most vocal libertarians or constitutionalists will say they want to retain the New Deal. But that commitment is for many only skin deep, and their underlying passive opposition comes through in what they say and, more important, what they do not say.

Reagan never had a problem saying that he believed it was society's obligation to take care of its weaker members. He did not have a problem saying that free trade works both ways, and that government should step in to protect American jobs when unfair competition threatened.

He did not have a problem saying that no one should be denied needed medical care because of a lack of funds, and that government had a role in helping those people out.

He did not have a problem saying those things, because in his heart he loved the average American. America was not great for him because it enabled great men to rise, although he admired men and women who showed ingenuity and initiative. America was great because it provided a home to let all people live free and dignified lives.

In his youth, tutored by his parents and his times, he found the answer to those beliefs in Franklin Roosevelt's New Deal. Government intervention and action seemed to be what Roosevelt told Americans it was, new means to implement old, traditional American values. In the world that existed before the New Deal—where a man could be fired for joining a labor union, or be left penniless if he lost his job, because there was no unemployment insurance—it was surely easy for Reagan, as it was for many millions of others, to see the New Deal as restoring an individual's freedom and dignity if he lacked bargaining power with his employer. When that era's conservatives said the world's problems were none of our concern even as Nazi Germany marched and Imperial Japan sailed to wage wars of conquest, it was easy to see Roosevelt's Democrats as both the voice and the arsenal of democracy.

If the Democratic Party had stopped there, Reagan probably would have remained a Democrat all his life. But it did not, because there was an undercurrent to Roosevelt's New Deal that did not simply seek to restore America but to transform it.

Starting with Henry Wallace's Progressive Party, some New Dealers believed America needed to be transformed, its individualist culture tamed to march to the beat of a centralized plan. Those who wanted a planned society also found it difficult to find communism as horrific or as threatening as did Reagan. For if America itself is something to be replaced, how can a regime whose central tenet was that America was inherently immoral be something to be loathed?

But as the Democratic Party left Reagan, he did not leave his core beliefs behind. His new conservatism did not pine for the days when men were men and employers could treat workers like beasts. He was *against* losing freedom by installments; he was *against* the rule of the many by the self-appointed few no matter what form that rule took. But he was also *for* human dignity. He was also *for* treating human beings with the respect they deserved and for giving each and every one of them a real fighting chance to live a decent life. He was *for* using government, when necessary, to accomplish these goals.

Barry Goldwater wrote in *The Conscience of a Conservative* that "the Conservative's first concern will always be: *Are we maximizing freedom?*"[76] But Ronald Reagan could tell Americans in his famous speech endorsing Barry Goldwater that conservatives were *for* Social Security, even though that curtailed the freedom of a person to, as Goldwater wrote, "be free throughout their lives to spend their earnings as they see fit."[77] He could say that conservatives were *for* telling senior citizens that no one should be denied medical care because of a lack of funds, even though that takes money "from fellow citizens who may have different ideas about their social obligations," against Goldwater's beliefs.[78]

In short, Reagan was *against* returning to the America before the New Deal. He was *for* interpreting Roosevelt's legacy in a way that maximized freedom and minimized bureaucratic control and the direction of Americans' lives.

Reagan could be for these things because he was for addressing "the realities of everyday life," not simply implementing an abstract theory. Can today's Republicans, especially those who proclaim his name the loudest, say the same?

So many people who invoke Reagan's name do not act or speak like him. Take Senator Cruz. No one quotes Reagan more and understands Reagan less.

Cruz treats conservatism as a singular creed with a single set of beliefs. Reagan treated conservatism as a set of principles about which there could be legitimate disagreement on particulars. Cruz treats Republicans who do not agree with him as the enemy, no better than Democrats. Reagan always sought to unify rather than divide Republicans and conservatives. Cruz would rather go down with flags flying, as he did in the attempt to shut down the government to defund Obamacare when Democrats controlled the Senate and the White House. Reagan always disliked the "ultra" who would rather lose without compromise than get part of a loaf and come back for more.

These differences extend to concrete policies too. Cruz was willing to risk national default on the debt ceiling bill to push conservative spending priorities. As president, Reagan strongly opposed conservative efforts to do that to him. He always insisted on a "clean" debt ceiling bill because the prospect of America welshing on its debts was hateful to him. Cruz is unwilling to raise even a dime in taxes no matter what spending cuts he might get in exchange. Reagan did make such deals, such as the one that has made Social Security solvent for the last thirty-five years. Reagan also was willing to raise taxes to provide new benefits: his catastrophic health insurance Medicare plan was financed by a surtax on wealthy seniors' income tax payments.[79]

Cruz also misrepresents Reagan's relationship with supply-side economics. In his presidential announcement speech, Cruz said "imagine it's 1979 and you and I were listening to President Reagan."[80] Aside from implying he was a very precocious eight-year-old, he claimed Reagan was calling then for reduction in tax rates from 70 percent to 28 percent. In a later *Wall Street Journal* op-ed touting his own tax plan, he called the supply-side guru Arthur Laffer "President Reagan's tax advisor."[81] Put this together and the implication is clear: Reagan was a supply-sider focused on cutting the top rate, just like me.

But we have seen that Reagan always disavowed the notion that he was a supply-sider. The tax plan Reagan presented in 1979 would have cut the top rate to only 50 percent, and he always spoke about that plan as cutting tax rates by 30 percent for everyone. You will look in vain for any major speech of Reagan's on taxes that makes the top tax rate the focus on his ideas. It wasn't. He spoke about reducing rates for all, with a particular emphasis on cutting the tax burden for the average American, from the time he endorsed this concept in 1958 all the way through his presidency. Cruz's focus on the top rate is the supply-side, Stockman way of talking about the tax code. But it was never Reagan's.

If Cruz is Reaganism's false prophet, others err in different ways. Take Ohio senator Rob Portman. In 2015, he wrote that cutting entitlement spending was a necessity to control the federal budget deficit.[82] When describing why Medicare needs to be cut, he wrote, "the typical couple retiring next year will have paid approximately $140,000 in lifetime Medicare taxes and premiums, yet will receive nearly $430,000 in Medicare benefits." Recall that this is the way David Stockman approached Social Security, as a forced savings program rather than a social guarantee that no American would experience poverty. But the whole point of programs like Social Security and Medicare is to use government as a vehicle to fulfill our society's commitment to all of its members.

Redistribution of this sort is a feature of these programs, not a bug. That's not to say that some people are getting benefits they don't need or are paying less than they should based on their assets or income. But to talk about the program that gives retirees a chance to keep on living as if it were an accounting exercise is the epitome of putting other people's money ahead of average people's lives.

Reagan did not talk that way even as he believed privately that entitlements needed to be cut. That is because when the chips were down, he cared more about life than money. As he said in 1958:

Certainly no thinking American would dispute the idea that there should be an economic floor below which no American should be allowed to live. In the last few decades we have indulged in a great program of social progress with many welfare programs. I'm sure that most of us in spite of the cost wouldn't buy back many of these projects at any price—they have represented forward thinking on our part.[83]

Would conservatives today say those words as Reagan did, with sincerity and enthusiasm?

The modern conservative use of the phrase "safety net" is another indication of the subtle yet crucial misunderstanding of the real Reagan that is rampant on the right. Conservatives regularly use the phrase "safety net" to refer to the panoply of means-tested government programs intended to raise people from poverty. Indeed, Ryan's 2014 antipoverty report includes the phrase four times, while the House Republicans' 2016 "A Better Way" antipoverty plan uses it eight times. The only problem is that Reagan actually used a different term. He spoke about the "social safety net."[84]

Leaving out that one little word speaks volumes about the mindset one approaches poverty with. Leave out the word "social" and you leave out the sense of obligation to the less fortunate that it conveys. Leave out the word "social" and you leave out the idea that many of these programs are part of "a great program of social progress." Leave out the word "social" and maybe you leave out the pride that was so evident in Reagan's voice when he spoke about "the forward thinking on our part." For Reagan, the word "social" implied that we could be truly self-governing, choosing freedom for ourselves *and* for the less fortunate of our neighbors.

The lack of a core idea of what government activity conservatives should be *for* holds back the cause of cutting government too. I've seen many conservative legislators come to state capitals or to Washington full of budget-cutting fervor. But without that idea of what government should do, they fall into one of two camps. The smaller camp is the legislator who, unable to distinguish between good and bad spending, votes no on everything. Ron Paul was that sort of congressman. That person never advances his or her ideas and always is on the short end of 434–1 votes.

The larger camp contains the people who start to vote yes on almost everything. If you don't have a view of what government should do, then anything that seems to have support in your district or contain a good-sounding idea is OK. You're opposed to "big spending" and "big government," but protecting your big employer's contract or supporting funding "for the children" or increasing health research no longer fits the idea of "big spending" or "big government." The reason so many conservative legislators turn into big spenders once they are in office awhile isn't because they get corrupted by lobbyists. It's that they don't have a strong enough sense of what government *should* do to let them act strategically to oppose what it should not.

This happens to the best of people. I should know, because I almost was one of them.

I ran for the California State Assembly when I was a mere twenty-four years old. During my unsuccessful campaign, I had a meeting that dramatized this problem, which has stuck with me for over thirty years.

One day I met with a man named Alan Alameda.[85] I was young and full of what I thought was a Reagan-inspired, antigovernment philosophy. As I explained to Mr. Alameda that I wanted to cut government and taxes, he asked me a simple question: "What do you want to cut?" I had never thought about that before. "Government" was an abstraction to me then, a thing that took freedom and money. But his question made me realize that I had to know what government did and then explain why such and such a program was not worth keeping if I was to actually cut government. What was in and what was out, and why? I had never considered that—and the only way to address that question without becoming like Ron Paul was to know what government should be doing, and why. I had to know what I was *for* to know what I should be *against*.

Reagan didn't know how to answer questions like Mr. Alameda's when he first declared for governor in 1966. But as he learned what the state government, and then the federal government, did, he was able to apply his philosophy to the specifics. That philosophy—support for programs that actually helped people who truly needed help to live decent, dignified lives; opposition to programs that either did not fit that requirement or that forced people to live in a way they did not want as a condition of getting the help—informed all the decisions he made during his governorship and his presidency.

If conservative Republicans adopted his philosophy as their own, they too could use it to inform the decisions they must make today and into the future. The Reagan philosophy would help us address the challenges of 2017, those of 2027, and those for years beyond. In doing so, we would also create the durable majority, the New Republican Party, which would shape the debate and move America in the direction of freedom and dignity.

This idea might seem a bit abstract, and one thing we know from Reagan is that conservatives should never be slaves to abstraction. I will never claim to know how Reagan would have solved the challenges we face today. His thinking was too subtle, his wisdom too profound, to know exactly how he would have applied his philosophy to a specific tax bill or what he would have specifically done on immigration or trade. But I do think we know enough about his ideas to hazard a guess as to how he might have approached some of the key challenges of our time.

Reagan would definitely have wanted to repeal Obamacare. Its rules and regulations put the government in the driver's seat in determining what care should be delivered, to whom, and at what price. This is exactly the sort of government-directed society that Reagan believed was opposed to American principles.

It's less clear what he would have wanted to replace it with. I think, however, it is pretty clear he would have wanted to ensure that people would not lose coverage that they had received as a result of Obamacare's exchanges and the Medicaid expansion. His consistent belief that it was OK for government to pay for needed medical care for those who could not afford it makes that plain. The details as to who should be covered, how much the government should pay, and what level of care they would be guaranteed would be up for discussion, but I can't imagine that Reagan would be more concerned about money than about life.

Reagan would probably think that individual tax rates were too high, but he would also be concerned about the effect a tax bill would have on those hurting the most. His bills often removed people from the tax rolls or targeted relief to people in the working and middle classes far beyond the simple reduction in rates. In one letter he suggested reducing a working person's Social Security taxes rather than giving him or her a government check; perhaps he would be open to exempting a certain amount of wages from all or part of the payroll tax. Or perhaps he would want to increase the amount of the personal exemption or the standard deduction to pull more people out of paying taxes at all. I doubt he would want to decrease the amount of the child tax credit, as some supply-siders suggest. The man who praised making it economical to raise families again when he signed the 1986 tax reform bill recognized that cutting the cost of human capital matters as much or more than cutting the cost of monetary capital.

Corporate taxes are a different challenge. Reagan did not talk much about the corporate tax code. We know he wanted to increase saving and investment, so ideas for immediate expensing of corporate investment might appeal to him. He might also be open to more direct measures to stimulate job creation and wage growth, such as tax credits for hiring American citizens or for increasing employees' wages. The bottom line would likely be what combination of all of the above was possible and was likeliest to increase economic well-being for average American citizens.

Trade and immigration are easier nuts to crack. Reagan was clearly for free trade and for fair trade. He did not hesitate to retaliate against what he thought were unfair trading practices; he was not a slave to the abstraction of free trade. He was proud when his sanctions helped Harley-Davidson recover its ability to compete against Japanese motorcycle imports. While he would never want to undo the global trading system that generally benefits all, he would not be idle when currency manipulation, lack of American access to markets, and dumping, or selling products for below cost, was closing American companies and losing Americans jobs.

Reagan was always concerned about America losing control of its borders. While he welcomed immigrants, he also knew that the country could not afford to include every economic migrant who wanted to come here for a better life. He surely would find a bill attractive that made real border control a priority while allowing some immigrants to come to our shores.

The man who increased gasoline taxes in a recession over conservative opposition to fund road building would probably not be averse to some new infrastructure construction. The federal gas tax has not been increased at all since 1993; Reagan would probably have approved of increasing it at least by the amount of inflation in the intervening twenty-four years. He might find innovative proposals like privatization or tolls attractive to fund the new projects. He might also find a move from gas taxes to a fee for every mile traveled of interest. Hybrid and electric cars like Priuses and Teslas cause as much damage to roads as their gas-engine competitors, but their much higher mileage means they pay a fraction of the cost to maintain the roads they drive. The comparatively wealthy owners of these cars could easily afford to pay for the roads they use; why not make them pay their fair share?

Reducing spending remains a large issue. While the annual budget deficit expressed as a percentage of the nation's economy is lower now than it was in any year in the Reagan presidency, it remains high.[86] America also borrowed a lot during the Obama and Bush presidencies; our total debt measured as a share of the economy is much higher than it was under Reagan's time.[87] I have no doubt that Reagan would want to cut the federal budget, especially since a number of programs he always tried to cut such as farm subsidies and the Export-Import Bank remain part of the federal government.

He would do so, however, carefully and with an eye toward need. His budget-cutting exercises always tried to protect federal spending on the truly needy. In his era, that always meant exempting core entitlement spending from cuts. Whether that would still mean that today for him is unknowable. But there are ways to cut spending within entitlements without endangering core social commitments.

One is by focusing on disability spending. Many of today's "disabled" are simply people over fifty-five with little education and some pain or depression. They collect benefits through the Social Security Disability Insurance program and the Medicare program. The federal government spends nearly $200 billion a year on disabled Americans in these programs; surely some people could be returned to work with the sort of requirements and assistance we provide welfare recipients.

Another is to increase means testing for Medicare and Social Security. Medicare premiums are highly subsidized even if you are Mitt Romney or Warren Buffett. Is this fair? The same goes for Social Security. Right now, only 50 percent of Social Security benefits are taxed if a senior citizen has substantially above an average income for a retiree outside of Social Security. The rest is tax free. Why not tax all Social Security benefits for the super well off?

I could go on and on, but the specifics are included only to point to the principle: benefits *should* go to people who *need* them. Treating all entitlement spending the same isn't fair. If conservative Republicans want to have the political mandate to change entitlement programs, they have to show that they value those programs for what they are: social guarantees from the better off among us to those less fortunate. That means putting average people's lives first and other people's money second.

I started this book with a personal story of my lifelong work in the conservative garden. I'm still at work in that garden, toiling away to help persuade Americans to choose to live a more free way of life. Many of you are also at work in that garden, whether as a policy maker, a journalist, a volunteer, or just someone who cares about his country and talks to his neighbors and friends. I'd like to end this book by talking directly to you.

Reagan and Roosevelt asked their audiences if they thought they were better off than they were in the past. I'm going to ask you a similar question: If conservative Republicans keep going on the course they have been on, do you think America will be better off in four or eight years? Do you think Americans will be freer from government restraints and commands? Do you think traditional values will be more respected by our public institutions? Do you think that America will be more respected in the world? Do you think more Americans will have joined our cause and that Republicans will consistently outnumber Democrats for the first time in eighty-four years?

I don't. I don't think America will be better off if we are simply louder and clearer about how much some conservatives don't like the New Deal. I don't think America will be better off if we put on new clothes and cosmetics, wink at social protections, and then show that what we really care about is the same old, same old. They say the definition of insanity is doing the same thing and expecting different results. I agree 100 percent.

For better and for worse, we live in Franklin Roosevelt's garden. The libertarian will be upset at this, but there is no evidence that more than a tiny portion of Americans want to tear that garden up and return to the wilderness of liberty that was pre–New Deal America. Our task as conservatives is what it has been for decades, to work to return that garden to what was promised us, a thing of beauty that enhances each of our lives, rather than let it become a collection of weeds and thorns that entwine and enslave us.

Ronald Reagan was loved by Americans because that was what he told them he wanted to do. He believed the garden he and the nation had been promised was just, but that without prudent gardeners it would inevitably become the weed- and thorn-filled hell that real socialism produces everywhere. Those gardeners were us, he said, because we are capable of genuine self-government.

We can meet our rendezvous with destiny, our time for choosing. We can choose to provide the security and the opportunity Roosevelt and Reagan told us we deserved. We can choose to treat every American with respect and dignity. We can choose to reverse America's decline and make conservative Republicanism the country's governing philosophy. We can choose to create the New Republican Party that gives people from every background, race, creed, and gender a real seat at our table.

Why do I think we can? Because I know in my heart that man is good, that what is right will eventually triumph, and that there's purpose and worth in each and every human life.

ACKNOWLEDGMENTS

The Liverpool soccer club's motto is "You'll never walk alone," and the Tottenham club's slogan is "To dare is to do." I think those two sayings nicely sum up what it is to write a book, as the writer takes the risk and creates the work while being supported by many people who help him along the way. My acknowledgments, therefore, will try to introduce you to the friends, companions, and coworkers with whom I walked while I dared and did.

This, my first sole-authored book, is the product of nearly a lifetime's fascination with and study of politics. So I'd like to acknowledge the early influences in my life who helped nurture the seed of interest into something that found root and grew. Bob Walker, Alan Heslop, Tony Quinn, and the late Alan Hoffenblum all took their time to teach me what they knew about practical politics and political analysis. Bob was particularly important to me when I was young, serving informally as my first mentor and as a good friend. I would never have taken the course I did in life that led to this book without their aid and friendship.

My interest in political theory arose later while I was attending Claremont McKenna College. The late Harry Jaffa, Bill Allen, Marlo Lewis, and Chicago law professor Richard Epstein were each teachers who forced me to think and dig more deeply into this phenomenon we call politics. Terry Hallmark, the late Pat Powers, and Colleen Sheehan were friends who continued to walk down the path of exploration and inquiry with me. They remain among my closest friends to this day.

I took a circuitous career route to becoming a writer, first working as a political consultant and a lawyer before entering the world of conservative think tanks. So I owe a particular debt of gratitude to the people who facilitated my midthirties career change, Don Eberly and Bill Boxx, who hired me to run the Commonwealth Foundation. I also owe a strong debt to Larry Mone, president of the Manhattan Institute, and Chris DeMuth, then president of the American Enterprise Institute, for bringing me to their institutions later in my career. Each step helped me mature and grow as a person and as a thinker, giving me exposure to a wide variety of people and strains of thought that kept pushing and challenging my understanding.

Most fifty-one-year-old family men don't leave a stable and rewarding job to pursue a dream and a new career, but that's exactly what I did in the summer of 2013 when I left the American Enterprise Institute to become a senior fellow at the Ethics and Public Policy Center, my current intellectual home. I will be forever grateful to the two men, my colleague Yuval Levin and our president, Ed Whelan, who decided that I could buck the odds and brought me on board the Ethics team to make a go of it. They were joined in their leap of faith by the Bradley Foundation, especially by then President Michael Grebe, Vice President Dan Schmidt, and his assistant Mike Hartmann; the Searle Freedom Trust and its head, Kim Dennis; and the Earhart Foundation led by Ingrid Gregg and assisted by Monty Brown. Along with other supporters, such as Thomas Smith and James Piereson of the Smith Foundation, each of these institutions saw merit in my book proposal and chose to dedicate the financial resources to make it possible. I owe each of them a debt that I can never fully repay.

Getting a publisher interested in your idea is much harder than it seems, or at least harder than I knew when I started this journey. So I am extremely grateful to my former AEI colleague Norm Ornstein, who saw value in my proposal and contacted people he knew in the publishing world on my behalf. Without his efforts I would never have made any progress, and I certainly would never have found my agents, Keith Urbahn and Matt Latimer, of the Javelin Group. With their help my core insights became a real book proposal, one that could actually see the light of day. Thanks to all of them for their help in bringing this book to fruition.

My editors at HarperCollins also contributed mightily to the product you have in your hands. Adam Bellow brought my idea to Harper-Collins and helped to focus my attention on bringing Reagan's early thoughts to the forefront. His successor as my editor, Eric Meyers, helped me turn a tome into a book, and Adam's successor as the head of Broadside Books, Eric Nelson, helped me craft a title that made the whole argument clear in one sentence. Along with their copyeditors and other assistants, they made the book what it is. Thanks for your insights and your efforts.

The archivists at the Reagan Presidential Library accommodated my unexpected arrival with professional aplomb. Their willingness to allow my unscheduled visit to proceed gave me access to Reagan's early years as a conservative. Without that access, this book would be incomplete, as only the longer versions of his early speeches provide the full depth and subtlety of his thought.

My parents, Henry and Dorothy, have been with me every step of the way, from the beginning to the present. From my youth when they encouraged and supported my early political interest through college (which they paid for) to the present day, letting me crash in their house for some final furious writing over Christmas vacation, their love for me has known no bounds. Thanks Mom and Dad for everything.

Two women deserve special acknowledgment. Karlyn Bowman was my colleague at AEI for over seven years and remains one of my closest friends. For years she has been studying the group of voters that quietly decide American national elections, the college dropouts and community college graduates whom pollsters label "some college." As I stumbled into learning the importance of the semi-skilled worker to the outcome of elections, Karlyn proved an able intellectual sparring partner and coach. Moreover, she always supported me as a colleague and as a friend through thick and through thin. I have often thought that were I a classical painter I would depict her in the form of Psephologia, the mythical Greek Muse of election study, her right hand holding a stylus writing and her left holding the ancient Athenian ballot, the pebble (*psephos* in Greek) from which the modern study of elections takes its name. As fanciful as that supposition might be, the truth is she has served as my muse throughout the last decade and her contribution to this book is profound and incalculable.

If Karlyn has been my muse, then my girlfriend, Audrey Mullen, has been my goddess. Her presence lightens my heart, her conversation challenges my mind, and her support fuels my life. The partner of any writer knows how burdensome sharing your life with a loved one's book can be. Audrey managed that challenge with aplomb, keeping me focused and afloat while keeping our relationship steady and deep. I couldn't have written any book without her, but I especially could not have written this book without her: her lifetime of work in the conservative movement helped her help me write a better book than I would otherwise have. Honey, this book's for you.

NOTES

CHAPTER I: REAGAN ENTERS, STAGE LEFT

1. Edmund Morris, *Dutch: A Memoir of Ronald Reagan* (New York: Random House, 1999), 123, 128, 205; Anne Edwards, *Early Reagan: The Rise to Power* (New York: William Morrow, 1987), 133, 149, 173, 177, 231.

2. Morris, *Dutch*, 128. Reagan's first wife, Jane Wyman, cited the same habit as a reason for their 1948 divorce (Edwards, *Early Reagan*, 355).

3. Edwards, *Early Reagan*, 172.

4. Lou Cannon, *Governor Reagan: His Rise to Power* (New York: Public Affairs, 2003), 93; Edwards, *Early Reagan*, 300; Kiron Skinner, Annelise Anderson, and Martin Anderson, eds., *Ronald Reagan: A Life in Letters* (New York: Free Press, 2003), 96.

5. Edwards, *Early Reagan*, 294.

6. Cannon, *Governor Reagan*, 119.

7. Ibid., 101. Anne Edwards states that Reagan secretly switched to backing Nixon by the end of the race (*Early Reagan*, 417–18). But this is contradicted by Reagan himself, who says he did not develop affection for Nixon until before the 1960 presidential campaign, and by a private letter Reagan sent in December 1952 in which he called Nixon "less than honest" and "an ambitious opportunist" undeserving of the vice presidency. See Ronald Reagan, *An American Life* (New York: Simon & Schuster, 1990), 133; Morris, *Dutch*, 292–93.

8. Edwards, *Early Reagan*, 457.

9. Skinner, Anderson, and Anderson, *Ronald Reagan: A Life in Letters*, 813.

10. Reagan, *An American Life*, 119, 135.

11. Reagan's final autobiography titled *An American Life*, was published in 1990. His first autobiography, titled *Where's The Rest of Me?*, after a famous line he uttered in the movie *King's Row*, was published in 1965 on

the eve of his first campaign for governor. The quotations concerning Reagan's father are taken from *An American Life*, 66.

12. See http://geoelections.free.fr/USA/accueil.htm. Indeed, Lee County remains so Republican that it voted for Barry Goldwater while he lost Illinois to Lyndon Baines Johnson by 19 percent. It also opposed favorite son Barack Obama in 2008 and 2012.

13. Anne Edwards says Reagan's mother, Nelle, was so committed to the Democratic Party that he held off on formally leaving the Democratic Party in part to avoid upsetting her (*Early Reagan*, 246). Reagan in fact did not formally reregister as a Republican until the last year of his mother's life, 1962.

14. Illinois, like every state in 1932, did not allow men or women to vote until they turned twenty-one years old.

15. Chicago, Detroit, Pittsburgh, Philadelphia, Cleveland, San Francisco, Saint Louis, and Baltimore were won by the Republican presidential nominee in at least six races from 1896 to 1932. Even Democratic bastions like New York and Boston voted Republican in some elections.

16. Franklin Roosevelt, acceptance speech at the 1932 Democratic Convention, 2 July 1932, accessed at https://publicpolicy.pepperdine.edu/academics/research/faculty-research/new-deal/roosevelt-speeches/fr070232.htm.

17. Franklin Roosevelt, "The Forgotten Man," 7 April 1932, accessed at https://publicpolicy.pepperdine.edu/academics/research/faculty-research/new-deal/roosevelt-speeches/fr040732.htm; see also Roosevelt's acceptance speech at the 1932 Democratic Convention.

18. Franklin Roosevelt, Address on Long-Range Planning, 31 October 1932, accessed at https://publicpolicy.pepperdine.edu/academics/research/faculty-research/new-deal/roosevelt-speeches/fr103132.htm.

19. Ibid.

20. Franklin Roosevelt, Oglethorpe University address, 22 May 1932, accessed at https://publicpolicy.pepperdine.edu/academics/research/faculty-research/new-deal/roosevelt-speeches/fr052232.htm.

21. Ibid.

22. Roosevelt, acceptance speech at the 1932 Democratic Convention.

23. Herbert Hoover, acceptance speech to the Republican Convention, 11 August 1932, accessed at http://millercenter.org/president/hoover/speeches/speech-accepting-the-republican-nomination3.

24. Ibid.

25. Herbert Hoover, campaign speech at Madison Square Garden, 21 October 1932, accessed at http://millercenter.org/president/hoover/speeches/campaign-speech-in-madison-square-garden.

26. Ibid.

27. Roosevelt, Address on Long-Range Planning.

28. Franklin Delano Roosevelt, "Commonwealth Club Address," 23 September 1932, found on Americanrhetoric.com/speeches/fdrcommonwealth .htm. All subsequent quotes or discussion concerning this speech are from the same source.

29. Roosevelt spoke directly to the people over the radio (television not being then invented) in what were called "fireside chats." Reagan listened to these religiously and praised FDR's warm, comforting presence even in his later years (Reagan, *An American Life*, 66). He regularly gave coworkers his impressions of FDR's chats (Edwards, *Early Reagan*, 149). For the text of Roosevelt's fifth chat, see Franklin Delano Roosevelt, fireside chat 5, "On Addressing the Critics," available at http://millercenter.org/president/speeches#fdrroosevelt. All subsequent quotations or discussions of Roosevelt's speeches, unless denoted otherwise, are from this source.

30. "Thomas Jefferson Memorial Construction," US National Park Service, www.nps.gov/thje/learn/historyculture/MemorialConstruction.htm.

31. Franklin Delano Roosevelt, 1944 State of the Union address, delivered by radio as fireside chat 28.

32. See Christopher J. Tassava, "The American Economy During World War II," EH.net, 10 February 2008, https://eh.net/encyclopedia/the-american-econ omy-during-world-war-ii.

33. Reagan, *An American Life*, 105.

34. Ibid., 90.

35. Lee Edwards, *Reagan: A Political Biography* (San Diego, CA: Viewpoint Books, 1967), 15.

36. Reagan, *An American Life*, 89.

37. Edwards, *Early Reagan*, 246.

38. Morris, *Dutch*, 158.

39. Edwards, *Early Reagan*, 324.

40. Reagan's father, Jack, was laid off from his job on Christmas 1931. He was unemployed for six months before he found public-sector employment by running government-financed relief operations in Lee County. His older brother had also been laid off his job as a manual laborer before he enrolled at Eurkea College.

41. Franklin Delano Roosevelt, 1941 State of the Union address, a.k.a. "The Four Freedoms Speech."

42. Franklin Delano Roosevelt, speech accepting the 1944 Democratic presidential nomination.

43. Cannon, *Governor Reagan*, 31.

44. Morris, *Dutch*, 209.

45. Ibid., 228.

46. Reagan always exempted people who, "through no fault of their own," could not fairly be expected to provide for themselves from this expectation, Reagan, *An American Life*, 185.

47. Ibid., 22, 28.

48. Franklin Delano Roosevelt, fireside chat 28, a.k.a. "The Economic Bill of Rights" speech.

49. Franklin Delano Roosevelt, fireside chat 7, "On the Works Relief Program and the Social Security Act."

50. Roosevelt, fireside chat 5.

51. Franklin Delano Roosevelt, Madison Square Garden Speech, October 1936.

52. Franklin Delano Roosevelt, fireside chat 6, "On Government and Capitalism."

53. Roosevelt, Commonwealth Club Address.

54. See Franklin Delano Roosevelt, fireside chat 11.

55. Edwards, *Early Reagan*, 324, quoting "Mr. Reagan Airs His Views," *Chicago Tribune*, 18 May 1947.

56. Reagan, *An American Life*, 28.

57. Edwards, *Early Reagan*, 200.

58. Ibid., 248.

59. Reagan, *An American Life*, 67.

60. Ibid.

61. Ibid.

62. Ibid., 119.

63. Ibid.

64. Progressive Party 1948 platform, available at www.davidpietrusza.com /1948-progressive-party-platform.html. All subsequent quotes and discussions of this platform come from this source.

65. 1948 Democratic Party platform, available at www.presidency.ucsb.edu. All subsequent quotes and discussion of this platform come from this source.

66. Cannon, *Governor Reagan*, 123.

67. Ibid.

68. Ibid.

69. Bill Boyarsky, *The Rise of Ronald Reagan* (New York: Random House, 1968), 75–76.

70. Reagan, *An American Life*, 132.

71. Ibid., 133. Truman died in December 1972.

72. See http://geoelections.free.fr/USA/elec_comtes/1948wall.htm; Kevin P. Phillips, *The Emerging Republican Majority*, (New Rochelle, NY: Arlington House, 1969), 65–66.

CHAPTER 2: RONALD REAGAN, ALL-AMERICAN

1. Kiron Skinner, Annelise Anderson, and Martin Anderson, eds., *Reagan in His Own Hand* (New York: Simon & Schuster, 2001), xiii.

2. Cannon, *Governor Reagan*, 115.

3. Boyarsky, *Rise of Ronald Reagan*, 28.

4. Steven Hayward, *The Age of Reagan: The Fall of the Old Liberal Order, 1964–1980* (New York: Crown Forum, 2001), 450.

5. Edward M. Yager, *Ronald Reagan's Journey: Democrat to Republican* (Lanham, MD: Rowman & Littlefield, 2006), 42.

6. Ibid., 30–31, 78–80.

7. Lou Cannon, *President Reagan: The Role of a Lifetime* (New York: Public Affairs, 1991), 435.

8. Reagan, *An American Life*, 133.

9. Morris, *Dutch*, 292.

10. Ibid., 292–93.

11. Dwight Eisenhower, *Mandate for Change, 1953–56* (Garden City, NY: Doubleday, 1963), 51, 441.

12. Phillips, *Emerging Republican Majority*, 69–70.

13. Ibid., 69.

14. William F. Buckley, Jr., "Our Mission Statement," *National Review*, 19 November 1955, www.nationalreview.com/article/223549/our-mission-statement-william-f-buckley-jr.

15. George Orwell, *1984* (New York: Signet Classics, 1961), 267.

16. Buckley, "Our Mission Statement."

17. Ibid.

18. E. J. Dionne, *How the Right Went Wrong* (New York: Simon & Schuster, 2016), 50, citing William F. Buckley, *Up from Liberalism* (New York: McDowell, Obolensky, 1959), 114.

19. Barry Goldwater, *The Conscience of a Conservative* (Shepardsville, KY: Victor Publishing Co, 1960), 3.

20. Ibid., 76.

21. Edwards, *Early Reagan*, 444.

22. Reagan, *An American Life*, 104–24.

23. Skinner, Anderson, and Anderson, *Reagan in His Own Hand*, 237.

24. Reagan, *An American Life*, 69.

25. Morris, *Dutch*, 230.

26. Edwards, *Early Reagan*, 363–70.

27. Ibid., 367.

28. Reagan, *An American Life*, 119.

29. Edwards, *Early Reagan*, 300.

30. Morris, *Dutch*, 229.

31. Ibid.

32. Ibid.

33. Ibid., 233.

34. Ibid., 234.

35. Ibid., 232–33.

36. Ibid., 237.

37. Edwards, *Early Reagan*, 324.

38. Ibid., 324.

39. 1948 radio broadcast sponsored by ILGWU for Truman-Barkley, listened to at the Reagan Presidential Library (henceforth, RPL), July 2016.

40. *United States v. Paramount Pictures, Inc.*, 334 US 131 (1948).

41. Edwards, *Early Reagan*, 166.

42. Ibid., 166.

43. Morris, *Dutch*, 209.

44. Edwards, *Early Reagan*, 254–55.

45. Ibid., 454.

46. Reagan, *An American Life*, 128.

47. Ibid., 129.

48. Yager, *Ronald Reagan's Journey*, 45.

49. Ronald Reagan, speech to Los Angeles County Young Republicans, November 1964, listened to at RPL, July 2016.

50. Yager, *Ronald Reagan's Journey*, 78.

51. Ronald Reagan, speech to California Fertilizer Association, 10 November 1958, listened to at RPL, July 2016.

52. Ibid.

53. Ibid.

54. Ibid.

55. Ibid.

56. Herbert Hoover, *The Consequences of the Proposed New Deal*, 21 October 1932, accessed from the Miller Center, http://millercenter.org/president/hoover/speeches/campaign-speech-in-madison-square-garden.

57. Reagan, speech to California Fertilizer Association.

58. Ronald Reagan, commencement address at Eureka College, 7 June 1957, accessed from PBS.org, www.pbs.org/wgbh/americanexperience/features/primary-resources/reagan-eureka. All further quotations in this and the following two paragraphs are taken from this source.

59. Reagan, speech to California Fertilizer Association.

60. Ronald Reagan, first gubernatorial inauguration address, 5 January 1967, http://governors.library.ca.gov/addresses/33-Reagan01.html.

61. John B. Judis, *William F. Buckley, Jr.: Patron Saint of the Conservatives* (New York: Simon & Schuster, 1990), 128.

62. Ronald Reagan, "Beyond the Lens," radio interview with Arnold Michaelis, 27 November 1958, listened to at RPL, July 2016.

63. "California 1958 Ballot Propositions," Ballotpedia, accessed at https://ballotpedia.org/California_1958_ballot_propositions.

64. Reagan, "Beyond the Lens."

65. Ben Moreel, "Address Delivered to the Pensacola, Florida, Chapter of ACA, Sept. 27, 1966," accessed from Stanford University, Hoover Library, https://searchworks.stanford.edu/view/3230389. For a description of the ACA, see http://dolearchivecollections.ku.edu/collections/press_releases/650526conc2p1.pdf.

66. Ronald Reagan, "Losing Freedom by Installments," speech to the Conservative League of Minneapolis, 29 January 1962, accessed from RPL, July 2016.

67. Roosevelt, fireside chat 6.

68. Skinner, Anderson, and Anderson, *Reagan: A Life in Letters*, 702.

69. Ibid.

70. Ibid., 703–4.

71. Ibid., 704–5.

72. Reagan, *An American Life*, 133.

73. Theodore H. White, *The Making of the President, 1960* (New York: Harper Perennial Classics, 2009), 198–202.

74. Ibid., 199.

75. Ibid., 204.

76. Nicole Hemmer, "Richard Nixon's Model Campaign," *New York Times*, 10 May 2012, http://campaignstops.blogs.nytimes.com/2012/05/10/richard-nixons-model-campaign/.

77. Craig Shirley, *Reagan's Revolution: The Untold Story of the Campaign That Started It All* (Nashville, TN: Thomas Nelson, 2005), 7.

78. Skinner, Anderson, and Anderson, *Reagan: A Life in Letters*, 753.

79. John Gizzi, "Gizzi on Politics: RIP, Joe Shell," *Human Events*, 21

April 2008, http://humanevents.com/2008/04/21/gizzi-on-politics
-april-2125/.

80. Edwards, *Early Reagan*, 480.

81. Morris, *Dutch*, 326–27.

82. Ronald Reagan, speech to the Phoenix Chamber of Commerce, 30 March 1961, accessed from RPL, July 2016.

83. Ibid.

84. Reagan, speech to Conservative League of Minneapolis.

85. Ibid.

86. Reagan, speech to Phoenix Chamber of Commerce.

87. Ibid.

88. Ibid.

89. Ibid.

90. Ibid.

91. Ronald Reagan, speech to California Realtor's Convention, 26 September 1963, accessed from RPL, July 2016.

92. Ibid.

93. See also the Kennedy adviser John Kenneth Galbraith's *The Affluent Society* (New York: Houghton Mifflin, 1958).

94. Ibid.

95. Arthur Schlesinger, "The Perspective Now," *Partisan Review* 14, no. 3 (1947), available at www.bu.edu/partisanreview/books/PR1947V14N3/HTML/files/assets/basic-html/page5.html.

96. White, *Making of the President, 1960*, 220.

97. Ibid.

98. From November 1964 speech to the Los Angeles County Young Republicans, listened to at RPL, July 2016.

99. Phyllis Schlafly, *A Choice, Not an Echo* (Alton, IL: Pere Marquette, 1964).

100. Barry Goldwater, Republican nomination acceptance speech, 16 July 1964, accessed from the Miller Center, http://millercenter.org/ridingthe tiger/republican-conventions-greatest-hits.

CHAPTER 3: "A TIME FOR CHOOSING": A STAR IS BORN

1. Reagan, speech to Los Angeles County Young Republicans.

2. Ronald Reagan, "A Time for Choosing," https://reaganlibrary.archives .gov/archives/reference/timechoosing.html. All subsequent quotes from or discussion of this speech are derived from this source.

3. Reagan, *An American Life*, 246.

4. Reagan, "A Time for Choosing," paragraph 2.

5. Ibid., paragraph 4.

6. Ibid., paragraph 6.

7. Ibid., paragraph 8.

8. Ibid.

9. Ibid., paragraph 7.

10. Edwards, *Early Reagan*, 425, quoting Ronald Reagan, "How Do You Fight Communism?," *Fortnight*, 22 January 1951.

11. Reagan, "A Time for Choosing," paragraph 22.

12. Ibid., paragraph 23.

13. Ibid., paragraph 26.

14. Ibid.

15. Reagan, speech to Phoenix Chamber of Commerce.

16. Reagan, "A Time for Choosing," paragraph 28.

17. Ibid., paragraph 29.

18. Ibid., paragraph 34.

19. Ibid., paragraph 38.

20. Ibid., paragraph 40.

21. Ibid.

22. See http://www.pbs.org/opb/thesixties/topics/politics/newsmakers_3.html.

23. The ad may be viewed online at www.youtube.com/watch?v=dDTBnsqxZ3k.

24. Reagan, "A Time for Choosing," paragraphs 44–45.

25. Ibid., paragraphs 46–47.

26. George F. Will, "The Cheerful Malcontent," *Washington Post*, 31 May 1998, www.washingtonpost.com/wp-srv/politics/daily/may98/will31.htm.

27. Cannon, *President Reagan*, 7.

28. Goldwater, *Conscience*, 11.

29. Ibid., 30.

30. Ibid., 3.

31. Ibid., 17.

32. Ibid., 6.

33. Ibid., 78.

34. Ibid., 56.

35. "Reagan Is Laid to Rest," CNN.com, 13 June 2004, www.cnn.com/2004/ ALLPOLITICS/06/12/reagan.main/index.html.

36. Goldwater, *Conscience*, 42.

37. Ibid., 43.

38. Reagan, speech to California Fertilizer Association.

39. Goldwater, *Conscience*, 56–57.

40. Ibid., 57.

41. Ibid., 68.

42. Ibid., 60.

43. Ronald Reagan, "The Myth of the Great Society," viewed at RPL, July 2016.

44. Skinner, Anderson, and Anderson, *Reagan: A Life in Letters*, 288.

45. As reprinted in Frank Rich, "Proud Loser," *New York*, 3 March 2013, http:// nymag.com/news/frank-rich/ronald-reagan-2013-3/. All subsequent quotes are taken from the same source.

46. See, for example, Reagan's 1961 letter to Lorraine Wagner re: running for governor.

47. In his first autobiography, *Where's the Rest of Me?*, Reagan wrote that the public response to his first political speech, one in favor of a "student strike" while he was at Eureka College, had been "heady wine." See Morris, *Dutch*, 74.

CHAPTER 4: THE CREATIVE SOCIETY, STARRING RONALD REAGAN

1. Ronald Reagan, Remarks at a White House Reception for Kennedy Center Honorees, 4 December 1983, accessed at www.presidency.ucsb .edu/ws/?pid=40833.

2. As quoted in Goldwater, *Conscience*, 3.

3. Reagan, speech to Los Angeles County Young Republicans.

4. Reagan, "Myth of the Great Society."

5. Cannon, *Governor Reagan*, 134; Edwards, *Reagan: A Political Biography*, 87.

6. Cannon, *Governor Reagan*, 134.

7. Ibid., 135.

8. Edwards, *Reagan: A Political Biography*, 89; Cannon, *Governor Reagan*, 138–39.

9. Edwards, *Reagan: A Political Biography*, 101.

10. Ibid., 105.

11. Ibid.

12. Ibid.

13. Reagan, *An American Life*, 32. Edmund Morris, Reagan's official biographer, notes that the theme of redemption through social assistance that leads to work is a central theme of *That Printer of Udell's*. The novel's hero, Dick Falkner, proposes his town's rich residents create a "dormitory-*cum*-lumberyard that will offer free shelter in exchange for full-time work" to the area's homeless. So redeemed, these men reenter society able to provide for themselves. Morris notes that this "prefiguring of Governor Reagan's welfare reform" is "surely more coincidental than prophetic." But it is a philosophy he deeply believed in throughout the rest of his life. See Morris, *Dutch*, 41–42.

14. Cannon, *Governor Reagan*, 137, 142, 145.

15. Edwards, *Reagan: A Political Biography*, 129.

16. Ibid., 116.

17. Ibid., 117.

18. Cannon, *Governor Reagan*, 122; Boyarsky, *Rise of Ronald Reagan*, 38, 148.

19. Cannon, *Governor Reagan*, 31.

20. Edwards, *Reagan: A Political Biography*, 117.

21. Reagan, speech to Los Angeles County Young Republicans.

22. Edwards, *Reagan: A Political Biography*, 123.

23. Ibid.

24. Judis, *William F. Buckley, Jr.*, 138–39.

25. Cannon, *Governor Reagan*, 31.

26. Ibid., 144.

27. Edwards, *Reagan: A Political Biography*, 165.

28. Ibid., 126.

29. Shirley Bebitch Jeffe, "A History Lesson on Part-Time Lawmaking," *Los Angeles Times*, 8 August 2004, http://articles.latimes.com/2004/aug/08/opinion/op-jeffe8.

30. Edwards, *Reagan: A Political Biography*, 153.

31. Ibid., 136.

32. Ibid., 137.

33. Ibid., 93–5.

34. Cannon, *Governor Reagan*, 157; Edwards, *Reagan: A Political Biography*, 154.

35. Edwards, *Reagan: A Political Biography*, 154.

36. Ibid.

37. Ronald Reagan, "The Creative Society," 19 April 1966, accessed at www.freerepublic.com/focus/f-news/742041/posts?page=1. All subsequent quotes or discussions of this speech are from this source.

38. Yager, *Ronald Reagan's Journey*, 80.

39. James Madison, no. 51, in *The Federalist*, ed. Michael Lloyd Chadwick (Washington, DC: Global Affairs, 1987), 281.

40. Reagan, speech to Conservative League of Minneapolis.

41. Skinner, Anderson, and Anderson, *Ronald Reagan: A Life in Letters*, 344.

42. Ibid., 347, 624–25.

43. "Inside Ronald Reagan," *Reason*, July 1975, http://reason.com/archives/1975/07/01/inside-ronald-reagan. All subsequent quotes from this interview are taken from this source.

44. Reagan, commencement address at Eureka College.

45. Reagan, speech to Los Angeles County Young Republicans.

46. Reagan, first gubernatorial inaugural address, accessed at http://governors.library.ca.gov/addresses/33-Reagan01.html.

47. Ronald Reagan, second gubernatorial inaugural address, 4 January 1971, accessed at http://governors.library.ca.gov/addresses/33-Reagan02.html.

48. Reagan, speech to Conservative League of Minneapolis.

49. William F. Buckley Jr., "Hunger and the Feds," 20 August 1983, in William F. Buckley Jr., *Right Reason* (Garden City, NY: Doubleday), 154–55.

50. Ibid., 155.

51. Ibid.

52. See Panama Canal Debate, 13 January 1978, broadcast on Buckley's PBS show *The Firing Line*; video is available online at www.youtube.com/watch?v=wYPY8El0Uew.

53. Reagan, "The Creative Society."

54. F. A. Hayek, *The Road to Serfdom* (Chicago: University of Chicago, 1944).

55. Cannon, *Governor Reagan*, 151.

56. Boyarsky, *Rise of Ronald Reagan*, 284; Cannon, *Governor Reagan*, 152 (Reagan got 38–40 percent of the Latino vote).

57. Boyarsky, *Rise of Ronald Reagan*, 152.

58. California Secretary of State, *Statement of the Vote and Supplement to the Statement of Vote, 1962 General Election*, 45, 48–49, accessed at https://archive.org/details/castatem196264cali; California Secretary of State, *Statement of the Vote and Supplement to the Statement of Vote, 1966 General Election*, 68, 71–73, accessed at https://archive.org/details/californiastate-196668cali.

59. *1962 Statement of the Vote*, 3; *1966 Statement of the Vote*, 6.

60. Cannon, *Governor Reagan*, 158.

61. Ibid.

62. Ibid., 159.

63. Ibid., 158.

64. Ronald Reagan, "1966: Year of Decision," listened to at RPL, July 2016.

CHAPTER 5: CALIFORNIA POLITICAL THEATER: RONALD REAGAN PRESENTS

1. Morris, *Dutch*, 345.

2. Cannon, *Governor Reagan*, 182. See also Boyarsky, *Rise of Ronald Reagan*, 173.

3. Reagan, first gubernatorial inaugural address.

4. Reagan, *An American Life*, 158.

5. See the discussion in chapter 2.

6. Cannon, *Governor Reagan*, 189.

7. Ibid., 194.

8. Ibid., 199.

9. Reagan, *An American Life*, 169.

10. Cannon, *Governor Reagan*, 200.

11. Ibid., 282.

12. Ibid., 283.

13. "Estimated Average Costs for California Residents, 2016–17," under "Admissions," http://admission.universityofcalifornia.edu/paying-for-uc/tuition-and-cost/, accessed 1 October 2016.

14. Edwards, *Reagan: A Political Biography*, 189.

15. Ibid., 190.

16. Cannon, *Governor Reagan*, 287.

17. Ibid., 186.

18. Ibid.

19. Skinner, Anderson, and Anderson, *Ronald Reagan: A Life in Letters*, 764.

20. Cannon, *Governor Reagan*, 255.

21. Ibid., 203.

22. Ibid., 263.

23. Ibid., 204.

24. Ronald Reagan, speech to California Republican Assembly, 1 April 1967, accessed at https://reaganlibrary.archives.gov/archives/speeches/govspeech/04011967a.htm. All subsequent quotes of this speech come from this source.

25. Reagan, *An American Life*, 171, 189.

26. CBS News, "What About Ronald Reagan?," 12 December 1967, viewed at RPL, July 2016.

27. Kent Steffgen, *Here's the Rest of Him* (Reno, NV: Forsight Books, 1968), 19; available online at https://archive.org/details/SteffgenKentHeresTheRestOfHim1968.

28. Ibid., 19–20.

29. Ibid., 53, 54, 57.

30. Ibid., 58.

31. Ibid.

32. Ibid., 139.

33. Ibid., 138.

34. Ibid., 137–40.

35. Ibid., 156.

36. Skinner, Anderson, and Anderson, *Ronald Reagan: A Life in Letters*, 613–14.

37. See Cannon, *Governor Reagan*, 206–14; Morris, *Dutch*, 351–52.

38. Reagan, speech to California Republican Assembly.

39. Steffgen, *Here's the Rest of Him*, 153.

40. One such man, S. I. Hayakawa, would be elected himself to the United States Senate in 1976.

41. Fred Barnes, "Unearthing the Eisenhower-Reagan Connection," *The Weekly Standard*, 10 October 2016, www.weeklystandard.com/unearthing-the-eisenhower-reagan-connection/article/2004653.

42. CBS News, "Town Meeting of the World," viewed at RPL, July 2016, https://www.youtube.com/watch?v=I1g8HaE4ArI.

43. Hayward, *Age of Reagan: Fall of the Old Liberal Order*, 170.

44. CBS News, "Town Meeting of the World."

45. "Helms Raps Reagan's Support of Duarte," *Daytona Beach Morning Journal*, 26 February 1982, accessed at https://news.google.com/newspapers?nid=1873&dat=19820226&id=_VAfAAAAIBAJ&sjid=8dEEAAAAIBAJ&pg=2896,5835603&hl=en.

46. William A. Link, *Righteous Warrior: Jesse Helms and the Rise of Modern Conservatism* (New York: St. Martin's Press, 2008), 245–51.

47. Russell Crandall, *The Salvador Option*, (New York: Cambridge University Press, 2016), 195; Roy Boland, *Culture and Customs of El Salvador*, (Westport, CT: Greenwood Press, 2001), 62.

48. "A Chance to Lead," *Time*, 16 August 1968, available on CNN.com, www.cnn.com/ALLPOLITICS/1996/analysis/back.time/9608/19/index.shtml.

49. Tom Wicker, "Nixon Is Nominated on the First Ballot," *New York Times*, 9 August 1968, https://partners.nytimes.com/library/politics/camp/680809convention-gop-ra.html.

50. Ibid.

51. Cannon, *Governor Reagan*, 324.

52. Reagan had opposed Kuchel's renomination when he was last on the ballot in 1962, while Lou Cannon says Rafferty's campaign was "run by ultraconservatives who had denounced Reagan for betraying the conservative cause when he raised taxes" (Cannon, *Governor Reagan*, 325). Rafferty beat Kuchel by 50–47 percent. See "Kuchel Loses to Rafferty in California," *Chicago Tribune*, 6 June 1968, http://archives.chicagotribune.com/1968/06/06/page/68/article/kuchel-loses-to-rafferty-in-california.

53. The dams in question were the Feather River and Dos Rios dams. See Cannon, *Governor Reagan*.

54. George Skelton, "The Man in the White Hat Who Saved the Sierra," *Los Angeles Times*, 28 July 1997, http://articles.latimes.com/1997/jul/28/news/mn-17071.

55. See Cannon, *Governor Reagan*, 310–14.

56. Ibid., 364.

57. Ibid., 336.

58. California Secretary of State, *Statement of the Vote and Supplement to the Statement of Vote 1970 General Election*, 10, 71, 74, accessed at https://archive.org/details/statementofvote197072cali.

59. See Cannon, *Governor Reagan*, 349.

60. Morris, *Dutch*, 368.

61. Ibid., 350.

62. Reagan, *An American Life*, 185.

63. Skinner, Anderson, and Anderson, *Ronald Reagan: A Life in Letters*, 200–1.

64. Cannon, *Governor Reagan*, 350.

65. Ibid., 351.

66. Reagan, second gubernatorial inaugural address.

67. At the same time, Reagan quietly opposed President Nixon's proposal to establish a minimum guaranteed income for every American. The Family Assistance Plan would have guaranteed every family of four $1,600 a year, plus $800 in food stamps, in exchange for work requirements. See Peter Passell and Leonard Ross, "Daniel Moynihan and President-Elect Nixon: How Charity Didn't Begin at Home," *New York Times*, 13 January 1973, www.nytimes.com/books/98/10/04/specials/moynihan-income.html.

68. Cannon, *Governor Reagan*, 359.

69. Skinner, *A Life in Letters*, 209.

70. Reagan, *An American Life*, 189.

71. Cannon, *Governor Reagan*, 360.

72. *Serrano v. Priest*, 5 Cal. 3d 584 (1971).

73. Cannon, *Governor Reagan*, 363.

74. *Ibid.*, 315.

75. *Ibid.*, 371–75.

76. Ronald Reagan, "Reflections on the Failure of Proposition 1," *National Review*, 7 December 1973, www.nationalreview.com/article/210999/re flections-failure-proposition-1-governor-ronald-reagan.

77. "Reagan's Proposition 1 Ads," YouTube video, posted by "danieljbmitchell," 16 July 1007, www.youtube.com/watch?v=kyYoaTmN5pU.

78. Reagan, "Reflections on the Failure of Proposition 1."

79. Ibid.

80. Ronald Reagan, *National Review*, December 1964, as reprinted in Frank Rich, "Proud Loser," *New York*, 11 March 2013.

81. See Howard Jarvis Taxpayers Association, "Proposition 13: A Look Back," hjta.org/propositions/proposition-13/proposition-13-look-back.

82. Skinner, Anderson, and Anderson, *Ronald Reagan: A Life in Letters*, 353.

83. Richard Nixon, presidential resignation speech, 8 August 1974, accessed at www.pbs.org/newshour/spc/character/links/nixon_speech.html.

84. The California Poll, "Reagan's Performance as Governor Rated Higher By California Public Than Pat Brown's Was," Field Research Corporation, release #829, 27 August 1974, accessed at ucdata.berkeley.edu/pubs/CalPolls/829.pdf.

85. Ronald Reagan, announcement, 20 November 1975, https://reaganlibrary.archives.gov/archives/reference/11.20.75.html.

86. Skinner, Anderson, and Anderson, *Ronald Reagan: A Life in Letters*, 241.

87. Ibid.

88. Ibid.

89. Ibid.

90. Cannon, *Governor Reagan*, 388–89.

91. Reagan, *An American Life*, 188–90.

CHAPTER 6: REAGAN'S "DEATH VALLEY DAYS"

1. "Inside Ronald Reagan."

2. Ronald Reagan, "Let Them Go Their Way," delivered to second CPAC convention, 1 March 1975, http://reagan2020.us/speeches/Let_Them_Go_Their_Way.asp. All quotes, paraphrases, and discussions of this speech are taken from or rely upon this source.

3. In research for this book, I discovered that the upperclassman came from

a very prominent political family in his state. His father had been a one-term member of the state legislature, where he gained a reputation as the most conservative member.

4. For the Libertarian Party 1980 platform, see http://issuepedia.org/US/Libertarian_Party/platform/1980; for the Libertarian Party 1972 platform, see http://www.presidency.ucsb.edu/ws/?pid=29615.

5. Cannon, *Governor Reagan*, 394.

6. Reagan, "Let Them Go Their Way."

7. In the interest of full disclosure, Manny is a personal friend whom I met when I was the speakers bureau director for the Yes on Proposition 36 campaign in California in 1984. Proposition 36 was another tax-limitation measure sponsored by a Proposition 13 cosponsor, Howard Jarvis, and Manny was our brightest and most articulate advocate. We have had many cordial and serious discussions about politics over the years, and he is never disagreeable even when disagreeing.

8. "Inside Ronald Reagan."

9. Klausner made clear the depth of this disagreement later in the interview. Reagan was arguing for a two-thirds supermajority to impose any taxes. Klausner responded by saying that libertarians "would like to go all the way to 100 percent requirement for taxes!" Reagan demurred, saying, "I don't know if that would work," but for a libertarian that was exactly the point.

10. In this case, one cannot exclude the possibility that Reagan's father's alcoholism weighed on his mind. Jack Reagan lost jobs or income regularly because of his affliction.

11. Reagan also explained how he came to his philosophy. Although he acknowledged reading "Bastiat and von Mises, and Hayek and Hazlitt"—all libertarian or libertarian-leaning economists—he told Klausner that he "developed his theory of individualism" by himself "by way of the mashed potato circuit." He explained how he was giving speeches about government censorship and discrimination against Hollywood only to discover many other businessmen had similar complaints. This is exactly what he wrote twenty-four years later in his autobiography. Libertarians interested in Reagan's views on Ayn Rand will be sorely disappointed. He told

Klausner that he had not read *Atlas Shrugged* and that he had not read anything by Rand since *The Fountainhead*. That book was published in 1943 and was developed by the studio which Reagan was under contract to, Warner Brothers, into a major A-list film released in 1949. One will always wonder if Reagan's interest in *The Fountainhead* was due less to an interest in Rand's ideas and more because Reagan coveted the starring role as the handsome, heroic, and virile hero, Howard Roark.

12. Gerhard Peters, "Federal Budget Receipts and Outlays," *The American Presidency Project*, ed. John T. Woolley and Gerhard Peters (Santa Barbara, CA: University of California Press, 1999–2012). Available from the World Wide Web: http://www.presidency.ucsb.edu/data/budget.php.

13. Cannon, *Governor Reagan*, 407–8.

14. Ibid.

15. Ibid. Reagan would later add sections to his stump speech to address concerns raised by this speech. The rough draft for those added sections mentions "ed., housing, community development, manpower training, revenue sharing & welfare." See Skinner, Anderson, and Anderson, *Reagan in His Own Hand*, 457.

16. Ibid.

17. Morris, *Dutch*, 397–99; Cannon, *Governor Reagan*, 407–15.

18. Cannon, *Governor Reagan*, 412; John Elmer, "Reagan Recants on $90 Billion, but Not Spending Cut," *Chicago Tribune*, 13 January 1976, http://archives.chicagotribune.com/1976/01/13/page/2/article/reagan-recants-on-90-billion-but-not-spending-cut.

19. Skinner, Anderson, and Anderson, *Reagan in His Own Hand*, 459.

20. Ibid., 458–59.

21. Ibid., 461.

22. Ibid., 462.

23. Reagan's biographer Edmund Morris notes that Reagan's practice of spelling "bureaucracy" this way was not an example of illiteracy or stupidity; rather, he was merely following the dictates of the "simplified spelling" approach employed in public schools when he was young. See Morris, *Dutch*, 704.

24. Skinner, Anderson, and Anderson, *Reagan in His Own Hand*, 463.

25. Ibid., 465–66.

26. Cannon, *Governor Reagan*, 411.

27. Reagan's view largely prevailed within conservatism and the Republican Party in the decades since this speech. The landmark welfare reform bill, passed in 1996, was essentially a Reaganesque turning over of federal funds to states with few regulations attached as to how state welfare programs were run. Today's GOP proposes applying this "block grant" approach to a host of social service programs in the very areas Reagan discussed over four decades ago.

28. Reagan, *An American Life*, 196–98. All subsequent quotations regarding his motivations for running in 1976 are taken from these pages.

29. On this point, see Reagan's letter to Lorraine Wagner, 13 July 1961. ("You won't find the threat of socialism spelled out in the bill—it never is. It comes through the rules and regulations the Department of Health, Education, and Welfare puts into effect to administer the bill.") (Skinner, Anderson, and Anderson, *Ronald Reagan: A Life in Letters*, 579.)

30. Ronald Reagan, "To Restore America," 31 March 1976, accessed at https://reaganlibrary.archives.gov/archives/reference/3.31.76.html.

31. Gerald Ford was a longtime Congressman from Michigan and the House Republican leader when President Richard Nixon appointed him pursuant to the Constitution's 25th Amendment to succeed Vice President Spiro Agnew after Agnew's resignation in October 1973. Ford became president when Nixon resigned on August 9, 1974.

32. Reagan, *An American Life*, 200.

33. Ford authorized a public-affairs campaign to mobilize anti-inflation sentiment, which included printing millions of "WIN" buttons people could wear on their clothes. I remember having one of those buttons myself as a middle schooler, but apparently adults thought they were a bit more foolish than a thirteen-year-old did, and they were quickly removed from circulation.

34. In the 2016 race, Texas senator Ted Cruz became the second major candidate to do this, selecting his former rival Carly Fiorina as his running mate in the days before the crucial Indiana primary.

35. Skinner, Anderson, and Anderson, *Ronald Reagan: A Life in Letters*, 589–90.

36. Ibid.

37. One Republican elector cast his ballot for Reagan.

38. Reagan, *An American Life*, 203.

39. Ibid., 203–4.

40. Ronald Reagan, "The New Republican Party," 6 February 1977, accessed at http://reagan2020.us/speeches/The_New_Republican_Party.asp. All subsequent quotes or paraphrases of this speech are taken from this source.

41. Skinner, Anderson, and Anderson, *Reagan in His Own Hand*, p. xiii.

42. The Italian prime minister Aldo Moro was kidnapped and murdered by the Red Brigade in 1978. See ibid., 128n.

43. Ibid., 23.

44. Ibid., 30.

45. See, for example, ibid., 101–2.

46. Ibid., 75–98 (seventeen commentaries opposing SALT II or arms control in general).

47. See, for example, ibid., 84, 118.

48. Ibid., 113.

49. Claremont McKenna College was then known as Claremont Men's College. The school went coed in 1976 but did not change its name until 1981.

50. Skinner, Anderson, and Anderson, *Reagan in His Own Hand*, 272.

51. Reagan, speech to California Fertilizer Association.

52. Reagan, speech to Phoenix Chamber of Commerce.

53. "Historical Inflation Rates: 1914–2017," Coin News Media Group LLC, www.usinflationcalculator.com/inflation/historical-inflation-rates.

54. See, for example, Ronald Reagan, "Losing Freedom by Installments," speech to the Conservative League of Minneapolis, 29 January 1962, listened to at RPL, July 2016.

55. Skinner, Anderson, and Anderson, *Reagan in His Own Hand*, 367.

56. Ibid., 371–73.

57. See, for example, Kurt Schuparra, *Triumph of the Right: The Rise of the California Conservative Movement, 1945–66* (Armonk, NY: M. E. Sharpe, 1998), 37; Skinner, Anderson, and Anderson, *Ronald Reagan: A Life in Letters*, 359 (letter to David Denholm of Californians for Right to Work explaining his opposition to right-to-work laws, 22 September 1970).

58. "Ronald Reagan Supported Right to Work 'Wholeheartedly,'" YouTube video, posted by "Right2WorkCommittee," 24 October 2011, www.you tube.com/watch?v=dxlFOR_Ro8w.

59. For Reagan's belief in the average American, see Skinner, Anderson, and Anderson, *Ronald Reagan: A Life in Letters*, 18 (the common American is in fact "very uncommon").

60. Ibid., 297.

61. Ibid., 263.

62. Reagan argued that these standards allowed "anyone unemployed" to collect checks without also forcing those people "to take any job which he or she is capable of performing." See ibid., 266.

63. Ibid., 268.

64. Ibid., 392–93.

65. Ibid., 390.

66. Ibid., 393.

67. Ibid., 271.

68. Ibid., 394–95.

69. Ibid., 10.

70. Reagan had been faced with abortion in 1967 when a bill legalizing the practice reached his desk. He agonized over the decision but ultimately signed the bill. For descriptions of that episode, see Morris, *Dutch*, 351–52; Cannon, *Governor Reagan*, 208–14.

71. Jon Nordhelmer, "Reagan Criticizes U.S. School Role," *New York Times*, 3 June 1976, www.nytimes.com/1976/06/03/archives/reagan-criticizes-us -school-role-makes-campaign-vow-to-get-federal.html.

72. Skinner, Anderson, and Anderson, *Ronald Reagan: A Life in Letters*, 366–67 (letter to Mr. Henri Lagueux, June 1976).

73. Skinner, Anderson, and Anderson, *Reagan in His Own Hand*, 351.

74. Skinner, Anderson, and Anderson, *Ronald Reagan: A Life in Letters*, 361 (letter to Luella Huggins, 5 February 1979).

75. www.upi.com/Archives/1984/10/07/EQUAL-RIGHTS-AMENDMENT -Reagan-Im-for-the-E-and/4346465969600/.

76. Skinner, Anderson, and Anderson, *Ronald Reagan: A Life in Letters*, 365 (letter to Reverend Gay).

77. See Gerard Magliocca, "Ronald Reagan and Gay Rights," 18 October 2010, Concurring Opinions, https://concurringopinions.com/archives /2010/10/ronald-reagan-and-gay-rights.html, which contains a copy of the op-ed Reagan wrote for the 1 November 1978 *Los Angeles Examiner*. Subsequent quotes and paraphrases of the op-ed are taken from this source.

78. Skinner, Anderson, and Anderson, *Ronald Reagan: A Life in Letters*, 210–11 (letter to Mr. Squires, 5 May 1979).

79. Ibid., 340–41 (letter to Mr. and Mrs. Fitzgerald, November 1980).

80. See ibid., 365, 366–67 (letters to Reverend Gay and Mr. Henri Lagueux).

81. Ibid., 257.

82. Ibid., 269 (letter to the Cleaver family, 16 December 1974).

83. Ibid., 578–79. All subsequent quotes and paraphrases of this letter come from this source.

84. Ibid., 344.

85. See Ronald Reagan, "Announcement for Presidential Candidacy," 13 November 1979, https://reaganlibrary.archives.gov/archives/reference/11.13.79 .html . All quotes or paraphrases of this speech come from this source.

86. Reagan, *An American Life*, 205.

87. Ibid.

88. Ibid.

89. Ibid.

90. Theodore H. White, *America in Search of Itself: The Making of the President, 1956–80* (New York: Harper & Row, 1982), 237.

91. Ibid.

92. Ibid., 240.

93. Ibid., 303–4. See also Cannon, *Governor Reagan*, 459.

94. Ibid., 31–32.

95. Ronald Reagan, acceptance speech at the 1980 Republican Convention, 17 July 1980, accessed at https://reaganlibrary.archives.gov/archives/refer ence/7.17.80.html. All subsequent quotes or paraphrases from this speech are taken from this source.

96. Reagan was the first Republican nominee to mention Roosevelt by name in his acceptance speech, positively or negatively, since FDR's death in 1945.

97. Franklin Delano Roosevelt, acceptance speech at the 1932 Democratic Party Convention, accessed at https://fdrlibrary.files.wordpress.com/2012/09/1932.pdf.

98. See http://issuepedia.org/US/Libertarian_Party/platform/1980.

99. "What About the Libertarian Party?", American Institute for Economic Research, *Research Reports* 47, no. 43 (27 October 1980), www.aier.org/sites/default/files/Files/Documents/Research/584/RR198043.pdf.

100. Joel Kotkin, "Libertarian Party," *Washington Post*, 31 March 1980, www.washingtonpost.com/archive/politics/1980/03/31/libertarian-party/51c8296b-b03c-4b2d-a093-5bfbe6602158/?utm_term=.1f3c71ba6ad8.

101. "Libertarian Candidate Clark Attacks Reagan and Carter Stands," *Harvard Crimson*, 10 October 1980, www.thecrimson.com/article/1980/10/10/libertarian-candidate-clark-attacks-reagan-carter.

102. Cannon, *Governor Reagan*, 487; Morris, *Dutch*, 409.

103. Cannon, *Rise to Power*, 491.

104. Hayward, *Age of Reagan: Fall of the Old Liberal Order*, 698–99.

105. See Reagan, *An American Life*, 221, for Reagan's description of the pent-up frustration that led to his restrained outburst.

106. Commission on Presidential Debates, Transcript of 28 October 1980 Debate, www.debates.org/index.php?page=october-28-1980-debate-transcript.

107. Ibid.

108. Roosevelt, fireside chat 5.

109. You can watch this for yourself at "NBC News Decision 1980 Reagan Wins," YouTube video, posted by "haiker16," 16 March 2009, www.youtube.com/watch?v=PsDe-8cOSYY.

110. John Anderson's independent campaign received 6.6 percent of the vote.

111. The states in question are Maryland, Delaware, Virginia, West Virginia, North Carolina, South Carolina, Florida, Georgia, Alabama, Mississippi, Tennessee, Kentucky, Louisiana, Arkansas, Missouri, and Texas. West Virginia was part of Virginia in 1861, but split from it to join the Union in 1863. Carter lost only Virginia among these states in 1976.

112. Reagan's extreme gain in Arkansas may have been partly due to President Carter's decision to house Cuban refugees at a military base near Fort

Smith. Tales of crimes committed by these refugees turned the state so heavily against national Democrats that voters even defeated the young Democratic governor running for reelection. Bill Clinton made his first comeback two years later, beating the Republican who had turned him out in 1980.

113. New York City Jews were particularly incensed by the Carter administration's vote in the United Nations to condemn Zionism as racism.

114. Reagan, *An American Life*, 221.

115. Michael Barone and Grant Ujifusa, *Almanac of American Politics, 1982* (Washington, DC: Barone & Company, 1981). By contrast, thirty-six of the fifty-four Republican senators received ACU ratings above 80 in 2014–15; eighteen had ratings above 90. For more information on ACU ratings, see the organization's website at http://acuratings.conservative.org/acu-federal -legislative-ratings/?year1=2015&chamber=13&state1=0&sortable=1.

116. Barone and Ujifusa, *Almanac of American Politics, 1982*. Only two Republicans (Lisa Murkowski of Alaska and Susan Collins of Maine) had ACU ratings below 50 in the most recent Congress. No Republican senator had an ADA rating above 50 in 2015. See www.adaction.org/media/ votingrecords/2015.pdf.

CHAPTER 7: PRESIDENT REAGAN

1. See Skinner, Anderson, and Anderson, *Ronald Reagan: A Life in Letters*, 511 (for legal immigration from Mexico) and 369 (for immigration quotas for people "coming to this country for economic betterment" "because that kind of immigrant is to be found in every corner of the world and there is no way we could, without limit, take all who want to come here").

2. Reagan, *An American Life*, 287.

3. Ronald Reagan, first inaugural address, 20 January 1981, accessed at https://reaganlibrary.archives.gov/archives/speeches/1981/12081a.htm. All subsequent quotes and paraphrases of this speech come from this source.

4. Ronald Reagan, Nationally Televised Address to the Nation on the Economy, 5 February 1981, accessed at https://reaganlibrary.archives.gov/ar chives/speeches/1981/20581c.htm. All subsequent quotes and paraphrases of this speech come from this source.

5. Ronald Reagan, Address before a Joint Session of the Congress on the Program for Economic Recovery, 18 February 1981, accessed at https://reaganlibrary.archives.gov/archives/speeches/1981/21881a.htm.

6. See Reagan, *An American Life*, 235.

7. Reagan's first words to Nancy after the shooting were, "Honey, I forgot to duck." He also asked his surgeon before going under if he was a Republican. "Today, Mr. President," the surgeon replied, "we are all Republicans." Reagan, *An American Life*, 260–61.

8. Douglas Brinkley, ed., *The Reagan Diaries* (New York: Harper Perennial, 2007), 21. Thus did he "reluctantly" include something he had proposed over two decades prior. See Reagan, *An American Life*, 286.

9. Reagan, *An American Life*, 285.

10. Reagan, Address to the Nation on the Program for Economic Security, 24 September 1981, accessed at https://reaganlibrary.archives.gov/archives/speeches/1981/92481d.htm.

11. Ibid.

12. William Greider, "The Education of David Stockman," *The Atlantic*, December 1981, www.theatlantic.com/magazine/archive/1981/12/the-education-of-david-stockman/305760/. All subsequent quotes and paraphrases are taken from this source.

13. Roosevelt used the phrase "leak through" to describe "trickle down" in his 1932 Democratic Convention acceptance speech. He used "trickle down" directly in an October campaign speech in Detroit (see www.presidency.ucsb.edu/ws/?pid=88393) and also used it in subsequent Fireside Chats.

14. Skinner, Anderson, and Anderson, *Ronald Reagan: A Life in Letters*, 212.

15. Ibid., 341.

16. Ibid., 318.

17. Ibid., 617.

18. Ibid., 318.

19. See Reagan, speech to the California Fertilizer Association. All three specific items mentioned in this paragraph were mentioned in that talk.

20. Reagan, *An American Life*, 231.

21. Cannon, *President Reagan*, 69.

22. Reagan, 1961 speech to Phoenix Chamber of Commerce.

23. Ibid.; 1958 Speech to California Fertilizer Association (approves of a different Herlong-sponsored tax bill).

24. David Stockman, *The Triumph of Politics: Why the Reagan Revolution Failed* (New York: Harper & Row, 1986), 50.

25. Cannon, *President Reagan*, 197.

26. Franklin Delano Roosevelt, Campaign Address at Detroit, Michigan, 2 October 1932, www.presidency.ucsb.edu/ws/?pid=88393.

27. Reagan, *An American Life*, 242.

28. Ibid., 255.

29. Ibid., 272.

30. Ibid.

31. Skinner, Anderson, and Anderson, *Ronald Reagan: A Life in Letters*, 401.

32. Reagan, *An American Life*, 315–24.

33. Ibid.

34. Kurt Anderson, "Thunder on the Right," *Time*, 16 August 1982, http://content.time.com/time/subscriber/printout/0,8816,950722,00.html.

35. Ibid.

36. Bill Peterson, "Viguerie Leaves Crane, Enters Connally's Camp," *Washington Post*, 8 August 1979, www.washingtonpost.com/archive/politics/1979/08/08/viguerie-leaves-crane-entnrs-connallys-camp/a0392210-99f3-44e5-b2b7-50ac063d79e9/?utm_term=.f7d62b35c070.

37. Brinkley, *Reagan Diaries*, 94–95.

38. Ibid., 96.

39. Skinner, Anderson, and Anderson, *Ronald Reagan: A Life in Letters*, 294. Writing to the San Diego Republican congressman Clair Burgener, Reagan said he opposed Kemp's idea of a tax cut without spending cuts. Americans would not believe, he wrote, that "lower taxes alone would generate additional funds and solve our deficit problems."

40. Ibid., 332 (letter to Mr. Lennie Pickard).

41. See Anderson, "Thunder on the Right."

42. Ibid.

43. Brinkley, *Reagan Diaries*, 99.

44. Ibid., 120–21.

45. Ronald Reagan, address to members of the British Parliament, 8 June 1982,

accessed at www.heritage.org/research/reports/2002/06/reagans-westmin ster-speech. All subsequent quotes and paraphrases from that speech come from this source.

46. Steven F. Hayward, *The Age of Reagan: The Conservative Counterrevolution, 1980–1989* (New York: Crown Forum, 2009), 256.

47. Reagan's diaries include three separate entries for 1983 and 1984 in which he notes that his staff directly or indirectly pushed him to increase taxes. Stockman is mentioned in each. See Brinkley, *Reagan Diaries*, 153, 210, 283.

48. "Legislative History: Summary of P.L. 98–21 (H.R. 1900), Social Security Amendments of 1983—Signed on April 20, 1983," prepared by the Social Security Administration, Office of Legislative and Congressional Affairs, 11/26/1984, www.ssa.gov/history/1983amend.html.

49. Fewer than half of the Republicans in the House backed the compromise on final passage, with the future presidential hopefuls Newt Gingrich, Jack Kemp, and Ron Paul all voting no or abstaining. See Social Security Administration, "Vote Tallies: 1983 Amendments," www.ssa.gov/history/ tally1983.html.

50. Skinner, Anderson, and Anderson, *Ronald Reagan: A Life in Letters*, 625.

51. Reagan, *An American Life*, 324–25.

52. Frank Newport, Jeffrey M. Jones, and Lydia Saad, "Ronald Reagan from the People's Perspective," Gallup Organization, June 7, 2004, www.gallup .com/poll/11887/ronald-reagan-from-peoples-perspective-gallup-poll-re view.aspx.

53. "Gallup Presidential Trial-Heat Trends," Gallup Organization, www.gallup .com/poll/110548/gallup-presidential-election-trialheat-trends-19362004 .aspx#4.

54. Reagan, *An American Life*, 326.

55. Reagan, Remarks at a Ceremony Commemorating the Fortieth Anniversary of the Normandy D-day Invasion, 6 June 1984, accessed at https:// reaganlibrary.archives.gov/archives/speeches/1984/60684a.htm. All quotes and paraphrases of this speech are taken from this source.

56. George W. Bush, transcript of remarks aboard the USS *Abraham Lincoln*, 1 May 2003, CNN.com, www.cnn.com/2003/US/05/01/bush.tran

script/. All subsequent quotes and paraphrases of that speech are taken from this source.

57. Ronald Reagan, State of the Union Address, 26 January 1982, accessed at https://reaganlibrary.archives.gov/archives/speeches/1982/12682c.htm. All quotes and paraphrases are taken from this source.

58. Ronald Reagan, "The Agenda Is Victory," address to the ninth annual CPAC conference, 26 February 1982, accessed at http://reagan2020.us/speeches/The_Agenda_is_Victory.asp.

59. Ronald Reagan, 1983 State of the Union Address, 25 January 1983, accessed at https://reaganlibrary.archives.gov/archives/speeches/1983/12583c.htm. All quotes and paraphrases of this speech are taken from this source.

60. "Gallup Presidential Trial-Heat Trends," Gallup Organization, www.gallup .com/poll/110548/gallup-presidential-election-trialheat-trends-19362004 .aspx#4.

61. Ibid.

62. Ronald Reagan, Acceptance Speech at the Republican National Convention in Dallas, Texas, 23 August 1984, accessed at https://reaganlibrary .archives.gov/archives/speeches/1984/82384f.htm. All quotes and paraphrases of this speech are drawn from this source.

63. Ronald Reagan, "Losing Freedom by Installments," address to the Conservative League of Minneapolis, 29 January 1962, listened to at RPL, July 2016. All subsequent quotes from or paraphrases of that speech comes from this source.

64. Brinkley, *Reagan Diaries*, 65.

65. Reagan, *An American Life*, 328.

66. Ibid., 329.

67. "Debating Our Destiny: 1984: There You Go Again . . . Again," Public Broadcasting System and McNeil/Lehrer Productions, https://web .archive.org/web/20001212070100/http://www.pbs.org/newshour/de batingourdestiny/dod/1984-broadcast.html.

68. Ronald Reagan, Second Inaugural Address, 21 January 1985, accessed at https://reaganlibrary.archives.gov/archives/speeches/1985/12185a.htm. All quotes and paraphrases of this speech come from this source.

69. Ronald Reagan, State of the Union Address, 6 February 1985, accessed at https://reaganlibrary.archives.gov/archives/speeches/1985/20685e.htm. All quotes and paraphrases of this speech are taken from this source.

70. Reagan, speech to Phoenix Chamber of Commerce.

71. Skinner, Anderson, and Anderson, *Ronald Reagan: A Life in Letters*, 348.

72. Reagan, speech to California Fertilizer Association.

73. Congressional Research Service, "H.R. 3838 (99th): Tax Reform Act of 1986," 18 September 1986, GovTrack, www.govtrack.us/congress/bills/99/hr3838/summary#libraryofcongress.

74. Ronald Reagan, Remarks on Signing the Tax Reform Act of 1986, 22 October 1986, accessed at www.reagan.utexas/.edu/archives/speeches/1986/102286a.html. All quotes and paraphrases of this speech are taken from this source.

75. Ronald Reagan, Address to the Nation on the Federal Budget and Deficit Reduction, 24 April 1985, accessed at https://reaganlibrary.archives.gov/archives/speeches/1985/42485b.htm. All quotes and paraphrases of this speech are taken from this source.

76. Reagan had opposed farm subsidies consistently throughout his early speeches. See, for example, his speeches to the Phoenix Chamber of Commerce and the Conservative League of Minneapolis.

77. Ronald Reagan, State of the Union Address, 4 February 1986, accessed at https://reaganlibrary.archives.gov/archives/speeches/1986/20486a.htm. All quotes and paraphrases of this speech.

78. Stockman, *Triumph of Politics*, 14.

79. For Stockman's Marxism, see ibid., 21–23; for his embrace of supply-side libertarianism, see ibid., 49.

80. Ibid., 8.

81. Ibid.

82. Ibid., 11.

83. Ibid.

84. Ibid., 11.

85. Ibid., 49–50.

86. Ibid., 49.

87. Ibid., 49–50.

88. Ronald Reagan, address to the National Association of Evangelicals, 8 March 1983, accessed at http://millercenter.org/president/speeches/speech-3409.

89. https://en.wikipedia.org/wiki/File:ReaganBeginsBombingRussia.ogg.

90. Reagan, *An American Life*, 612.

91. Ibid., 614–15.

92. Ibid., 636.

93. Ibid., 641.

94. "Crude Oil Prices—70 Year Historical Chart," 2 March 2017, Macrotrends LLC, www.macrotrends.net/1369/crude-oil-price-history-chart.

95. See Reagan, *An American Life*, 675. (Gorbachev tells Reagan the USSR reneged on a deal to buy American wheat "because of falling oil prices, which meant fewer Soviet dollars for wheat.")

96. Ibid., 664.

97. Ibid., 677.

98. Ibid.

99. Ibid., 678.

100. Ibid., 686.

101. Ibid., 683.

102. Ibid., 696.

103. See the 22 May 1987 issue of *National Review*, available at www.unz.org/Pub/NationalRev-1987may22.

104. Lee Edwards, *William F. Buckley, Jr.: The Maker of a Movement* (ISI Books, 2014). See also Reagan's written reply to Buckley in Skinner, Anderson, and Anderson, *Ronald Reagan: A Life in Letters*, 418 ("I have not changed my belief that we are dealing with an 'evil empire'").

105. Skinner, Anderson, and Anderson, *Ronald Reagan: A Life in Letters*, 384.

106. For Gorbachev's sincerity, see ibid., 386; for Gorbachev being different, see ibid., 414.

107. Ibid., 414–15.

108. Ibid., 420.

109. Rudy Abramson, "Senate Approves INF Treaty 93–5," *Los Angeles Times*, 28 May 1988, http://articles.latimes.com/1988-05-28/news/mn-3390_1_senate-democrats.

110. Skinner, Anderson, and Anderson, *Ronald Reagan: A Life in Letters*, 387.

111. The Right Honorable Theresa May, Speech to Conservative Party Conference, 5 October 2016, accessed at http://press.conservatives.com.

CHAPTER 8: THE TIME IS NOW: REAGAN

1. Ronald Reagan, Explosion of the Space Shuttle *Challenger* Address to the Nation, 28 January 1986, accessed at http://history.nasa.gov/reagan12886.html.

2. See "In Their Own Words: Obama on Reagan," *New York Times*, www.nytimes.com/ref/us/politics/21seelye-text.html.

3. Trends in Party Identification, 1939–2014, Pew Research Center, 7 April 2015, accessed at www.people-press.org/interactives/party-id-trend.

4. CNN National Exit Poll, accessed at CNN.com, www.cnn.com/election/results/exit-polls.

5. See state-level exit polls at CNN.com, www.cnn.com/election/results/exit-polls/wisconsin/president; www.cnn.com/election/results/exit-polls/pennsylvania/president; and www.cnn.com/election/results/exit-polls/michigan/president.

6. The classic skit can be listened to at www.youtube.com/watch?v=-tVzdUczMT0.

7. See William Schneider, "An Insider's View of the Election," *The Atlantic*, July 1988, www.theatlantic.com/past/politics/policamp/insider.htm.

8. Bill Clinton, 1995 State of the Union Address, accessed at http://millercenter.org/president/clinton/speeches/speech-3440.

9. William J. Clinton, "Text of Clinton Government Shutdown Address," 14 November 1995, CNN, www.cnn.com/US/9511/debt_limit/11-14/transcripts/clinton.html for his statement announcing the government shutdown.

10. David Horowitz, "I'm a Uniter, Not a Divider," *Salon*, 6 May 1999, www.salon.com/1999/05/06/bush_2/.

11. Richard Oppel and Jim Yardley, "The 2000 Campaign," *New York Times*, 20 March 2000, www.nytimes.com/2000/03/20/us/2000-campaign-texas-governor-bush-calls-himself-reformer-record-shows-label-may.html.

12. Stephen Buttry, "Candidates Focus on Christian Beliefs," *Des Moines Register*,

15 December 1999, accessed at http://archives.cnn.com/1999/ALLPOLITICS /stories/12/15/religion.register.

13. "Newspaper: Butterfly Ballot Cost Gore White House," 11 March 2001, CNN.com, www.cnn.com/2001/ALLPOLITICS/03/11/palmbeach.recount.

14. Jeanne Sahadi, "Bush's Plan for Social Security," CNN/Money.com, 4 March 2005, http://money.cnn.com/2005/02/02/retirement/stofunion_ socsec/.

15. Sean Sullivan, "The Most Aired Campaign Ad of the Past Decade," *Washington Post*, 8 April 2014, www.washingtonpost.com/news/the-fix/ wp/2014/04/08/watch-obama-hit-mccain-in-the-single-most-aired-cam paign-ad-of-the-past-decade/?utm_term=.f5c1b7b322de.

16. Barack Obama, "Keynote Address 2004 Democratic National Convention," 27 July 2004, www2.gwu.edu/~action/2004/demconv04/obama072704spt .html. All quotes and paraphrases of this speech are taken from this source.

17. See 2008 exit poll, accessed on CNN.com, www.cnn.com/ELECTION/2008 /results/polls/#val=USP00p5.

18. Statewide election results are available on CNN.com: www.cnn.com/ ELECTION/2008/results/polls/#val=IAP00p1 (Iowa); www.cnn.com/ ELECTION/2008/results/polls/#val=MIP00p1 (Michigan); www.cnn .com/ELECTION/2008/results/polls/#val=NHP00p1 (New Hampshire); www.cnn.com/ELECTION/2008/results/polls/#val=INP00p1 (Indiana).

19. See 2008 election poll results on CNN.com, www.cnn.com/ELEC TION/2008/results/polls/#val=OHP00p2.

20. The next four paragraphs are taken from Henry Olsen, "Obama's Young Garden," *National Review*, 23 January 2017. This material is used with permission.

21. Jackie Calmes, "Spotlight Fixed on Geithner, a Man Obama Sought to Keep," *New York Times*, 12 November 2011, www.nytimes.com/2011/11/13/ us/politics/spotlight-fixed-on-geithner-a-man-obama-fought-to-keep.html.

22. The three candidates I have in mind are Sharron Angle in Nevada, Ken Buck in Colorado, and Christine O'Donnell in Delaware.

23. Henry Olsen, "Day of the Democratic Dead," *National Review Online*, 1 November 2010, https://eppc.org/publications/day-of-the-democratic -dead/.

24. See "A Roadmap for America's Future: The Challenge, The Responsibility, The Opportunity," accessed at www.wispolitics.com/1006/_080521_Ryan_roadmap.pdf. All subsequent discussion of the plan's details come from this source.

25. "A Roadmap for America's Future 2.0," January 2010, p. 44 (copy on file with author).

26. See www.taxhistory.org/thp/presreturns.nsf/Returns/9F81699BC7D6DE238525798F0051C35F/$file/M_Romney_2011.pdf.

27. "Roadmap 2.0," 17.

28. See "The Path to Prosperity: A Blueprint for American Renewal," 45–56, accessed at http://budget.house.gov/prosperity/fy2013.htm.

29. The idea was not forgotten. In one televised debate for the 2012 nomination, former House Speaker Newt Gingrich criticized Romney for not lowering capital gains taxes enough, saying offhandedly "we all know the optimal capital gains rate is zero."

30. "The Path to Prosperity," 35–44.

31. Ibid., 66.

32. Ibid., 52–53.

33. Pew Research Center, "Beyond Red vs. Blue Political Typology," 4 May 2011 (copy on file with author).

34. Ibid., 109.

35. Ibid.

36. Ibid.

37. Ibid., 106.

38. Ibid.

39. Ibid., 13.

40. Ibid., 108.

41. Ibid., 109.

42. Ibid.

43. Ibid., 28.

44. Ibid., 100.

45. Ibid., 108.

46. Ibid., 54.

47. Ibid., 31.

48. Ibid., 110.

49. Ibid., 111.

50. Ibid., 110.

51. See Ron Elving, "GOP's 'We Built This' Theme Both Puzzling and Telling," NPR, 31 August 2012, www.npr.org/sections/itsallpolitics /2012/08/31/160370383/gops-we-built-it-refrain-is-both-puzzling-and-telling.

52. Michael Shear and Michael Barbaro, "In Video Clip, Romney Calls 47% 'Dependent' and Feeling Entitled," *New York Times*, 17 September 2012, http://thecaucus.blogs.nytimes.com/2012/09/17/romney-faults-those-de pendent-on-government.

53. Information in this paragraph is taken from a 2012 CNN exit poll, available at www.cnn.com/election/2012/results/race/president/.

54. "Growth and Opportunity Project," Republican National Committee, 2013, accessed at http://goproject.gop.com/rnc_growth_opportunity_ book_2013.pdf.

55. See Page Gardner, "The Rising American Electorate: Game Changers in 2016 Elections," *Huffington Post*, 29 June 2015, www.huffingtonpost.com/ page-gardner/the-rising-american-elect_b_7688610.html.

56. John Judis and Ruy Teixeira, *The Emerging Democratic Majority* (New York: Scribner, 2002).

57. "Growth and Opportunity Project," 7–8.

58. Robert Jones and Daniel Cox, "2013 Hispanic Values Survey," Public Religion Research Institute, executive summary, www.prri.org/research/his panic-values-survey-2013.

59. "Expanding Opportunity in America," House Budget Committee, 24 July 2014, accessed at http://budget.house.gov/uploadedfiles/expanding_op portunity_in_america.pdf.

60. Paul Ryan, "Renewing the American Idea," 15 July 2014, delivered at the Kirby Center of Hillsdale College, accessed at http://paulryan.house.gov/ news/documentsingle.aspx?DocumentID=387848#.U9FLh_mwJvC.

61. Paul Ryan, "A Better Way Up From Poverty," *Wall Street Journal*, 15 August 2014, www.wsj.com/articles/paul-ryan-a-better-way-up-from -poverty-1408141154.

62. Sahil Kapur, "Ted Cruz to GOP: Shut Down the Government or You're

Voting for Obamacare," *Talking Points Memo*, 23 September 2013, http://
talkingpointsmemo.com/dc/ted-cruz-to-gop-shut-down-the-government
-or-you-re-voting-for-obamacare.

63. Burgess Everett, "Cruz Warns McConnell on Debt Ceiling," *Politico*,
20 October 2015, www.politico.com/story/2015/10/default-republicans-
cruz-mcconnell-214978.

64. Fred Barbash, "Bad Blood: John Boehner and His Tormentor Ted Cruz,"
Washington Post, 28 September 2015, www.washingtonpost.com/news/
morning-mix/wp/2015/09/28/bad-blood-john-boehner-and-the-tormenter
-he-called-jackass-ted-cruz/?utm_term=.c046ceddd799.

65. Tony Lee, "Ted Cruz Urges Boldness in Acceptance Speech for Claremont
Institute's Churchill Award," Breitbart.com, 19 March 2014, www.breitbart
.com/big-government/2014/03/19/ted-cruz-receives-claremont-institute-s
-churchill-award-urges-boldness-over-timidity-in-troubled-times.

66. Ted Cruz, Claremont Institute address, quoted in Henry Olsen, "Forget
the Alamo," *National Review*, 20 October 2014, www.nationalreview.
com/article/390811/forget-alamo-henry-olsen. Material from this article
is used in this and the following paragraph with permission.

67. See Olsen, "Day of the Democratic Dead."

68. The material discussing the impact of the Muslim ban and the role of the
concepts of citizenship and nationalism in Trump's appeal is taken from
Henry Olsen, "Trump's Faction," *National Review*, 9 May 2016, accessed
at https://eppc.org/publications/trumps-faction (used with permission).

69. Bush dealt with this criticism by saying the nominee had to be willing to
"lose the primary to win the general" election. Peter Sullivan, "Jeb Bush:
Republicans Have to 'Lose the Primary to Win the General,'" The Hill.
com, 2 December 2014, http://thehill.com/blogs/ballot-box/225681-jeb
-bush-lose-the-primary-to-win-the-general.

70. See the 2016 exit polls for Iowa, Michigan, Ohio, Pennsylvania, and Wisconsin on CNN.com, www.cnn.com/election/results/exit-polls.

71. Henry Olsen, "Setting the Record Straight About the White Working
Class," 17 October 2013, *The American*, accessed at www.aei.org/publica
tion/setting-the-record-straight-about-the-white-working-class.

72. See the national exit polls for 2012 and 2016 on CNN.com, www.cnn

.com/election/2012/results/race/president/ (2012) and www.cnn.com/
election/results/exit-polls (2016).

73. Between 2006 and 2016, the working-class counties that backed Trump
had supported the Democrats Debbie Stabenow and Jennifer Granholm
in Michigan, the Democrat Tammy Baldwin in Wisconsin, and the Republican Joni Ernst in Iowa. Demographically similar counties in other
states had also backed women such as the Democrat Heidi Heitkamp in
North Dakota, the Democrat Amy Klobuchar in Minnesota, and the Republicans Olympia Snowe and Susan Collins in Maine.

74. The counties in question are Dunn, Pepin, Buffalo, Trempealeau, Jackson,
Lincoln, Price, Sawyer, Forest, Door, Vernon, Crawford, Grant, Richland,
Adams, Sauk, Columbia, Lafayette, Racine, Kenosha, and Winnebago.

75. David Nir, "Daily Kos Elections' Presidential Results by Congressional District for the 2016 and 2012 Elections," 19 November 2016, DailyKos.com,
www.dailykos.com/story/2012/11/19/1163009/-Daily-Kos-Elections-presi
dential-results-by-congressional-district-for-the-2012-2008-elections.

76. Goldwater, *Conscience*, 8 (emphasis in original).

77. Ibid., 6.

78. Ibid., 66.

79. Martin Tolchin, "Retreat in Congress; The Catastrophic-Care Debacle—A
Special Report; How the New Medicare Law Fell on Hard Times in a Hurry,"
9 October 1989, *New York Times*, www.nytimes.com/1989/10/09/us/re
treat-congress-catastrophic-care-debacle-special-report-new-medicare-law-fell
.html.

80. Ted Cruz, presidential announcement speech, accessed at www.wash
ingtonpost.com/politics/transcript-ted-cruzs-speech-at-liberty-university
/2015/03/23/41c4011a-d168-11e4-a62f-ee745911a4ff_story.html?utm_
term=.dbc9aef4bd39.

81. Ted Cruz, "A Simple Flat Tax for Economic Growth," *Wall Street Journal*,
28 October 2015, www.wsj.com/articles/a-simple-flat-tax-for-economic
-growth-1446076134.

82. Rob Portman, "Heading Off the Entitlement Meltdown," *Wall Street
Journal*, 21 July 2014, www.wsj.com/articles/rob-portman-heading-off-
the-entitlement-meltdown-1405983479.

83. Reagan, speech to California Fertilizer Association.
84. David E. Rosenbaum, "Reagan's 'Safety Net' Proposal: Who Will Land, Who Will Fall; News Analysis," 17 March 1981, *New York Times*, www .nytimes.com/1981/03/17/us/reagan-s-safety-net-proposal-who-will-land -who-will-fall-news-analysis.html.
85. Mr. Alameda, a funeral home operator, passed away earlier this decade.
86. Christopher Chantrill, "Annual Federal Deficit Fiscal Years 1900 to 2020," *US Government Debt*, www.usgovernmentdebt.us/spending_ chart_1900_2020USp_XXs2li011tcn_G0f_Annual_Federal_Deficit.
87. Christopher Chantrill, "Combined Gross Public Debt Fiscal Years 1900 to 2020," *US Government Debt*, www.usgovernmentdebt.us/spending_ chart_1900_2020USp_XXs2li011tcn_H0sH0lH0f_Combined_Gross_ Public_Debt.

INDEX

Great Depression, 150
 FDR's New Deal and, 6, 11
 GDP during, 5
 government "relief" and, 6
 Hoover's opposition to federal action
  and, 6–7
 poor Republican leadership and,
  5, 6
 presidential election of 1932 and, 3
 Reagan's family and, 11
 social safety net lacking and, 5, 6
 stock market crash of 1929, 5
 unemployment in, 5
 voter shift to FDR-led Democrats,
  xii, 4, 5
Great Society, xiv
 AFDC and, 95
 California's Medi-Cal and, 102,
  106–7
 Reagan on "the Republican
  approach" versus, 76
 Reagan's attack on and "The Myth
  of the Great Society" (1965),
  73–74
 Reagan's Creative Society contrasted
  with, 83–92
 Reagan's undoing of, xvii, 134, 211
 as Reagan's "welfare state," 211–12
Greece, 16
Greider, William, 192
 "The Education of David
  Stockman," 192–93
Grenada, 205, 209

Haig, Alexander "Al," 201
Hamilton, Alexander, 8
Harley-Davidson company, 265
Harrison, William Henry, 152
Hart, Gary, 209
Hayakawa, S. I., 288n40
Hayek, Friedrich, *The Road to Serfdom*,
 91
Hayward, Stephen, *The Age of Reagan*,
 20

health care, xiii, 5, 46, 48–49, 111
 California's Medi-Cal, 95, 102,
  106–7, 122, 123
 Clinton's national health care bill, 231
 Kerr-Mills Act, xiii, xvi, 49, 87, 111,
  145, 155, 168, 178
 McCain's plan, 237, 241–42
 Obamacare, 239, 250, 260, 264
 Reagan and, xiii, xvi, 48–49, 87,
  102, 104, 106–7, 111, 113, 145,
  155, 163–64, 168–69, 178, 187,
  211, 216, 264
 Reagan on state control of, versus
  federal, 145–46
 Reagan's catastrophic health
  insurance, 169, 187, 216, 260
 Ryan's Roadmap agenda and, 241
 socialized medicine, 11, 49, 111,
  113, 168, 169
 See also Medicaid; Medicare
Heitkamp, Heidi, 310n73
Helms, Jesse, 116, 148, 200, 202, 222
Here's the Rest of Him (Steffgen), 110
Herlong-Baker tax bill, 47–48, 195
Hinckley, John, 191
Hispanic voters, 247–48
 Mexican Americans for Reagan, 93
 Public Religion Research Institute's
  2013 Hispanic Values Survey, 248
 Romney and, 248
Hodges, Jo, 14
Hollywood
 Communism in, xii, 2, 17, 21, 28,
  30–32, 33
 Conference of Studio Unions (CSU)
  in, 31–32
 government antitrust lawsuit against
  the movie industry, 21–22,
  33–34, 35
 Reagan filming in Labor-governed
  London, 28, 29–30
 Reagan's career in, 1, 14, 19, 27,
  33–34, 128, 291–92n11
 See also Screen Actors Guild (SAG)

ABOUT THE AUTHOR

HENRY OLSEN is a senior fellow with the Ethics and Public Policy Center, a DC think tank. An incisive political analyst, he is a regular contributor to such leading publications as *The National Review*, *The Weekly Standard*, *National Affairs*, *Commentary*, *The National Interest*, *The American Interest*, and *The Claremont Review of Books*. He has also published op-eds and book reviews in *The Wall Street Journal*, *The Washington Post*, *The Washington Times*, and *The Washington Examiner*. He is the coauthor, with Dante J. Scala, of *The Four Faces of the Republican Party: The Fight for the 2016 Presidential Nomination*.